BEYOND THE GIBSON GIRL

Beyond the Gibson Girl

Reimagining the American New Woman,
1895–1915

MARTHA H. PATTERSON

UNIVERSITY OF ILLINOIS PRESS
URBANA AND CHICAGO

Publication of this book was made possible in part
by a grant from McKendree College.

The Library of Congress cataloged the cloth edition as follows:
Patterson, Martha H., 1966–
Beyond the Gibson Girl : reimagining the American new woman,
1895–1915 / Martha H. Patterson.
p.   cm.
Includes bibliographical references and index.
ISBN-13: 978-0-252-03017-8 (acid-free paper)
ISBN-10: 0-252-03017-6 (acid-free paper)
1. American fiction—Women authors—History and criticism.
2. Feminist fiction, American—History and criticism.
3. American fiction—19th century—History and criticism.
4. American fiction—20th century—History and criticism.
5. Feminism and literature—United States.
6. Women and literature—United States.
7. African American women in literature.
8. Women in literature.
I. Title.
PS374.F45P37   2005
813'.52093522—dc22   2005009424

Paperback ISBN 978-0-252-07563-6

In memory of my father

Robert Allen Patterson

1928–1999

To my parents

Robert Allen Patterson

Helen Hansen Patterson

CONTENTS

ILLUSTRATIONS

ACKNOWLEDGMENTS

This book has had such a long gestation that it is difficult now to acknowledge properly the impetus for its origins, but I would like to begin by thanking my mentors at the University of Iowa: Linda Kerber, Kim Marra, Teresa Mangum, Kathleen Diffley, and Tom Lutz. I would especially like to thank Tom Lutz for his keen suggestions and irreverent sense of humor as he guided me through the many iterations of this project.

My work has benefited greatly from conversations with friends and colleagues who read drafts of chapters or offered research advice: Susanna Ashton, Debra Blake, Martha Jane Brazy, Michael Tavel Clarke, Margaret Davis, Sue Everson, Teresa Faden Alto, Jo Forstrom, Ned Stuckey-French, George Gilmore, Betsy Gordon, John Greenfield, Christine Jespersen, Mike Johnson, Michael McClintock, David Sauer, Carol Roh Spaulding, Michele Stacey-Doyle, Carol Wallace, John Young, Mark Young, and Nancy Beck Young. I would like to thank Stephanie Girard, in particular, for her support, lunchtime brainstorming, and astute editorial suggestions. To complete the book, I have relied on numerous child-care providers, but Debbi Boone's excellence in this capacity stands out; I thank her for giving me the peace of mind to write. Julie Pannier juggled a demanding schedule at McKendree College to serve well as my research assistant, while Sarah Robinson was kind enough to copy an enormous amount of material for me. My students at the University of Iowa, the University of Michigan, Grinnell College, Spring Hill College, and McKendree College have not only spurred my work in new directions but also inspired me with their enthusiasm for the material. I am indebted to my three readers, contracted by the University of Illinois Press, for their insightful suggestions and queries, which have made this a better book. One of those readers, Elsa Nettels, introduced herself to me at a conference, and I am grateful to her for her support for this and subsequent projects. Stretching a small-college library budget, the library staff at Spring Hill College and McKendree College were an invaluable help to me in completing my research. With graciousness and due diligence, Brett Heim, Phyllis Compretta, Becky Bostian, LeAnn Noland, and Liz Vogt responded to numerous requests. My editor, Laurie Matheson, shepherded me through the review and revision process with an unflagging commitment to the project. I am grateful to her for her support and editorial advice. Copyeditor Ann Youmans helped me polish the manuscript in the final stages.

Several grants and fellowships have made this work possible. At an early stage, I benefited from the Frederick P. W. McDowell Scholarship for work in American literature from the University of Iowa. A Woodrow Wilson Grant in Women's Studies encouraged me to think of my work as evolving toward a book. The Frederick F. Seely Fellowship for Teaching and Research from the English department at the University of Iowa allowed me to vet my ideas about the New Woman with a group of lively students while giving me time to do additional research. A Helm Fellowship at the Lilly Library in Bloomington, Indiana, in 1996 allowed me to complete some of my research on Edith Wharton. Research grants from Grinnell College and Spring Hill College, including a Mitchell Faculty Scholarship and a Teagle Summer Fellowship from the latter, helped to give me the necessary time in recent summers to do the bulk of my revisions. A Newberry Library Short-Term Fellowship in 2002 enabled me to return to and expand my research on Charles Dana Gibson as well as explore Willa Cather's work in *McClure's*. The staff there was particularly helpful to me during my brief stay. And, finally, McKendree College offered generous assistance at a critical juncture in the book's publication. I am grateful to Dennis Ryan and Gerald Duff for their enthusiastic support of my scholarship.

I would like to thank *ATQ: Nineteenth-Century American Literature and Culture* and *Studies in American Fiction* for permission to reprint revised versions of two chapters: a portion of chapter 1 appeared as "'Survival of the Best Fitted': Selling the American New Woman as Gibson Girl" in *ATQ* in June 1995, and an earlier form of chapter 4 appeared as "Incorporating the New Woman in Edith Wharton's *The Custom of the Country*" in *Studies in American Fiction* in Autumn 1998.

My family—Cheryl, Craig, Steve, John, and Colleen—have steadfastly encouraged me to complete this project, even as they have razzed me about its long tenure. I want to thank my parents, Robert Patterson and Helen Hansen Patterson, for their vision and love. Without their support (in so many forms), I would not have been able to complete this book. My husband, Bill Thomas, has been my most generous, thoughtful, and gentle critic. I am more indebted to him than I can possibly acknowledge. My young sons, Mark and Walter, remind me daily of the joys of language and the deepest pleasures of life. Their enthusiasm for the countless weekend trips to "Mommy's office" has mitigated the poignancy of my lost time with them.

INTRODUCTION

I hate that phrase "New Woman." Of all the tawdry, run-to-heel phrases that strikes me the most disagreeably. When you mean, by the term, the women who believe in and ask for the right to advance in education, the arts, and professions with their fellow-men, you are speaking of a phase in civilization which has come gradually and naturally, and is here to stay. There is nothing new or abnormal in such a woman. But when you confound her with the extremists who wantonly disown the obligations and offices with which nature has honored them, you do the earnest, progressive women great wrong.
—Emma Wolf, *The Joy of Life* (1896)

The "new woman" has been the subject for illustration and description more or less in earnest. She is described as smoking, drinking, and demanding what she calls liberty. This seems to be not the liberty of law, but of license; the right to live without restraint. . . . There is a new woman, the product of evolution, the result of domestic, social and commercial changes.
—Lillian W. Betts, "The New Woman," *Outlook* (1895)

She has christened herself the "new," but when her opponent speaks of her by that name she replies with characteristic contrariety that the New Woman, like the sea-serpent, is largely an imaginary creature. Nevertheless, in the next sentence, she will refer to herself by her favorite cognomen.
—Ella Winston, "Foibles of the New Woman," *Forum* (1896)

If the so-called New Woman, who is so eager to support herself and to be a barber and a day laborer and everything that man is, had any sense of humor, she would see in the mirror of these anthropologic and historic facts that she is in reality a very old-fashioned, primitive and crab-like sort of a woman. Like the squaw and the peasant woman, she has taken to smoking again, and, in some respects she is even more mannish than the savage woman, for that woman in most cases leaves at least hunting and politics to the men.
—Henry T. Finck, "The Evolution of Sex in Mind," *Independent and Weekly Review* (1901)

The Negro woman is really the new woman of the times, and in possibilities the most interesting woman in America. This is the woman who is destined to play an important part in the future business man's career.
—Fannie Barrier Williams, "The Woman's Part in a Man's Business," *Voice of the Negro* (1904)

This new element in reform which seems to be poking the fire from
the top, this New Woman, does not know how to wait. Haste! That is
surely the danger which walks at the elbow of our most noble instinct
of social responsibility.
—Margaret Deland, "The Change in the Feminine Ideal,"
   Atlantic Monthly (1910)

Christened in 1894 during a debate between Sarah Grand and Ouida in the *North American Review,* the New Woman immediately inspired censure and applause on both sides of the Atlantic. Within the dominant white press, she was either what her detractors called an unattractive, browbeating usurper of traditionally masculine roles, or she was what her champions proclaimed an independent, college-educated, American girl devoted to suffrage, progressive reform, and sexual freedom. While the New Woman debate is most often constructed as just such a dramatic dichotomy—a new revolution overthrowing old ideas—such oppositional rhetoric provides only a cursory understanding of what was at stake in claiming the New Woman label. Even as the popular press used the term more often as an accusation than as an accolade, its capaciousness allowed a diverse range of writers to deploy it strategically, playing on its ability to evoke a host of cultural anxieties and modern desires. Signifying at once a character type, a set of distinct goals, and a cultural phenomenon, the New Woman defined women more broadly than the suffragette or settlement worker while connoting, even in its seemingly more socially conservative deployments, a distinctly modern ideal of self-refashioning. Not simply shorthand for a commitment to changing gender roles, the phrase could signal a position on evolutionary advancement, progressive reform, ethnic assimilation, sexual mores, socioeconomic development, consumer culture, racial "uplift," and imperialist conquest.

At the same time, writers who deployed the New Woman trope often situated her figure among a series of distinct character types classified by their ability to thrive in an economy increasingly dependent on consumer demand, technological advances, professional expertise, and capital coalitions. All of these writers make their case for those who could best adapt to the new economy while expressing their fears about populations that might either hinder its progress or founder in its wake. Indeed, if the New Woman were new, other policies and people were necessarily old, an old occasionally venerated as worthy or picturesque but often maligned as a fundamental impediment to progress. At the same time, the coalitions these writers imagine their New Woman protagonists making, and those that they do not, reveal the extent to which the logic of the "new" and the "old" was informed by increasing anxiety about the "other": the Jew, Negro, Chinese,

Bohemian, and Mexican, the socialist agitator, the tramp, and the homosexual. My study, then, is less celebratory of the important sociopolitical and economic demands the emergence of the New Woman represented and is more concerned about the ways in which defining and deploying the trope carried with it both possibilities and pitfalls, change and status quo.

As Jennifer Fleissner argues, however, while the trajectory of recent criticism on white women writers of the period has rightly sought to uncover the reinscription of white racial hegemony in their literary texts, it has too often neglected the real struggles these writers faced by focusing on the disciplinary effects of these works' rationalized discourse. So, for example, readings of Gilman's *Herland* that unequivocally criticize the novel for its rationalized approach to maternity neglect to consider the degree to which "nineteenth-century 'social purity' feminists' support for a rationalized body and psyche" was a direct response to popular claims of men's uncontrollable sexual impulses that "made marital rape acceptable, coercive 'seductions' of young girls excusable, and women's own sexual adventuring cause for immediate condemnation" (100).[1] Fleissner's point is an important one, and in hopes of creating such a dialectical analysis, I situate the New Woman in a wide range of social, economic, aesthetic, and political discourses to make my case. The growing demands of women's rights activists for new personal freedoms, social reforms, and political equality in conjunction with the increasing impact of evolutionary theory, incorporation, consumer culture, and electrification and other new technologies; realist, naturalist, regionalist, and modernist aesthetics; "new" immigrants, disaffected labor, Jim Crow, xenophobic legislation, and imperialist missions at home and abroad all work to define the New Woman and the narrative forms in which she appears. While critics have looked at the New Woman in conjunction with some of these historical developments (most notably the rise of socialism, sexology, applied evolutionism, imperialism, the New Thought movement, and consumerism),[2] they have generally not explored how a broader array of social changes defined the New Woman and the ideologies of woman's rights from which her figure emerges. All of these social and political developments provided the ideological threads from which the New Woman was and, to some extent, continues to be woven. The figure that emerges in my study is one of proscription as much as of liberation or transgression, and it changes depending on the racial/ethnic, economic, political, regional, and aesthetic locations of the writer.

I argue, then, that once we broaden our focus to include the web of historical events from which the New Woman emerges and evolves, that figure becomes, in her dominant form, an anxious and paradoxical icon of modern American power and decline; co-opted by writers deemed Other, the New Woman can signal at once a protest of, anodyne for, and an appeasement to the ideological imperatives of the dominant icon. At the same time, as one of the foremost symbols of feminist ambition, the New Woman reflects the synthesis of the personal and the political for a transformation politics reinvoked in subsequent generations. As Rosemary Hennessy notes, "[T]he figure of the New Woman is interesting for feminists now because the discourses out of which she emerged continue to intervene in contemporary ideologies of the feminine. How we read this figure—as instance of generational difference among feminists, as ideological containment of feminine excess, or as one of the many interlinked subjects serving the new relations of empire—is in part the effect of debates over history and the social which emerged in the late nineteenth century" (135). Better understanding the New Woman's origins and evolution—what is old in the new and new in the old—becomes, then, imperative if we are to vitalize a feminist movement too few see as relevant, inclusive, or necessary in the twenty-first century.

During the period from 1895 to 1915, Margaret Murray Washington, Pauline Hopkins, Edith Wharton, Sui Sin Far, Mary Johnston, Ellen Glasgow, and Willa Cather all deployed versions of the New Woman while popular illustrators such as Charles Dana Gibson depicted her visually.[3] As she appeared in their work, she both promised and threatened to effect sociopolitical change as a consumer, as an instigator of evolutionary and economic development, as a harbinger of modern technologies, as an icon of successful assimilation into dominant Anglo-American culture, and as a leader in progressive political causes. None of these writers, however, espoused the radical feminism associated with Greenwich Village and *The Masses,* where Floyd Dell and Max Eastman advocated voting rights, birth control, job equality, and educational opportunities for women in conjunction with free love (Sochen 70–80). I see the ambivalence of the writers examined here toward the New Woman both as a discomfort with the controversial nature of her image and a realization of their more or less tenuous stake in the literary marketplace. All of these writers conceived of themselves or were positioned as representatives of a larger group; they were "speaking for" just as they were "speaking of" and "speaking to." Embracing the dominant image of the New Woman could betray the sociopolitical goals of their respective communities but could also relegate their own artistic practice to the even more marginal and generally less lucrative realm of popular political fiction. With the exception of Edith Wharton and Margaret Murray Washington, each of these writers depended on her writing as the primary source of her income. They feared then losing whatever stake they had managed to claim in their respective branches of the turn-of-the-century literary marketplace.

The historical context that shaped the New Woman's conception and construction is complex but most closely associated with the suffrage movement. In 1895, the *Woman's Tribune,* a leading women's suffrage newspaper, wryly reported that before a gathering of Baptist ministers, Chicago preacher Dr. Henson accused the New Woman of being the child of the devil and National Woman Suffrage Association leader Elizabeth Cady Stanton ("The New Woman" 90). While only two of the writers I examine—Mary Johnston and Ellen Glasgow—directly campaigned for full women's suffrage, the issue informs all of these writers' constructions of the New Woman. With the formation of the National American Woman Suffrage Association (NAWSA) in 1890 to the passage of the Nineteenth Amendment in 1919, the influence of the movement grew steadily, albeit without the hoped-for long string of political victories. From 1893 to 1917, the membership in the NAWSA increased from 13,150 to 2 million (Kraditor 7). And yet the NAWSA's policy of expediency worked to exclude the participation of black women, seeming to confirm W. E. B. Du Bois's 1907 complaint about the "narrowness" of American [white] women: "The Negro race has suffered more from the antipathy and narrowness of women both South and North than from any other single source" (Du Bois 127). Partially in response to white exclusionary practices, African American women formed their own suffrage associations, often as part of women's clubs, and broadened the suffrage appeal to include increasingly disenfranchised black men. As Rosalyn Terborg-Penn notes, thousands of black women joined clubs for which women's suffrage and, by extension, the reenfranchisement of black men, was a key goal (9).

Membership in women's clubs among all women, but especially middle-class women, grew exponentially during this period, with a peak in the early 1920s of an estimated 2 million clubwomen, organized generally along racial, class, religious, and/or political lines (Gere 5). In fact, two of the most significant coalitions of club members were formed in the late nineteenth century: the General Federation of Women's Clubs in 1890 and the National Association of Colored Women (NACW) in 1895. According to Anne Ruggles Gere, the focus of these clubs was to enhance literacy, thereby enabling greater engagement in issues of national debate. While native-born white women often faced derision for their membership in independent clubs, black women seemed to face less community opposition, a difference that may be due to the cross-gendered appeal of their racial-uplift agenda. Indeed, as Anne Meis Knupfer notes, African American clubwomen's advocacy of Christian moralism, municipal housekeeping, and Republican motherhood was in keeping with both Booker T. Washington's industrial education model and W. E. B. Du Bois's talented-tenth leadership ideal (15–17, 159–60 nn. 1–2). Such a difference in reception of women's club work is also borne out in my study. While Wharton and Cather satirize clubwomen as only superficially intellectual, Hopkins and Washington celebrated clubwomen as respected community leaders and role models.

The activity that arguably effected the greatest politicization of women, Prohibition, figures significantly in my study given that drinking—which the New Woman of this period, especially the New Woman of color, typically eschewed—was generally associated with vice and sexual entrapment.[4] Mary Johnston spoke on behalf of temperance and both she and Glasgow in their fiction highlight the dissipating effects of alcohol on either a male protagonist or society at large. Writing for *Gall's Daily News Letter* in Jamaica in 1897, society columnist Fire

Fly (Sui Sin Far/Edith Eaton) offers a defense of the female bicyclist, the divided skirt, and the bicycle generally as "the greatest temperance reformer of the present day, for no man can drink and bicycle."[5] Other New Women writers, however, viewed the temperance movement as teetotaling zealotry. In Gertrude Atherton's *Patience Sparhawk and Her Times* (1897), the "intellectual anarchist" and New Woman Patience calls the movement "narrow-minded and an unwarrantable intrusion" (86, 282). How, she asks the shrilly pious Miss Beale, "do you reconcile your animosity to alcohol with the story of Christ's turning the water into wine at the wedding feast?" (282). While the female drinker does figure in some representations of New Woman liberation during this period, most strikingly Edna's cocktail scene in Kate Chopin's *The Awakening,* such scenes are much more central to the flapper image of the 1920s after nationwide Prohibition was constitutionally enacted in 1919.

Other social changes during this period shape the New Woman's characterization more demonstrably. By 1900, the divorce rate had risen to one out of twelve couples (one out of nine by World War I), while the birth rate had fallen to 3.5 children per mother (Riley 53). Divorce figures prominently in the narratives I examine, and it reflects a turning point, but towards what depends greatly on the social position of the writer and character. For Edith Wharton, divorce generally represents a distinctly American gilded-age opportunism. For Sui Sin Far, although divorce offers a necessary escape, it is associated with a selfishness coded as white and American (her Chinese American male protagonists, by contrast, exhibit more spousal loyalty).

None of the fiction writers I examine had children, and few of their New Woman characters in this period have them. And yet, given that, maternal status is central to their vision of the New Woman. In the work of African American writers, maternal rights and responsibilities in large part define the New Negro Woman's authority. Indeed, given the legacy of slavery, black women's maternal rights would be central both to defining the New Negro Woman's ambition and her purview, one that would extend to the uplift of the entire race.[6] To Edith Eaton writing as Sui Seen Far, the Chinese woman in America may be a New Woman in her dress and love of adornment and gossip, but she also accepts patriarchy without question, praying that she may bear a son and having "perfect confidence in her man" ("Chinese" 64). For Sui Sin Far, however, the Chinese New Woman's maternal devotion offered a critique of American New Woman selfishness. The southern white writer Ellen Glasgow, on the other hand, contrasted the enervating selflessness of the child-laden "true woman" with the self-assured dynamism of the childless New Woman. If her New Woman protagonist does have children, the exigency of providing for them, especially after they have been abandoned by their father, becomes for their mother a source of motivation towards economic and emotional independence. Suggesting the influence of Charlotte Perkins Gilman, who demonstrated so vividly in "The Yellow Wallpaper" the ways in which a postpartum rest cure silenced a woman already infantilized within a patriarchal marriage, virtually all of the white women writers who crafted New Woman protagonists define at least some of them by the oppression they face as wives and/or mothers. At the end of *The Awakening,* Edna sees her children as "antagonists . . . who had overpowered and sought to drag her into the soul's slavery for the rest of her days" (113). And yet, as Alison Berg points out, while Gilman "predicated racial advancement on women's prior emancipation," Chopin and Wharton "concede the primacy of race as an ineluctable limitation on white woman's freedom" (17). For Berg, even as *The Awakening* presents reproduction as the greatest limitation to white women's freedom, by emphasizing the Other's "natural" reproductive role, the novel reveals a "eugenic anxiety about the repercussions of white middle-class feminism" (72).

Not surprisingly, then, birth control is also a prominent New Woman theme, even though artificial birth control was regarded by some feminists as merely a means by which men could more easily objectify and sexually exploit their partners (Jeffries 159). This view is reflected arguably in the unbowdlerized version of Dreiser's *Jennie Gerhardt.* To persuade a faltering Jennie to be his mistress, the self-serving Lester Kane assures her, "I understand a number of things that you don't yet. It can be arranged. You don't need to have a child unless you want to" (158). Mary Johnston's Hagar avoids such victimization by forming a distinctly nonsexual union with the suggestively named John Fay. The lower birthrate, especially among native-born, middle-class, urban white women, was due to a number of factors: growing concerns for child welfare, desires for more autonomy, aspirations for a middle-class lifestyle, as well as access to information about birth control, albeit in defiance of Comstock laws (Kennedy 45–46). Yet the drop was often blamed on women's greater participation in higher education. The British evolutionary theorist Herbert Spencer argued in *The Principles of Biology* (1898), for example, that the "deficiency of reproductive power among" upper-class women may be "reasonably attributed to the overtaxing of their brains" (512–13), a trend that showed no signs of abating: "By 1910, when approximately 5 percent of college-age Americans attended college, 40 percent were female" (Riley 47).

In Cather's work, a woman's pursuit of advanced study becomes one marker of female exceptionalism that child rearing would only discourage. Given racist pseudoscientific arguments about the inferiority of Native, Jewish, and African Americans; prevailing patriarchal social codes; and tensions between community needs and individual rights, higher education becomes a personal pursuit with profound communal ramifications. When Zitkala-Ša delivered a stirring address advocating indigenous rights in an 1896 otherwise all-white, all-male college oratorical contest, the opposing team displayed a large white flag with a caricature of an Indian girl under which was printed "squaw" (Fisher 12; Zitkala-Ša 79). Although she ended up winning second place in the contest, symbolically defeating bigotry, she was left feeling profoundly alienated, unable to connect her academic success with her Dakota heritage. Disapproving of her "attempt to learn the white man's ways," her mother, writes Zitkala-Ša, was "far away on the Western plains . . . [holding] a charge against me" (76, 80). By contrast, Mary Antin, in her best-selling autobiography *The Promised Land* (1912), offers a more celebratory portrait of American educational opportunities, in large part because, even though she battled patriarchal religious traditions, her family eventually supported her educational goals. In the beginning of her autobiography, Antin describes her frustration with patriarchal privileges, especially educational privileges, enjoyed by men in Russian Jewish culture. While all Russian Jewish boys were sent to Hebrew school and could be Torah scholars or rabbis, girls could not: "A girl's real schoolroom was her mother's kitchen. . . . And while her hands were busy, her mother instructed her in the laws regulating a pious Jewish household and in the conduct proper for a Jewish wife; for, of course, every girl hoped to be a wife. A girl was born for no other purpose" (34). Antin's narrative of uplift and assimilation, with its keen class consciousness, offers education as the ultimate remedy for gender, race, and class inequity crippling the nation.[7]

All of these factors contribute to what perhaps is the most demonstrable change in women's lives, especially white women's lives, that the New Woman represents: greater involvement in the paid workforce. By 1900, an estimated 5 million women, or one out of every five, were employed in a number of different and mostly low-paying fields, namely textile manufacturing, clerical labor, sales, housekeeping, domestic service, primary education, nursing, and agriculture (Riley 54–55). Yet the work patterns were strikingly different for white and black women. In 1900, only three out of every hundred married white women were paid employees, primarily in domestic service, and in 1920 only six out of every hundred were employed. This modest increase indicates the extent to which white women tended to stop working after they married. Roughly 40 percent of all black women, however, were paid employees for their entire adult lives (Katzman 81–82). Many New Woman narratives emphasize how economic exigencies forced their female protagonists to gain employment outside the home. For Sui Sin Far, Wharton, and Hopkins, the pursuit of such work is often less a sign of personal fulfillment than economic necessity. Indeed, most of these writers emphasize the hazards in paid employment—be they effects on family life, personal safety, physical health, or emotional well-being. And many New Woman narratives of the period stress the peripatetic lifestyles such work demands. Edna Ferber's popular *Roast Beef Medium* series features the lady drummer and single mother Emma McChesney, who declares, "I got my divorce ten years ago, and I've been on the road ever since. . . . I'm pulling down a good, fat salary and commissions, but it's no life for a woman" (43). In her autobiographical writing, Sui Sin Far describes a working career characterized by a similar rootlessness—"I roam backward and forward across the continent"—but one also motivated by a profound sense of biracial dislocation: "I give my right hand to the Occidentals and my left to the

Orientals, hoping that between them they will not utterly destroy the insignificant 'connecting link'" ("Leaves," 132). For white women writers, the "home" is most often marked by patriarchal domination or fecklessness and leaving home serves as a marker of necessary independence, while for African American characters "home" is generally a site of external colonization and working outside the home is as much for personal safety or racial uplift as economic exigency. Marie Louise Burgess-Ware's story "Bernice, the Octoroon," which appeared in the *Colored American Magazine* in 1903, for example, describes the tragic mulatta story of Bernice. College-educated, wealthy, and engaged to the most eligible of white bachelors, Bernice leaves home to become a teacher among Negroes after being exposed as mixed race by her jealous "white" cousin Lenore.

For most women—and especially for immigrant and African American women—working conditions were poor to abysmal with wages far lower than their male counterparts, hours long, advancement opportunities few, and safety measures almost nonexistent. To alleviate poor working conditions, tens of thousands of women joined settlement houses or labor organizations. Hull House founders Jane Addams and Ellen Gates Starr campaigned for reforms such as better garbage collection, child labor laws, and public health programs (Riley 38–39). For her work on behalf of miners in the Pittsburgh United Mine Workers' strike, Mary Harris "Mother" Jones, the *National Labor Tribune* declared, was the best type of New Woman and would "go down in history as one of the martyrs to the cause of oppressed humanity" ("The New Woman"). While foreign-born socialist women tended to favor more traditional gender roles as they worked to insure their family's cohesiveness in the face of increasing xenophobia, native-born women forged a distinct socialist vision apart from their male counterparts (Buhle xvi). For Johnston, socialism and women's emancipation were inseparable issues, so her working-class character's socialist vision parallels and informs her New Woman protagonist's liberation. Writers such as Mary Wilkins Freeman and Edith Eaton took a more moderate approach. In *The Portion of Labor* (1901), Freeman presents the native-born, working-class protagonist Ellen Brewster as one who asserts a radical commitment to social justice even as she fulfills the dictates of the domestic narrative by marrying the upper-class factory owner Robert Lloyd.[8] While "Canadian Fire Fly" Edith Eaton declares, "I am no Socialist," she did advocate industrial education for Jamaican blacks.[9]

Yet the historical developments that had the most pronounced impact on these writers' conception of the New Woman were the growing dominance of consumer capitalism, corporate culture, and evolutionary discourse. The period between 1895 and 1915 witnessed a revolution in the display and marketing of manufactured goods in American culture. New electrically lit department stores and more aggressive advertising strategies worked together to create new desires among primarily female consumers. Indeed, in 1901 James Collins writes in *Printers' Ink*, the foremost advertising journal of the period, that even though, as compared to man, woman is without reason, common sense, thrift, or foresight, "she does all of his buying and the whole world is built pretty much to her tastes, whims and prejudices" (3). Consequently, the wise advertiser should "take her into strict account when he deals with her in space and dollars and cents" (3). With women as the primary consumers in mind, department stores worked to seduce them into purchasing. Large plate-glass windows encouraged customers to gaze at sumptuously decorated displays; main doorsteps were removed and revolving doors were installed to invite customers in; floodlights, spotlights, prismatic lights, electric lights of all sorts saturated interior shopping spaces; newly installed elevators and later escalators moved customers closer to goods; and a growing number of female store clerks graciously helped their customers navigate the increasingly complex but sensuous purchasing process. Orientalism, with its notion of a feminized, primitive Asia and its accompanying "exotic," sensual products—Indian silks, Turkish carpets, Japanese ceramics, and Chinese florals—became one of department stores' favorite aesthetics.[10]

Yet consumers' relationships to the products on display were invariably mediated by a necessarily conflicted relationship to modes of production. The history of consumption, as Richard Godden reminds us, "should be set within the history of the riotous unrest which the logic of its development provoked" (5). The Pullman strike of 1894, the Triangle Shirtwaist Fire of 1911, the rise of the Socialist Party, Jim Crow and Yellow Peril restrictions and violence, tenement living conditions, child labor, and voracious corporate trusts, not to mention the personal socioeconomic concerns of these writers, all shaped directly or indirectly the ways in which they viewed the emerging consumer culture of which their work and their protagonists were a part. Indeed, all of these writers explore the exigencies of a marketplace where many are victimized and only a few prosper. While creating protagonists who attempt to compete in or transform the marketplace in which they maneuver, each of these women writers reveals how marketplace dynamics construct interpersonal relationships, political reform movements, and the ways in which women present themselves. To sell their books and their characters, these writers also had to embrace an ethic of profitable exchange contrary to other more progressive themes in their novels. On the one hand, the fact that the "consuming" practices of ethnic Americans were viewed as highly suspect—either they were attempting to forge crass imitations of white originals or their exoticism proclaimed a commitment to maintaining economies of vice—suggests, in part, why Sui Sin Far, Hopkins, and Washington present such ambivalent images of the New Woman as the consummate purchaser of new goods. On the other hand, despite the prevailing racist images within advertising of the period, transformation through consumption seemed to bypass the more reified hierarchies within evolutionary theory. One means of demonstrating a willingness to assimilate was to buy those goods that signified a commitment to the demands of bourgeois culture. Compounding the complexity of these necessarily conflicted positions are the advertisements and illustrations, which positioned both the authors and their characters for greatest sales appeal. I examine the specific workings of these market-driven dynamics in the production of each writer's work and ask whether these writers deem it possible, or even preferable, to leave behind women's "condition as commodities."[11]

From 1897 to 1904, one third of all companies vanished in mergers with other companies, and by 1905 less than 1 percent of manufacturers employed more than one fourth of all manufacturing employees (Painter 177). Even as trusts strived to control entire industries, an emerging corporate culture, with some values coterminous with progressivism, began to emerge. As Martin Sklar has observed, the new corporate ideals valued interconnectedness (versus localism), bureaucratic organization, mass production, technological innovation, professionalization, and, in certain cases, federal regulation (*United* 24–25, 70–77). Indeed, corporations depended on the kind of stable and broad workforce that many progressive sociopolitical movements would help to provide. Labor-law reform, women's suffrage, women's higher education, settlement work, and higher wage demands—causes associated with the New Woman—could be viewed as merely helping to ease diverse workers into an often more alienating work environment.[12] But if the emerging corporate culture necessarily co-opted reform efforts, its logic could be adopted to legitimize new freedoms, reforms, and coalitions. Johnston and Glasgow, for example, seemed to support the corporate logic of necessary interconnectedness—where unions of urban and rural capital mitigated sectional conflicts—to sanction new coalitions across gender and class but not, significantly, across racial boundaries. At the same time, however, all of these writers claimed their rightful place in the hierarchy of their profession and consequent social circles, a model of social stratification that they legitimize in their fiction. One point at which these necessarily "conflicting stories" converge is in their support of progressive reforms that would enable more women, but not all women, to enjoy a greater stake in the emerging corporate-capitalist economy.

To legitimate the New Woman and the new social stratification her ascendancy necessarily created, each of these writers relied on evolutionary discourse. Considering the dismal prospects most evolutionary theorists offered for women's advancement, it was, in some respects, an unlikely discursive strategy. As Cynthia Eagle Russett notes, the overwhelming consensus among evolutionary theorists was that women were fundamentally different from men, not only anatomically and physiologically but also emotionally and intellectually. Childlike in body and mind, women lagged behind the more courageous and intellectually sophisticated men, much as the "primitive" peoples lagged behind Europeans (*Sexual* 11–12). Indeed, in *Descent of Man and Selection in Relation to Sex* (1871), Darwin writes, "The chief distinction in the intellectual powers of the two sexes is shewn by man's attaining to a higher eminence, in whatever he takes up, than woman can attain—whether requiring deep thought, reason, or imagination, or merely the use of the sense and hands" (327). While Darwin claimed that evidence of the highest state of evolution was altruism, a trait that women were more likely to possess, women had a host of other qualities associated with the "lower races." For women, the "powers of intuition, of rapid perception, and perhaps of imitation, are more strongly marked than in man; but some, at least, of these faculties are characteristic of the lower races, and therefore of a past and lower state of civilization" (565–66). The social theorists who informed these writers' works—such as Havelock Ellis, Thorstein Veblen, and Lester Ward, as well as evolutionary theorists such as Henri Bergson, Patrick Geddes and J. Arthur Thomson, Vernon Kellogg, and Francis Galton, generally positioned women and races as subject to an inexorable and hierarchical evolutionary logic. Progress in these narratives was possible, but it was not assured.

All of these writers modified significantly or selectively embraced such arguments concerning women's role in the evolutionary narrative. With the exception of Hopkins and Wharton, they echoed Charlotte Perkins Gilman's argument in *Women and Economics* (1898) that the appearance of the New Woman was a definitive sign of overall race progress. Less a sudden apparition than a logical product of improved family and social conditions, this "stronger and healthier" New Woman reflected a largely positive vision of technological change and social reform at the turn of the century. To legitimate their desires for progressive reform, most of these writers preferred either a neo-Lamarckian approach to evolutionary change, in which natural selection was a secondary force in evolution and characteristics acquired during one's lifetime might be inherited, or a reform Darwinist perspective similar to Lester Ward's (or a combination of the two).[13] The rise in popularity of neo-Darwinists such as Francis Galton, who founded the eugenics movement, would require a shift in tactics for those committed to progressive reform (Russett, *Sexual* 198–201).[14] Because biology increasingly seemed to determine destiny, showcasing protagonists who had a Gibson Girl vitality if not social ethics became one means of demonstrating the New Woman as an evolved type. With her statuesque form and northern European features, the Gibson Girl's status on the evolutionary ladder was assured—she was racially as well as culturally superior.

Although wary in many respects of neo-Darwinism, Wharton, Glasgow, and Cather nonetheless construct New Woman protagonists who thrive in competitive environments where the "unfit" are inevitably weeded out. For Wharton, the New Woman's ascendance signified a changing economy, one in which the primitive Darwinian logic of unmitigated struggle was being replaced by a growing corporate ethic in which coalitions of like-minded investors were best equipped for survival. For Johnston and Glasgow, the rise of the New Woman that brought with it a new understanding of who would be deemed "unfit" was one way of creating common ground with white northern readers. By assuming their natural leadership roles and by reaffirming new racial hierarchies within the progressive movement, their New Woman protagonists promise to solve the "race problem." For Cather, the white New Woman thrives while her darker and "degenerate" cousin is punished. Subject to overwhelmingly pessimistic pronouncements of their place on the evolutionary ladder, Washington, Hopkins, and Sui Sin Far employed the rhetoric of racial uplift as a means of revising the criteria on which the racial hierarchies were based. Their New Women have an earned moral authority, which supersedes the genetic legacy, that white New Women had been given but had not earned. As Kevin Gaines has demonstrated, however, the rhetoric of racial uplift reflected a legacy of internalized racism (*Uplifting* 6). Because Washington, Hopkins, and Sui Sin Far reconfigured, but did not ultimately reject, the dominant logic of race development along an evolutionary model, their model of communal liberation contained elements that were self-condemning.

In all of these socioeconomic developments that shaped the various expressions of the New Woman trope, region and class are determining factors. Mary Johnston and Ellen Glasgow's white New Women of the New South have a distinct spiritual investment in the heroics of the lost cause and the agrarian plantation economy upon which that cause was based that their northern counterparts eschew. Their protagonists, however, either voluntarily or by circumstance, must abandon that class—but not race—privilege in order to further their evolution and to create connections with the dangerous but vital northern element associated with an urban paid workforce. Willa Cather, a self-described "American of the Apache period," used the western landscape with its wide expanses, history of hardscrabble immigrant experience, and desert ruins—evidence of a connection to a "purer" indigenous past—as a canvas for a generally middleclass white New Woman's sexual liberation. Sui Sin Far would capitalize on the celebration of the West as a site of ethnotourism with still-remaining frontier opportunities even as she would herald the Far East as offering the spiritual, physical, and moral regeneration the United States desperately needed. Her Chinese New Woman protagonists are markedly middle class with a kind of stability and moral probity that countered stereotypes of the period. At the same time, while explicitly criticizing the unacknowledged class privilege of the most visible proponents of white New Woman reforms, she would implicitly unveil the hypocrisy of xenophobia in a movement supposedly devoted to the emancipation of all women. Edith Wharton, as a member of the old New York elite, constructs a New Woman who represents a threat to an old order, which, though stifling in its social codes, valued an aesthetic of genuineness as opposed to what she saw as the overwhelming sham of fin-de-siècle commercialism. Pauline Hopkins, although she was born in Portland, Maine, and spent the entirety of her professional life in Boston, worked to defy regional identification in an effort to make Jim Crow degradations a national rather than regional crisis. Her "New Negro Women" protagonists are marked by a class privilege that qualifies them to lead the race, forging interregional, interracial, and ultimately international alliances to end oppression. By contrast, for Margaret Murray Washington, whose energies were focused on Tuskegee, the crucial race work was to be done in the South, a place that must increasingly be identified less with the degradations of slavery and more with the possibilities of uplift.

At the same time, the intertwined histories of the "New Woman," "New Negro Woman," "New Negro," "New China," "New South," and "New Empire" suggest how the trope of the New Woman also worked to define American identity during a period of rising nativist sentiment, intense racial conflict, and imperialist conquest. As Walter Benn Michaels has noted in "The Souls of White Folk," after *Plessy v. Ferguson* in 1896, "white" and "American" increasingly became adjectives describing an essentially spiritual character more than a potentially indeterminate skin color. This new racial identity "transcended color while at the same time invoking its biological authority" (191). All of these writers reveal their awareness that the dominant version of the New Woman, particularly in her Gibson Girl incarnation, represented a white, native-born, "Christian" American nation. Her stature and inviolability signified the authority of a nation embarked on imperialist "civilizing" missions both at home and abroad. The new model of American identity that the Gibson Girl offered, however, also suggested the possibility that one might "perform" American identity, a performance subject to variable interpretations. Sui Sin Far, Pauline Hopkins, and Margaret Murray Washington, for example, even though they use religious discourse to criticize American racism and greed, they also promote a professional "performative" model of American identity to make their case for full acceptance as citizens. Working within the Chinese American communities on the West Coast, Sui Sin Far assumed a position as cultural interpreter, offering a Chinese American endorsement of a "New China," a China that adopts Western economic reform. One way in which Sui Sin Far represented the possibility of this New China is in her depiction of the "real" New Woman, a Chinese American woman able to negotiate between Chinese and American cultural practices and thereby able to facilitate the economic assimilation of Chinese men. Hopkins was influenced by the black nationalist rhetoric of John E. Bruce, Anna Julia Cooper, and W. E. B. Du Bois, and she hailed not only the "new era" when all Americans acknowledge their Ethiopian roots but also the era when Ethiopians', and hence black Americans', amenability to a bourgeois work ethic would be duly recognized. In her essays describing the work of the black women's club movement, Washington created a "New Negro Woman," who effects a kind of internal colonization by enforcing white bourgeois ideals yet who nevertheless has a new authority of social probity behind her. The assurances these writers give of their characters' ability to assimilate are part of an understandable, albeit flawed, strategy in an enormously hostile working environment.

Each of the writers that I have chosen to focus on deploys a different representative trope of the New Woman to define her own sociopolitical reform objectives.

Many other American fiction writers in this period, of course, either directly or indirectly weighed in on the New Woman debate. Mary Austin, Kate Chopin, Theodore Dreiser, Alice Dunbar-Nelson, Mary Wilkins Freeman, Charlotte Perkins Gilman, William Dean Howells, Henry James, Sarah Orne Jewett, Jack London, Frank Norris, Gertrude Stein, Mark Twain, and Zitkala-Ša, for example, all crafted New Woman protagonists (though they may not have explicitly used the terminology), and their work informs my arguments. Gertrude Stein's ambivalence towards the New Woman, for example, is similar to Cather's and suggests a parallel in queer vision—a focus on gender-role subversion in conjunction with same-sex intimacy—that the other writers in my study, for the most part, eschew. While Stein would defend the cause of college education for women in a speech she gave shortly after her first year in medical school, she presented a more ambivalent portrayal of the New Woman in her novella *Fernhurst* (1904–05), which she would later incorporate into *The Making of Americans* (1934).[15] Based on a scandalous Bryn Mawr love triangle between a married professor, his female colleague, and the college president, M. Carey Thomas, *Fernhurst* demonstrates both a fascination with the New Woman's ambition and energy and a critique of her insularity from the vicissitudes of daily struggle. "I wonder," says the narrator Philip Redfern, "will the new woman ever relearn the fundamental facts of sex. Will she not see that college standards are of little worth in actual labor" (4).

I focus on women writers because I am interested in the tension between the writer's own professional status (all of these writers would, by definition, be considered New Women) and their construction of New Woman characters. I chose these particular writers because they either used the rhetoric of the New Woman explicitly in their fiction or essays, or because that rhetoric directly informed their construction of particular female protagonists. With the exception of Johnston's *Hagar,* I do not concentrate on American popular novels, college-girl fiction, club women, or suffrage or socialist texts that focused exclusively on the social consequences of the New Woman's emergence and necessarily shaped the dialogue in which the writers I discuss participated.[16] Nor does my study include an indepth discussion of the New Woman's predecessors—for example, Fanny Fern's resourceful heroines, Mark Twain's rebellious women, Henry James's American girl, Sarah Orne Jewett's female doctor, and so forth[17]—in part because the image of the New Woman has too often been conflated with the significantly different vision of the 1880s American Girl, which Henry James and William Dean Howells imagined. Both Daisy Miller and Penelope Lapham are more naive and "pert" than the savvy, statuesque New Woman in the marketplace. Writing for the *Ladies' Home Journal* in 1904, Winfield Scott Moody compares Daisy Miller and Theodosia, the "modern" American girl of Gibson's creation: Daisy was "unsophisticated, innocent, and thus vulgar only because she lacked culture." Theodosia, by contrast, was "most sophisticated, highly educated in all that the schools teach" and although knowledgeable about polite behavior, chooses to be

"a hoyden and a tomboy . . . slangy, incredibly self-assured, and serenely indif-
ferent to the rights of others."

I have worked, instead, to illustrate the important regional, ethnic, and political
differences of the American New Woman trope in what has become, with a few
exceptions, canonical turn-of-the-century American literature. I wish to make
cross-cultural connections while remaining attuned to the historical specificity
of each work's mode of production, thereby emphasizing the complexities of the
New Woman trope against the reductive treatment it has received in the past. The
New Woman in all of her incarnations—degenerate, evolved type; race leader or
race traitor; brow-beating suffragette, prohibitionist, mannish lesbian, college girl,
savvy professional woman, barren spinster, club woman, lady drummer, restless
woman, wheelwoman, or insatiable shopper—represented a complex response
to an emerging, feminized conception of modernity and, even in her positive
formations, cannot be read as an accurate reflection of women's experience. But,
as Rita Felski notes, there is also no realm of "authentic femininity" outside of
the "textual and institutional logics of the modern" (21). Indeed, as Felski cautions, we must resist viewing women's experience as a "pre-given ontology" in
favor of exploring how it

> is constituted through a number of often contradictory, albeit connected strands,
> which are not simply reflected but are constructed through the "technologies of
> gender" of particular cultures and periods. Such an understanding of history as
> *enactment* situates femininity in its multiple, diverse, but determinate articula-
> tions, which are themselves crisscrossed by other cultural logics and hierarchies
> of power. Gender is continually in process, an identity that is performed and
> actualized over time within given social constraints. (21)[18]

The often contradictory and evolving deployments of the New Woman, which
work to normalize some behaviors and populations while pathologizing others,
highlight the performative aspects of this gendered trope. To appropriate Judith
Butler's definition of gender as performance, the New Woman is always a doing, "though not a doing by a subject who might be said to preexist the deed"
(*Gender* 25). There is then no New Woman as such during this period but rather
patterns of performing an often ethnically, regionally, socially, and politically
distinctive trope.

The dominant image of the American New Woman, which has emerged out of
contemporary literary and cultural studies, however, is much more monolithic.
Most cultural critics use the term to describe white, well-educated, frequently
single, and politically progressive women, while New Woman literary critics have
tended to privilege and homogenize the voices of politically "progressive," white,
generally realist women writers. Indeed, the work of Willa Cather, Kate Chopin,
Charlotte Perkins Gilman, Ellen Glasgow, Edith Wharton, and, to a lesser extent,
Mary Austin, Sarah Orne Jewett, and Mary Wilkins Freeman has come to define

New Woman realist writing in this period. Only recently has the term been used more accurately to describe works produced after 1894, although its expiration date still varies considerably, and to include women writers of color. To call a writer a New Woman has most often meant to grant her privileged status in the canon of turn-of-the-century, left-leaning women writers with a "female consciousness." Whether she is viewed by contemporary critics as sexually transgressive or devoted to radical political movements, progressive reform efforts, suffrage, or artistry, her image is most often represented in celebratory terms.[19]

Cultural historian Carroll Smith-Rosenberg provides in *Disorderly Conduct: Visions of Gender in Victorian America* (1985) perhaps the most oft-quoted and influential analysis of the New Woman, defining her as a second-generation champion of women's rights able to challenge fundamentally naturalized gender relations and notions of female sexuality (245). Smith-Rosenberg explains the source of the New Woman's political agency: "Her quintessentially American identity, her economic resources, and her social standing permitted her to defy proprieties, pioneer new roles, and still insist upon a rightful place within the genteel world. Repudiating the Cult of True Womanhood in ways her mother—the new bourgeois matron—never could, she threatened men in ways her mother never did" (245).

In her essay on the New Woman for the *Columbia Literary History of the United States* (1988), Cecelia Tichi offers a narrower definition of the New Woman—so narrow as to exclude popular New Woman suffrage and socialist texts—while casting her in celebratory terms. Claiming that the New Woman's "radicalism was a matter of personal decision" rather than a commitment to an organized reform movement, Tichi sees the New Woman as individualistic in her subversiveness (592). Lois Banner, Martha Banta, Patricia Marks, and Rosemary Hennessy focus on some of the permutations of the New Woman's image in bourgeois popular culture and the social anxieties or theoretical images those images suggest.[20] June Sochen and Mary Jo Buhle position her within left-wing political movements, while Rosalind Rosenberg explores how her ascendancy depended on progressive intellectual discourse.[21]

Other literary critics who frame at least part of their analysis as a study of American New Woman writers have focused on the cultural anxiety surrounding the disruptive sexuality of white women during the period. Sandra Gilbert and Susan Gubar, Marianne DeKoven, Laura Doan, Ellen Kay Trimberger, and Esther Newton have all used the term to celebrate a white, often privileged New Woman's transgressive sexuality, especially as it challenged the traditional marriage plot.[22] Elaine Showalter has explored the racialized and socioeconomic threat that white New Woman sexuality posed to the turn-of-the-century English bourgeoisie. Marianne DeKoven does not use the "New Woman" terminology directly, but she, like Showalter, explores the fear that white male and female modernists had concerning the period's threat of revolutionary changes in gender, race, and class relations. She claims Chopin's *The Awakening* as a modernist text signifying the fear of punishment many female modernists faced for desiring such revolutionary change.

Only recently, however, has the term become ethnically and racially inclusive in women's cultural history and literary criticism. Kathy Peiss, Susan Glenn, and Marjorie Wheeler, for example, give the term essential class, ethnic, and regional specificity.[23] In her essay for Adele Heller and Lois Rudnick's *1915: The Cultural Moment* (1991) and in her book *Conflicting Stories: American Women Writers at the Turn into the Twentieth Century* (1992), Elizabeth Ammons extends beyond dominant white version of the New Woman.[24] In *Conflicting Stories,* she includes an analysis of Jewish, black, Asian, and Native American texts that "reflect an emerging, shared, and often defiant confidence in the abilities and rights of women that historians associate with the 'new' middle-class American woman of the period" (4). Ammons, however, then ultimately links these diverse texts through a preestablished, dominant New Woman paradigm—artistic agency. As opposed to the "professional" writers of an earlier generation, these writers were artists, who, according to Ammons, often radically experimented with narrative form and shared a broad interest in exposing oppressive networks of power. Ammons's assessment, however, implies equal access to "artistic" agency by quite diverse writers. Writers such as Pauline Hopkins, Sui Sin Far, and Mary Johnston could not position themselves as "artists"—in the same way that Edith Wharton, Ellen Glasgow, or Willa Cather did, for example—because their work was viewed as melodramatic, regional, political, or historical fiction, relatively "minor" literary forms. While more attentive to the historical context from which the terms True Woman and New Woman emerged, Martha Cutter in *Unruly Tongue: Identity and Voice in American Women's Writing, 1850–1930* (1999) celebrates the New Woman's "unruly tongue" even as she critiques the inability of the writers she examines to move beyond the binary logic of dominant discourses. Most recently, in *Women, Compulsion, Modernity* (2004), Jennifer Fleissner reveals how the question of the New Woman is in fact central to what is widely considered a hyper-masculine genre, naturalism. Because of a new belief that all human beings were affected by physical forces as well as social ones, women, generally understood as solely determined by their bodies, could, in effect, enter public life without having to prove they left nature behind (22). For Fleissner, compulsive activities in these texts—rocking, cleaning, eating—show the negotiation between the physical and the social in such a way that nature, traditionally viewed as the locus of a static feminine force, is questioned and historicized. Edna's final swim in *The Awakening,* then, is no longer a retreat from reality but a questioning of what nature is, perhaps "meaningless endlessness" (242). Fleissner's work may well demonstrate an important shift in New Woman criticism as it asks us both to consider how our interpretations of these texts reinscribe our own cultural biases and to develop a better understanding of the cultural dialectic that informs early feminism. It is in that vein that I enter this project with the aim of yet further complicating and elucidating the New Woman's literary and cultural history. By moving beyond the New Woman as accolade and epithet to examine how a wider array of regionally and culturally distinct New Woman rhetorics serve to proscribe as well as to liberate, I hope to do just that.

Indeed, the protest elements in these works that appear as modern innovations of realist or sentimental literary style and theme are often partially contained by the consumer, corporate, technological, and evolutionary logic of the New Woman's emergence. In *New Women, New Novels: Feminism and Early Modernism* (1990), Ann Ardis lists what she sees as the significant literary innovations employed by British New Woman novelists. They include a number of characteristics that can readily be applied to many American New Woman texts: challenging the "inevitability of the marriage plot" with sexually active or abstemious heroines, creating rogue heroines who distinguish their voice from that of the male narrators, and collapsing conventional distinctions between popular culture and high art as well as creating moments of ideological self-consciousness and intertextuality (3). Yet, as Felski demonstrates, analyzing the shifting "axes of power" in texts may reveal the "potential contradictions between different power hierarchies" (Felski 32).[25] Johnston's associative sentence fragments of cultural tumult signify a northern and masculine moral chaos that the New Woman of the New South, with her more evolved spiritual authority, will help to rectify. Sui Sin Far's "trickster" figures defy racial categories and hierarchies but at the same time often affirm Western corporate ideals of worker productivity and efficiency. Hopkins's intertextuality reminds readers of a long history of abandoned American democratic principles as well as African American resistance, but at the same time that intertextuality is framed by an uplift ideal that undermines possibilities for full community empowerment.

In addition, the arguably wider range of American New Woman texts that make up the American New Woman canon make it difficult to establish an analogous unifying stylistic paradigm. The common stylistic thread that links the white American New Woman novels is that of wave imagery. If the desiring body is what fuels the engine of modern life, then the turbulent, ravenous appetites of the modern woman appear as most threatening. As feminist critics have demonstrated, associating water with a dangerous feminine desire is a defining aspect of fin-de-siècle culture. Most notably, Marianne DeKoven sees female desire "imaged as turbulent flood, either of water as a general element or, more specifically, as unleashed red flood of all that dangerous, repressed sexual-political matter . . . *simultaneously* the *red* flood of socialist revolution and of menstruation and childbirth" (34; emphasis in original).

This feminized water wave imagery so characteristic of the period, however, is also linked to images of sound, light, and electric waves, and together these overlapping motifs define the New Woman's social force and the social, economic, and political turbulence with which she is associated. Streams of "new immigrants," charged currents of female sexual desire, the "restlessness" of the modern woman, the nervous dis-ease with the demands of American culture, the pleasure and danger of female consumption, the struggles and victories within a social Darwinist marketplace, the ebb and flow of capital in corporate America, all serve as defining factors for the New Woman as a powerful, potentially erratic force. As the New Woman served as a vehicle for this wave energy, she was at once a threat to a masculinized gear and girder technology, a source of vitality to a moribund old-moneyed elite, a less threatening and more tractable force than ethnic Others, but, most importantly, as a conduit for electric energy, she was modern and new, faster and more powerful than forces of old.

Even though popular use of electricity began in the 1870s and 1880s, it was not until the 1890s and the introduction of alternating current, which allowed long-distance power transmission, that industrial, commercial, and then residential use of electricity began to be used on a grand scale. With the harnessing of Niagara Falls for alternating current direct to Buffalo in 1896, and the similarly powered Electric Tower at the Buffalo Pan-American Exposition in 1901, Americans were made aware of the tremendous electric power potential of a distinctly feminized water motion. In Evelyn Rumsey Cary's publicity poster for the exposition, Niagara is an allegorical female nude standing with arms outstretched, veiled by the water of which she is a part; industrial Buffalo appears in a half-moon segment behind her (LaChiusa). The electric generator offered a semblance of control to such a notoriously chaotic element. Indeed, as David Nye notes, the exposition promoted the mastery of electricity in sexualized terms—male science over erratic female force (151). Rather than a disruptive force to be feared, the feminized wave forces could now be harnessed, even wooed for the benefit of all. Writing for the *Independent* in 1901, George Walsh begins by heralding the successful harnessing of the Niagara and then cheerfully expounds that "scientists are studying the power problem with every promise of success, and inventors are coqueting with the tides of the rivers and bays, and with the currents of air that sweep over our heads, and even with the waves of the ocean" (Walsh 556).

At the same time, electricity was celebrated as a new liberating force for women. Writing for the *Independent* in 1902, one editorialist exclaims that rather than fighting for the ballot, women should fight to control the "new power": "Woman must now become an electrician. This achieved, and she passes into control of the force that not only does house work and farm work, but the force that controls the age" ("New Power" 357). In a 1912 article for *Good Housekeeping*, Thomas Edison makes even greater claims about the power of electricity to transform women's lives. He describes the "housewife of the future" as more a "domestic engineer than a domestic laborer, with the greatest of all handmaidens, electricity, at her service" (436). With a bevy of new electric appliances at her command, he continues, woman is developing a "real sex independence" and is newly free to exercise her mental energy, which will in turn build "new fibers, new involutions, and new folds" in the brain (440, 444). With electricity enabling this brain work, the newly evolved woman in "perfect partnership" with the already evolved man will help to redirect the nation's eugenic fears: "We shall stop the cry for more births and raise instead a cry for better births" (444). Charlotte Perkins Gilman likewise saw electricity as a technology intrinsic to women's liberation from domestic servitude. In her serial novel *What Diantha Did* (1909–1910), Gilman presents entrepreneur Diantha Bell who commissions a feminist hotel designed to professionalize domesticity. Taking a tour of the hotel, Diantha "blazed with enthusiasm over the great kitchens, clean as a hospital, glittering in glass and copper and cool tiling, with the swift, sure electric stoves" (242). And for the Washingtons, harnessing electricity was both a crucial skill needed for industrial education and for managing the home, where the woman's influence was paramount, a distinct marker of success among the black professional elite. In Booker T. Washington's *Up from Slavery*, he writes, "My plan was not to teach them to work in the old way, but to show them how to make the forces of nature—air, water, steam, electricity, horse-power—assist them in their labour" (87). The Washingtons' celebrated home, the Oaks, was the first in Macon County, Alabama, to have steam heating and electricity (National Park Service).[26]

And yet the "new power" was also a source of anxiety for writers of the period. As Tim Armstrong argues in his reading of *Sister Carrie*, embracing new electrical technologies brought with it a concomitant acceptance of their dehumanizing potential. Steadfastly linked to gaslight, Hurstwood's suicide is rationalized, and under the direction of the Thomas Edison–like character, Ames, "Carrie is more than simply a human being, a body; she becomes a desiring-machine" (Armstrong 26). For Henry Adams, the new forces were awesomely powerful and yet mysterious, a "symbol of infinity," having the power of the Virgin without the sex. Like the American astronomer and inventor Samuel Pierpont Langley, who, according to Adams, saw the new forces, especially radium, as "anarchical. . . . little short of parricidal in their wicked spirit towards science" (381), Adams saw them as defying measurement and morality. Cather too was anxious about electricity's seemingly immoral force, but especially as it served as an expression of a kind of phallic commercialism. Her social protest story "Behind the Singer Tower" (1912) condemns inadequate fire-safety features for commercial buildings, the exploitation of immigrant laborers, and, most pointedly, the rapacious robber-baron spirit of the age. The narrator looks out "at the great incandescent signs along the Jersey shore, blazing across the night the names of beer and perfumes and corsets, . . . a single name, a single question, could be blazed too far. Our whole scheme of life and progress and profit was perpendicular" (*Twenty-four Stories* 280). For Wharton, likewise, the electric light, which defines Undine Spragg's beauty and power, is "blazing" and "crude" with a "decomposing radiance" that threatens to destroy the subtler shades of Old World refinement she encounters (*Custom*

of the Country 15). At the end of *The House of Mirth,* an exhausted Lily Bart tries
desperately to find refuge in sleep but cannot: "It was as though a great blaze of
electric light had been turned on in her head, and her poor little anguished self
shrank and cowered in it" (250).

And yet for the white writers, riding the electrical current, so to speak, also
became a powerful means of rewriting the "fantasy of feminine evil" so prevalent
in the "restless woman" script. Even if they critique the harsh splendor of the new
medium, Wharton, Johnston, and Glasgow make electric wave energy a defining
principle of the New Woman, while Cather refigures it. The writers of color, by
contrast, create their New Woman protagonists as part of a spiritual, stabilizing
force, not antimodern per se but offering guidance sorely needed in the new
modern age. Sui Sin Far, for example, constructs Mrs. Spring Fragrance, the title
character of her short-story collection, as less an exotic Other to be consumed
and more a rejuvenating "natural" light to refocus; Mrs. Spring Fragrance's re-
freshing presence offers the dominant white culture an opportunity to regain a
clarity in moral vision clouded in modern life.

To explore how each of these writers reconfigures the dominant trope of the
New Woman, I read that discourse in relationship to the other circulating "new"
tropes that these writers appropriated. Those who claimed positive conceptions
of the "New Woman," "New Negro Woman," "New China," and "New South"
risked eliding politically painful pasts in favor of proclaiming their relevance to
the new economy. Accordingly, my project begins with the genesis of the terms
"New Woman" (1894) and "New Negro Woman" (1895) and with the first folio
printing of Charles Dana Gibson's work (1894), and it ends roughly when the
dominant image of the New Woman shifts from Gibson Girl to that of the flapper, which one writer suggests occurred in 1913, and when a new modern consciousness began to emerge with the onset of World War I.[27] While the rhetoric
of the "New South" had a longer tenure, the rhetoric of the "New China" arose
at roughly the same time as the New Woman. All four of these terms would be
used in conjunction with the New Woman and would consequently define her
image as she defined theirs. My study examines the dialogics of these sociopolitical trends as they signaled hope for and anxiety about political and economic
change in a new century.

To establish the rhetorical and visual context within which I will interpret these
women writers' literary production, my first chapter, "Selling the American New
Woman as Gibson Girl," explores the ideological implications of Charles Dana
Gibson's immensely popular visual depictions of American white women. While
rarely depicting women "working" in the marketplace, his images frequently
satirize women as voracious consumers in a marketplace where a "survival of
the best fitted" ethic now prevailed. To subsidize their shopping, Gibson Girls act
as sirens, luring their diminutive fathers and awestruck suitors to their financial
doom. While Gibson's images sanction women's participation in athletics and in

a heterosocial environment, they would seem to undermine New Woman efforts to gain political and economic reform. Intent on acquisition of the latest man or the latest fashion, the Gibson Girl may play tennis, but she never plays politics. Nevertheless, several of the writers I examine appropriated the popular Gibson Girl image for themselves or their characters in order to sanction "progressive" political activities.

In my second chapter, "Margaret Murray Washington, Pauline Hopkins, and the New Negro Woman," I examine how Pauline Hopkins and other writers in the *Colored American Magazine,* including Margaret Murray Washington (Booker T. Washington's third wife), responded to and recast the rhetoric of the "new." The "New Negro" in the dominant white press was the black male rapist, who, without the "civilizing" influence of slavery, revealed his "true" racial inheritance; the "New Negro Woman" was a degraded parody of a legitimate original. Washington recast the image of the New Negro Woman as bourgeois homemaker. In the face of racist oppression, the struggle for subjectivity among black men and women could only begin, according to Washington, after the "new negro woman" established herself at "home," selectively purchasing those objects that signify a new bourgeois class status. For Washington, the primary purpose of the black women's club movement was to help more black women buy and make homes, thereby refuting racist arguments ridiculing black upward mobility. Pauline Hopkins, however, was more ambivalent about appropriating the New Woman trope. She questioned whether the New Woman's focus on individual accomplishment and personal freedom undermined the allegiances men and women must make to fight race, class, and gender oppression. While Hopkins's fictional characters in her last novel, *Of One Blood,* claim bourgeois domesticity, their domestic security depends upon their "new" pan-African consciousness. Hopkins, then, called for a renewed historical, racial, Christian, and social vision seemingly at odds with Margaret Murray Washington's "New Negro Woman," but she was also committed to a vision of black women as race leaders, albeit through indirect influence.

While Edith Wharton depicted the double binds faced by ambitious women in an American culture increasingly devoted to commodity fetishism, she appeared to criticize the demands of those New Women characters who sought to control the commodity exchange. In my third chapter, "Incorporating the New Woman in Edith Wharton's *The Custom of the Country,*" I explore the significance of Wharton's construction of Undine Spragg, the voracious New Woman protagonist of *The Custom of the Country.* With her continually fluctuating desires, Undine, as her name suggests, embodies the wave current of the new age. Devoted to the "new ethic" of quick marriages and easy divorces, flagrant money grubbing, and crass pleasure taking, she is both vibrant and empty, a product of her nouveau riche father's ambition and her mother's dullness. In terms of the popular neo-Darwinist discourse of the times, in which Wharton herself was immersed while writing *The Custom of the Country,* Undine appears as a tremulous new species nominally independent and fiercely imitative, a species that thrives in the mutable marketplace and withers in the domestic sphere. As such, Undine does not simply represent Wharton's anxieties about American culture's moral decay but the need for a shift from an entrepreneurial to a corporate-capitalist ethic. Wharton ultimately transforms the central protagonist of her novel from a roving entrepreneur to a well-managed employee.

My fourth chapter, "Sui Sin Far and the Wisdom of the New," explores how, through the rhetoric of the "new" and the trope of the New Woman, Sui Sin Far worked to combat racism toward Chinese Americans while exploring the consequences of Americanization. On the one hand, Sui Sin Far heralded traditional Chinese values of filial duty and "communal consciousness" while questioning the "new" American values of individual advancement and sexual freedom. This critique of American culture confirmed popular anxieties about modernization and new social roles for women. Yet, in stories like "Mrs. Spring Fragrance" and "The Inferior Woman," Sui Sin Far crafted favorable images of Chinese American characters successfully competing within the American marketplace. These American-identified characters assured readers that Americanization is both possible and preferable, an argument used by progressive imperialists to justify developing American interests in China. While Sui Sin Far gave voice and authority to her American-identified characters, her Chinese-identified characters are curiously voiceless. In "The Wisdom of the New," for example, she foregrounded the difficulty, if not impossibility, of a Chinese-identified woman adopting "new" American cultural and commercial values. While Sui Sin Far may have critiqued aspects of the "new" American culture and New Woman that thwarted the formation of politically necessary alliances between Chinese American men and women, she readily accepted the western influence necessary for the formation of a "New China" and the "New Chinese."

Sui Sin Far's attitude toward the Chinese New Woman, then, is necessarily a vexed one because each word in the phrase is at the center of a contested sociopolitical debate. While she links the Chinese American woman with the term New Woman, she does so uneasily, acutely aware, it would seem, like Hopkins, that the trope carries with it connotations of intersex tension and increasingly racialized sexual transgression even as it represents a personal freedom counter to popular stereotypes of Chinese women's inherent subservience. Rather than spearheading specific reforms, Sui Sin Far's Chinese American female protagonists act as cultural interpreters who offer readings of American culture that are most validated if they demonstrate bicultural influence. Likewise, the dominant version of the white New Woman promises social disruption unless her position is moderated by a Chinese or Chinese-like influence.

In my fifth chapter, "Mary Johnston, Ellen Glasgow, and the Evolutionary Logic of Progressive Reform," Mary Johnston and Ellen Glasgow cast a New Woman with varying degrees of commitment to feminism, socialism, progressivism, and mysticism as the figure best able to assuage the racial and economic anxieties of the developing New South. While Johnston and Glasgow were writing their novels of the New South, they, like Wharton, relied on the various philosophical and social scientific arguments about race, gender, and evolution. But they also incorporated a number of related discourses, all of which had as a foundation both the changing economic order that Wharton addressed and the special place of the South in that order and in the national rhetorics of progress. Even as Johnston and Glasgow crafted similar extended metaphors, such as electricity (as a spiritual harbinger of the modern) and spirituality (as an electric reinvention of tradition), they deployed them in somewhat different ways. Their arguments about the "new" contradicted some of the conclusions of their northern counterparts.

Defined principally by their genteel status and their desire for both economic independence and gradual social reform, Johnston and Glasgow's New Woman protagonists promise none of the social upheaval of an Undine Spragg. Even Johnston's character Hagar's open advocacy of women's enfranchisement, socialism, and transcendental mysticism arouses only immediate family tension rather than the specter of widespread class conflict or social chaos. Johnston and Glasgow express far less ambivalence about the emergence of a New Woman than do Wharton, Hopkins, or Sui Sin Far because their new southern women retain a spiritual commitment to a southern agrarian past, which sustains worthy vestiges of the old social order, even as they work to eliminate some of its worst abuses. Johnston and Glasgow offer their readers the promise that when visionary new (white) women make allegiances with like-minded new (white) men, the genteel white leadership, threatened during Reconstruction and more recent trends in immigration, would be strengthened.

In my final chapter, "Willa Cather and the Fluid Mechanics of the New Woman," I examine the ways in which Willa Cather makes a case for the white New Woman even as she warns of her danger. Defined principally by their gender and sexual transgressions, Cather's New Women are associated with a fluid element that threatens to rupture the very "gear-and-girder" foundations of the new economy. By displacing the anxiety that the white New Woman's transgressive behavior creates onto safer targets—a western landscape already marked as the site of social-political transgression and a group-identified ethnic Other—Cather sanctions her emergence. At the same time, however, the ascendancy of the New Woman in Cather's fiction exposes the fault lines of the emerging corporate culture.

Cather's construction of Alexandra Bergson, for example, deflects many of the arguments against the New Woman—that she was mannish and destined to become a lesbian if her "bold and tom-boyish" behavior went unchecked—by suggesting that her emergence was essential to the development of agricultural technology in an era of professionalization, to the maintenance of white racial hegemony in the face of immigrant threats, and to the creation of social order during a period of sexual transgression. Yet professionalization, bourgeois class identity, whiteness, and compulsory heterosexuality are critiqued even as they appear to triumph: codes of professionalism aligned with Protestant prohibitions create coldness and alienation; the Taylorist work ethic of tireless efficiency crushes human life; white characters continually seek a psychic release offered by marginalized ethnic communities; middle-class consumption hides personal insecurities; seemingly happy marriages conceal destructive turbulence. Even as Cather's white New Women characters promise safe economic development and social control in exchange for their transgressions, the costs of such socioeconomic stability remain high indeed.

Under closer scrutiny, then, a seemingly celebratory term like the New Woman becomes not only a trope of progressive reform, consumer power, and transgressive femininity but also one of racial and ethnic taxonomies, social Darwinism, and imperialist ambitions. As critics, then, we must consider how multicultural and feminist literary studies can obscure differences even as they highlight them. By locating these writers in their historically shifting cultural and political positions while looking for those moments when they each employed "new" rhetoric, I explore the ways in which these writers co-opted, rejected, transformed, and/or reiterated the contested rhetoric of the "New Woman," "New Negro Woman," "New Negro," "New South," and "New China." I aim to reveal the web of New Woman discourse unique to each writer and region but connected by shared cultural anxieties and social aspirations. While these writers may not have read each other's work, they did have overlapping audiences and concerns, a fact that is rarely sufficiently investigated in studies that bring these writers together. Most of the previous critics who have discussed Edith Wharton and Pauline Hopkins together, for example, either treat them as inhabiting separate spheres that overlap historically or as writers sharing the canonically sanctioned, bourgeois individualist ideals of artistic agency or personal independence. While it seems unlikely that Pauline Hopkins read Edith Wharton and even less likely that Wharton read Hopkins, we know both writers read popular novelist Robert Grant's satire of the New Woman in *Unleavened Bread* (1900). Their different anxieties over the New Woman would relate directly to the kind of threat that the popularization of her image posed to their respective communities. Such a historically grounded point of comparison uncovers, I would suggest, a stronger and more revealing fabric than those pre-woven in the political aesthetics of the dominant literary canon. Given how contested the rhetoric of the New Woman was and its continued cultural currency, exploring the nature and ramifications of key New Woman performances becomes imperative as feminism faces new reactionary assaults and co-optive deployments—where a new body and a new image offer all the empowerment one should imagine.

CHAPTER 1

Selling the American New Woman as Gibson Girl

She is loveliness personified. In every way the ideal American beauty—
the woman every girl wanted to be.
—advertisement for Franklin Heirloom Dolls, "The Gibson Girl
 Bride Doll" (1992)

Single, white, affluent, politically and socially progressive, highly educated, and athletic, the dominant version of the New Woman was a liminal figure between the Victorian woman and the flapper, a "pioneer [of] new roles" able to "insist upon a rightful place within the genteel world" (Smith-Rosenberg 245). Considering the relatively small number of women at the turn of the century who could or would lay claim to these attributes, her prototypes sparked tremendous debate. While liberal critics might concede that her appearance was a sign of progress, most others worried that she represented the fundamental erosion of time-honored sex roles.

As a suffragette, for example, the New Woman might be called unattractive, barren, neglectful, and manly, doomed to the rank of spinster, shrewish wife, neglectful mother or housekeeper. In an article for the *New York World* entitled "Here Is the New Woman" (1895), the newspaper presents a "composite made from the photographs of twelve of the most advanced women of the day" including Elizabeth Cady Stanton, Susan B. Anthony, Francis Willard, Belva Lockwood, and the minister and suffrage leader Anna Howard Shaw. In the accompanying article, the writer concedes that the composite face is "strong" and "intellectual" but laments its "stern, unyielding" aspect, later playfully speculating whether "the Old Man . . . would like to marry the woman he sees pictured here," especially one that does not give "greater promise of masculine independence after the ceremony" ("Here Is the New Woman"). And in "*Life*'s Suffragette Contest" (1910), the magazine offered to pay $300 for the "best reason, or reasons, why any man should not marry a suffragette." Reason number twelve was "A suffragette has succeeded in making herself a man, but she has not succeeded in making herself a gentleman" (1050). Gibson warned of the dangers of women's growing demands for empowerment in a sketch featuring a Gibson Girl judge and military leader. A plaintive boy with wings and a tin cup wears a placard reading "I'm Not Blind," while the caption reads "In Days to Come Who Will Look after This Boy?" And in "Ho! For the Suffragettes!" (1911), a line of vermin—including a buffalo bug, red ant, blue fly, cockroach, and flea—carry signs with slogans such as "The New Woman For Us," "Microbes Club / We Vote for Suffragettes," and "Anti Soap Club."

Working as a self-professed artist, the New Woman might be found wanton and a traitor to the delicacies of her sex, or subject to the same criticism as the suffragette. Mary Austin's *A Woman of Genius* (1912)—which celebrated Olivia Latimore's rejection of "true woman" morality in favor of temperamental artistic genius, including a "new" ethic of individualism and sexual expression—apparently offended the wife of one of Austin's publishers at Doubleday, and consequently the book received little endorsement (Austin, *Earth* 320). Kate Chopin's depiction of the sexually transgressive artist Edna Pontellier in *The Awakening* (1900) received similar censure from many contemporary literary critics. Frances Porcher, for example, writes in *The Mirror* (1899) that one would rather beg for "sleep unending . . . than to know what an ugly, cruel, loathsome monster Passion can be when, like a tiger . . . it yawns and finally awakens."

As a college student, the New Woman might be accused of exercising her mind at the expense of her reproductive capabilities, or, like the women active in social-reform movements or the woman's club movement, she could be found guilty of disavowing the heterosexual union by forming unseemly alliances with other women. While sexologist Havelock Ellis seemed to be on the side of sexual liberation in his support of marriage reformer Ellen Key and birth control advocates Margaret Sanger and Marie Stopes, he warned of the rise in "sexual inversion" among young emancipated women.[1] Along with Richard von Krafft-Ebing's work that pathologized "masculine"-behaving women, Ellis's arguments became a powerful tool to those opposed to women's higher education (Smith-Rosenberg 275–80). This fear of the inverted New Woman and her unseemly relationship to other women within the homosocial environment of the women's club is epitomized in an 1897 Cassel cartoon for *Life*. The cartoon features two women at a table playing cards, one in boots, bloomers, and bow tie grimly smoking, spittoon nearby as she lays down her cards. The sign above them reads "New Woman's Club Rules: No Swearing Allowed. Fighting is Prohibited." The caption, in the voice of her card partner, reads, "Naw you don't, my fair and beauteous maid! In this club the queen is high, and your king is the lowest card in the deck."

If the New Woman's proponents celebrated her as just one positive development in a series of exciting cultural changes—"The New Man, New Woman, and New Ideas"—or hailed her as an anodyne to existing social problems, one of her most visible detractors recreated her in a popular, consumable image. Tall, distant, elegant, and white, with a pert nose, voluminous upswept hair, corseted waist, and large bust, Charles Dana Gibson's pen-and-ink drawings of the American girl,

"NAW YOU DON'T, MY FAIR AND BEAUTEOUS MAID! IN THIS CLUB THE QUEEN IS HIGH, AND YOUR KING IS THE LOWEST
CARD IN THE DECK."

Cassel, "Naw You Don't, My Fair and Beauteous Maid!" Cartoon in *Life* (December 2, 1897): 464. Courtesy of the Newberry Library.

the Gibson Girl, offered a popular version of the New Woman that both sanctioned and undermined women's desires for progressive sociopolitical change and personal freedom at the turn of the century. On the one hand, some of Gibson's images pointedly depict the need for progressive reform. In "Going to Work: Dedicated to the Employers of Children" (*Everyday People*), Gibson indicted child-labor practices: a thin child trudges to work in a sea of weary adults. In "The Streets of New York," he calls for better sanitation measures: Gibson Girls hold their noses as sewage pipes are presumably being installed (*Sketches and Cartoons*). Gibson's "Studies in Expression/When Women Are Jurors" pictures an all-female jury whose members sport expressions representing a range of female types: the showy wide-eyed open-mouthed wonderer, the portly, mannish deliberator, the world-weary old woman, but most strikingly the flirtatious Gibson Girl (*Social Ladder*). Such an image suggests the inevitability of national suffrage even as it perpetuates long-held gender stereotypes used by antisuffragists. The fabulously rich in Gibson's images are often unhappy—bloated with self-indulgence or pinched with envy—while the young poor suggest all the promise of undiscovered Gibson Girls.

On the other hand, Gibson's commitment to some progressive reforms did not include an endorsement of women's political organizing, a fact that Fairfax Downey recalled in his celebratory biography of the illustrator: "'In a mass of women, you lose entirely the irresistible appeal of the individual,' Gibson remarked. 'They are rather terrifying *en masse*. You don't get the usual feeling but a chilly sensation and you think you ought to see a doctor,' he added with a grin. 'Architecturally women don't fit into a parade. They lack the swing of soldiers, and the careful selection a stage manager uses in picking a chorus is impossible'" (318). Gibson portrayed those women who did engage in public politics as humorless, severe, and portly. In "A Suffragette's Husband" (1911), for example, Gibson depicted a bespectacled double-chinned woman casting a stern gaze on her beleaguered but resigned husband, whose dog sits nearby in mute sympathy (*Other People*). The primary vehicle for his images, the humor magazine *Life*, offered even more pointed critiques of suffragists, socialists, and women club workers.[2] In 1910, for example, it ran a fictional column describing the trials of an ambitious suffragette by "a practical pragmatist, a theoretical Socialist, but as yet . . . not . . . a connubialist, 'Miss Priscilla Jawbones,'" whose visage—gaptoothed, dowdy, and bespectacled—accompanied many of her columns ("A New Member" 429).

A SUFFRAGETTE'S HUSBAND

Charles Dana Gibson, "A Suffragette's Husband." *Other People* (1911). Courtesy of the University of Iowa.

And yet Gibson did present women dominating the mating game and less frequently smoking, drinking, swimming, golfing, or posing as college girls and jurors. In "Girls Will Be Girls" (1897), a group of Gibson Girls casually smoke and drink after a day of horseback riding and golfing. With golf clubs strewn about them and pictures of a boxing match and a bulldog behind them, these Gibson Girls seem little concerned with having entered a male domain. Even though picturing women drinking and smoking was uncharacteristic of Gibson, his images almost invariably promoted a measure of women's personal independence, self-actualization, and sexual assertiveness. The tremendous proliferation and appeal of her image, and the bevy of imitations her success sparked, makes her image the most influential version of the New Woman.[3] Meanwhile, the tremendous popularity of vaudeville among women, whose eccentric female performers were frequently "fat, dark-skinned or 'too mannish,'" challenged dominant conceptions of feminine beauty and behavior (Kibler 14). Popular icons such as George DuMaurier's Trilby and actresses Lillian Russell and Mae West likewise offered the American public, in some respects, a significantly different vision of popularized feminism. And yet it was the Gibson Girl and her imitators—Howard Chandler Christy, James Montgomery Flagg, and Harrison Fisher—that dominated the marketplace and hence became the foremost visual icon interpolating gendered, classed, and racialized subjects.[4]

Her figure is also the common element linking these regionally, ethnically, and politically distinctive writers of new womanhood in the period. Charlotte Perkins Gilman, for example, lauded the Gibson Girl as a New Woman representing women's legal, social, mental, and physical progress, a symbol of their growing freedom from the sexual-economic relationship with men:

> The Gibson Girl and the Duchess of Towers,—these are the new women; and they represent a noble type, indeed. The heroines of romance and drama today are of a different sort from the Evelinas and Arabellas of the last century. . . . The false sentimentality, the false delicacy, the false modesty, the utter falseness of elaborate compliment and servile gallantry which went with the other falsehoods,—all these are disappearing. Women are growing honester, braver, stronger, more healthful and skillful and able and free, more human in all ways. (*Women and Economics* 148–49)

One of Edith Wharton's earliest stories, "Mrs. Manstey's View" (1893), was illustrated by Gibson, and arguably her most vibrant female protagonist, Undine Spragg, was the most Gibson Girl–like of all.[5] John H. Adams's New Negro Women, especially Gussie, the last image and only full-length portrait, is in the style of Christy, and the prototype for the New Negro Woman, Margaret Murray Washington, was explicitly compared to a Gibson Girl. In the second decade of the new century, *McClure's*, a primary magazine vehicle for Jane Addams and Willa Cather, featured Gibson Girls on a series of its covers. And even though

ιved over *Trilby,* F. Graham Cootes's illustrations for her novel *Alexander's*
the "Bohemian Girl" by Sigismond de Ivanowski, and the frontispiece
Pioneers! by Clarence Underwood emphasized the feminine power of the
ιle-class American Girl rather than the working-class, boyish Bohemianism
of Trilby. Writing for *Harper's Bazaar,* Julia Magruder imagined "The Typical
Woman of the New South" as a Christy Girl, and Johnston's New Woman of the
New South, in particular, represented a similar pinnacle of evolutionary development. And, finally, Sui Sin Far indirectly invoked the Gibson Girl's signature
love of shopping and adornment while making the case that the Chinese woman
was, in fact, the original new woman.

At the same time, however, Gibson's images often co-opted the desire for
sociopolitical change into a desire for new material goods. During a period of
intense social and political turmoil, his images worked to create a stabilized modern American identity by not only reiterating the bourgeois individualist ideals
upon which the emerging corporate culture was based but also by asserting the
primacy of Anglo-Saxon womanhood. The Gibson Girl embodied the values
necessary to sustain a consumer-based economy: insatiable demand, purchasing
power, and commodity discernment. As a definitive sign of a modern ethos, the
legitimization of personal preference, be it in shopping for men or a mate, is often
a central theme in Gibson's illustrations. In an article for the *Atlantic Monthly*
(1901), Caroline Ticknor envisions a meeting between the Steel-Engraving Lady
and the Gibson Girl. Ensconced in domestic and spiritual bliss, the Victorian
Steel-Engraving Lady eagerly awaits the return of her adoring husband when
the Gibson Girl bursts in wearing "a short skirt and heavy square-toed shoes,
a mannish collar, cravat, and vest, and a broadbrimmed felt hat tipped jauntily
upon one side." The two types debate their respective virtues, the Gibson Girl
proclaiming,

> we are so imbued with modern thought that we have done away with all the
> oversensitiveness and overwhelming modesty in which you are enveloped. We
> have progressed in every way. When a man approaches, we do not tremble and
> droop our eyelids, or gaze adoringly while he lays down the law. We meet him
> on a ground of perfect fellowship, and converse freely on every topic . . .
>
> Whether he *likes* it or not makes little difference; *he* is no longer the one whose
> pleasure is to be consulted. The question now is, not "What does man like?" but
> "What does woman prefer?" That is the keynote of modern thought. (106)

The Gibson Girl's desire for political equality—the "ground of perfect fellowship"—is transformed in this narrative into the desire to exert personal preference. Rather than disavowing Victorian ideals of patriarchal authority, deferring
to a woman's preference becomes an act of chivalry in a modern age.

With her corseted waist and discerning aspect, the Gibson Girl also foregrounded the need for the management skills necessary for the development of corporate

bureaucracies and imperialist ventures. Yet even as Gibson's illustrations extolled the virtues and rewards of emulating the Gibson Girl image—reminding viewers that by both consuming goods and managing the body, one could produce a better self—his images also evoked what William Leach describes as one of the principal anxieties of the advertising age: that "pecuniary (or market values)" now defined one's worth. "Increasingly, the worth of everything—even beauty, friendship, religion, the moral life—was being determined by what it could bring in the market" (7–8). For women positioned increasingly as commodities and consumers within this culture, the task of seeking new rights and freedoms associated with the New Woman meant exploiting and being exploited by the complex ideology the Gibson Girl images promoted.

Everywhere ready to emulate, her image appeared in popular magazines, novels, and theatrical productions, as well as on a plethora of objects to be owned by or exchanged among women (Koch 72). New technologies that allowed for the mass reproduction of lithographs helped to circulate her image to millions of readers. Gibson illustrated for best-selling novelists such as Richard Harding Davis, Anthony Hope, and Robert Chambers; for popular magazines, most notably for *Life, Collier's,* and *McClure's;* and for a series of folio volumes, many devoted exclusively to his images. Dances, songs, and clothing styles were named after the Gibson Girl. Tableaux vivants of Gibson Girl drawings became entertainments at social gatherings (Banner 154). Calendars, decorator plates, postcards, pyrographic glove boxes and plaques, dresser sets, brooches, flasks, and cigarette cases featured her image in various poses. Her image became so popular that, as Lois Banner writes, "Observers noted that women on the streets all seemed to look like Gibson girls. 'Fifth Avenue,' wrote Mark Sullivan, 'is like a procession of Gibsons'" (154).

Debates in the popular press about Gibson's original model for this new vision of American beauty signified the extent to which the Gibson Girl's popularity crossed class, regional, and ethnic lines. Rumored at first to be the image of Irene Langhorne (the Virginia socialite who would become Gibson's wife), the Gibson Girl was later believed to be either the likeness of Minnie Clark, a professional model of Irish descent and working-class background, or the likeness of a personal maid to the popular dancer Loie Fuller. Daughter of a French father and a Cuban mother, Fuller's maid appeared proof to some American journalists that assimilation could, in fact, prove successful (Banner 158). The wide circulation of the Gibson Girl image and the debates over her origins allowed women who did not have the ethnic or class signifiers of Gibson Girl status to redeploy her image, in effect taking on the role of the Gibson Girl as masquerade. With at least some of the trappings of the Gibson Girl look, women of color could demonstrate their amenability to assimilation and their consequent right to the franchise and social esteem. Black women, for example, might adopt her image to suggest that the legacy of slavery in no way permanently affected the progress of the race. Working-class women could embrace Gibson Girl images as they sanctioned unchaperoned heterosocial environments. While engaging in emerging forms of commercial entertainment, these women could experiment "with new cultural forms that articulated gender in terms of sexual expressiveness and social interaction with men, linking heterosocial culture to a sense of modernity, individuality, and personal style. Creating this style was an assertion of self, a working-class variant of the 'New Woman'" (Peiss 6).

The major distributors of the Gibson Girl image, however, worked to control the ways in which her image would be deployed. Upon introducing the Gibson Girl to *Collier's Weekly* in 1902, Robert Grant distinguished seven distinct types of Gibson Girls: the Beauty, the Boy-girl, the Flirt, the Sentimental, the Convinced, the Ambitious, and the Well-balanced. Readers were encouraged to identify their own "type," and Grant quotes one testimonial from a woman writer who glorifies them all: "We love her already, as we adored her original; we worship her exalted beauty, and if it were given unto women to make themselves over according to their own desires, the world would, almost without an exception, be peopled with charming magnificent Gibson types" (Grant, "Charles Dana Gibson" 8–9). As women were encouraged to distinguish among various types of female beauty and to fight for the rights to lay claim to their status, they were also increasingly encouraged to distinguish between and vie for various similar products. Yet even while encouraging women to identify themselves with an advertiser's prepackaged conception of selfhood, these types did offer women a degree of freedom from the strictures of Victorian femininity. Women might claim previously unsanctioned subject positions like the "Boy-girl," "Flirt," and "Ambitious." Who knew what the "Ambitious Boy-girl" might do?

While any woman could appropriate her image, as Charles Dana Gibson conceived her, the Gibson Girl was an essentially "white" bourgeois ideal representing the pinnacle of evolutionary accomplishment and serving as the foundation for American dominance on a world stage. In 1913 Walter Tittle presented on the cover of *Life* a Gibson Girl figure in a white dress, her torso thrust forward, left arm akimbo, a monkey perched on her shoulder. The caption reads "Evolution." Fellow illustrator Howard Chandler Christy claimed that the American Girl "will become a veritable queen of the kingliest of races" (12). According to Christy, she united the best of Western European characteristics and stood with her mate not only as the culmination of American progress, but also as the ultimate justification for imperialism:[6] "She has stood shoulder to shoulder in subduing the wilderness; hand in hand with them she has blazed her way through the forests; alternately with them she has stood on guard against their savage foes; she has even borne, by the aid of her superb physique, a nearly equal share in their Titanic labor of carrying forward into the wilds the standard of civilization" (15–16). Even though Gibson's images by themselves were rarely overtly nationalistic and *Life* was anti-imperialist,[7] Gibson's images of the American girl were quite similar to

Vol. 61, No. 1589. April 10, 1913
Copyright, 1913, Life Publishing Company

Walter Tittle, "Evolution." Cover of *Life* (April 10, 1913). Courtesy of the Newberry Library.

FORE!
THE AMERICAN GIRL TO ALL THE WORLD.
(1900)

Charles Dana Gibson, "Fore! The American Girl to All the World." Illustration in *Americans* (1900). Courtesy of the University of Iowa.

Christy's—the Independence Day 1903 *Life* explicitly featured the Gibson Girl as Columbia—and played a crucial role in promoting white supremacy and imperialist conquest. Three years after the Gibson Girl's debut in *Life,* the Chicago Columbian Centennial of 1893 featured statuesque Gibson Girl types as emblems of national power, wealth, and liberty.[8] Statues such as the monumental version of Columbia and Daniel Chester French's representation of the Republic presiding over the Court of Honor prompted one visitor to remark, "To our eyes, those statues look rather like monumental versions of the Gibson Girl" (quoted in Banner 326 n. 33). Compared to the White City's numerous ethnographic exhibits, which reminded viewers of the world's exotic, "pre-civilized" racial types, Columbia would serve as an emblem of white racial pride and imperialist imperative. In an image resonating perhaps even greater such ideological imperatives, "Fore! The American Girl to All the World" featured a Gibson Girl holding a golf club in one hand while the other is outstretched in caution. She both hails and warns the world of her ascendance (Gibson, *Americans*).

Yet nowhere is the linkage between New Woman independence and imperialist conquest more direct in Gibson's work than in the illustrations he did for his

long-time friend Richard Harding Davis, after whom the Gibson Man was modeled (Downey 102). In Davis's novel *Soldiers of Fortune* (1897), the New Woman
protagonist, Hope Langham, becomes engaged to the swashbuckling American
mercenary Clay, who quells a fictional Latin American revolution. As Amy Kaplan
argues, Davis's plot was characteristic of popular historical romances of the day,
which make the New Woman essential to the formation of the New Empire: "The
heroines prove their own modernity by at once freeing themselves from traditional hierarchies and voluntarily subduing themselves to some 'real live man,'
just as imperial subjects . . . prove their capacity for liberation through their alliance with American power" (*Anarchy of Empire* 108). Yet the illustrated *Soldiers*
refigures that conquest as feminine—the cover of the novel features a Gibson Girl
striding confidently forward alone, and in the final illustration Hope is noticeably
taller, almost eclipsing a more subdued Clay—which both soft sells the violence
of conquest and destabilizes the patriarchal authority of its assertion.

As "queen of the kingliest of races," the American Girl's most important duty
was a maternal one. Noting the "obvious fact" of the "law of heredity" and environmental "daily influence," the Rev. Henry C. Potter urged the female readers
of *Harper's Monthly Magazine* in 1901 to consider their civic responsibility to be
good mothers (101, 103): "Somebody has said that the Founders of the Republic
bred great offspring because, though burdened beyond the conception even of
the modern mothers, the women gave themselves, first of all and before all, to the
rearing of their children. We are in danger, some of us, of getting a little too fine
for that, and it is a peril that should be taken very seriously" (104). In a 1903 article
for *Good Housekeeping,* William Allen White likewise cautioned women that they
had tremendous responsibilities as the producers of little men: "If the boy sees
an ill-kept house, slovenly housekeeping, and a grunty, slouchy, whiney mother
. . . the world is going to have a miserable time teaching that boy to work and get
ahead and be forehanded and keep out of the poorhouse . . . So much advice is
given to boys and so little to mothers of boys, who are the real man-makers in this
world" (406). How would the mother who does not keep her home and herself
well-managed, White suggests, ever successfully produce the men equipped to
run the nation? Such injunctions reached a peak with the passage of President
Wilson's Mother's Day resolution in 1914, which called on Americans to display
the American flag while expressing "love and reverence for the mothers of our
country." According to Anne Ruggles Gere, Wilson's resolution promoted "an
ideology of motherhood that undercut the new woman by publicly celebrating
the importance of the private domestic relationship to the nation" (139).

While the New Woman as college student too often deferred or outright rejected her maternal obligation, the Gibson Girl offered assurances of eventual
marriage and children. Many late-nineteenth-century physicians conceived of the
body as a closed energy system in which a certain amount of nervous energy was
subject to a strict bodily economy. People could either lose their nervous energy

gh moral or economic profligacy, or they could wisely reinvest their limited
ɪnt of nerve force by engaging in "productive" labor (Lutz 3). Productive
_ r for men meant engaging in bouts of physical exertion to compensate for
the feminizing effects of brain work in an increasingly urban environment. For
white middle-class women, however, who were naturally frail and hypersensi-
tive to begin with, such mental exercise could prove disastrous to their reproductive capabilities: "The woman who favored her mind at the expense of her
ovaries—especially the woman who spent her adolescence and early adulthood
in college and graduate school—would disorder a delicate physiological balance.
Her overstimulated brain would become morbidly introspective. Neurasthenia,
hysteria, insanity would follow. Her ovaries, robbed of energy rightfully theirs,
would shrivel, and sterility and cancer ensue" (Smith-Rosenberg 258). The Gibson Girl seemed to assure consumers that that "delicate physiological balance"
would be maintained. Rarely a college student and always more concerned with
finding a mate, the Gibson Girl showed none of the signs of a nervous disposition. The "well-balanced" Gibson Girl type was, in fact, according to Robert
Grant, "the artist's favorite, for it is she who comes nearest to the ideal of young
American Womanhood. The Well-balanced Girl is all harmony, she is loved by
many men, she refuses many offers of marriage and still retains the friendship
of the men" ("Charles Dana Gibson" 8). As series such as *The Education of Mr.
Pipp* reassure, neither her selection in men nor her production of children were
infinitely delayed.

The Gibson Girl also transformed the threat of the New Woman as masculine
woman, who in continuing to defy conventional gender roles not only risked endangering her reproductive capabilities but also risked becoming an androgyne
or manly woman. In plays such as Laura Parson's *The New Woman's Reform Club*
(1902), female guards presiding over a club meeting admonish, in this case with the
proverbial battle-axe, an unwelcome male intruder and spy. In Edith Wharton's
novella *Sanctuary,* the heroine must successfully oppose Clemence Verney, who is
"'patently of the new school': a young woman of feverish activities and broad-cast
judgments, whose very versatility [makes] her hard to define" (84). With the figure
of "young St. John of Donatello's" and a decidedly masculine ambition, Verney
thinks it glorious to "go crashing through obstacles, straight up to the thing one is
after," and she poses a threat to the higher moral vision of the male protagonist's
conventionally feminine mother (95). The Gibson Girl, whose "dainty femininity
is one of her chief charms" (Grant, "Charles" 8), certainly attempted to put to
rest any fears of the growing masculinization of American women, even though
she too would likely go "crashing through obstacles" for what she wanted. While
her stature connoted formidability, her large bust, cinched waist, and voluminous
hair would come to define feminine allure and fecundity.

It was the specter of what Theodore Roosevelt popularized as "race suicide"
that encapsulated most dramatically the threat that the New Woman's activities

posed. Rising divorce and declining birth rates among middle-class, native-b
white women only exacerbated fears that the New Woman's emergence was a
sign that the "kingliest of races" was in trouble. By presenting images of essentially white women who devoted nearly all of their energies to maintaining their
image in order to acquire a suitably vigorous mate, the Gibson Girl helped to alleviate fears that "race suicide" was being committed by educated white women
(Gibson, *Everyday People*). Although Gibson seldom pictured her with offspring,
the Gibson Girl at least promised fertility, if not maternal devotion, given her
single-minded devotion to securing a mate.

Like Gibson, Charlotte Perkins Gilman promoted the Gibson Girl as an evolved
type who would assuage eugenic fears about racial degeneration. But while Gibson
assured his audience that the fundamental concern of white bourgeois women
was success in the mating dance—hence the joke of "Race Suicide"—rather than
sociopolitical liberation, Gilman's deployment of the Gibson Girl suggested that
women's sociopolitical liberation would mean that they could dictate the outcome
of that dance. The growing physical, economic, and social autonomy of white
women was to provide a substantial racial payoff because women would choose
their mates more wisely. Indeed, the Gibson Girl represented a definite marker
of progress not only because she was "more human," and thus encouraged a

RACE SUICIDE.

Charles Dana Gibson, "Race Suicide." Illustration in *Everyday People* (1904). Courtesy
of the University of Iowa.

cooperative ethic essential to modern industrial society, but also because she was more in charge of sexual selection. While men neglected their duty to select a mate "for points of racial superiority," choosing, instead, to please themselves with a superficially attractive mate, women, as mothers of the race, would work to ensure racial progress (Gilman, *Man-Made World* 31). Patriarchy, then, not only indicated a lower stage of evolutionary development—"[p]ractically all our savages are decadent, and grossly androcentric"—but also threatened the very progress of the race (Gilman, "Personal Problems"). As Louise Newman writes, "Gilman held that the solution to the problem of 'race suicide' was to make (white) women economically independent of men so that (white) women could once again resume control over sexual selection" (*White Women's Rights* 138).

Gibson did not unequivocally celebrate woman's role as sexual selector because he also emphasized the anxiety this new social dynamic would provoke. As an image from *The Weaker Sex* series (1903) demonstrates, the Gibson Girl's need to choose the best mate—the mate best able to provide—meant that her image could never be comfortably consumed by a male viewer. The Gibson Girl acts in this image as both exacting in her duty as sexual selector and alluring as desirous object, an ambivalent position that might well make her suitor feel "the latest victim of some fair entomologist." Or, in a 1903 Valentine's Day issue of *Life,* the Gibson Girl literally juggles her miniaturized suitors, begging both the question, "Which one of them will she drop?" and the even more unsettling thought, "Will she drop any at all?" As an entomologist or a juggler, these images emphasize male anxieties when the American Girl, at once demanding and capricious, controls the market in men and consumer goods. Might the Gibson Girl's fastidious inspection discover too many inadequacies? Might she, as Undine Spragg managed to do so successfully in Edith Wharton's *The Custom of the Country* (1913), juggle her suitors even after her juggling days were supposedly over? Might she not keep preferring when she seems to have preferred?

Lasciviousness was, however, along with virilization, the most common charge brought against the New Woman. The New Woman's sexuality—supposedly free from social or moral restraints—was viewed as a threat both to the marital fidelity necessary to insure rightful paternity and to the maternal devotion necessary to insure racial progress. In "Is the New Woman Really New?" (1896), for example, Maurice Thompson laments the road that the "irresponsible" New Woman in literature has taken, a road "paved with erotic poetry and the fiction of free love and marital infidelity, beginning her new life by posing as a victim bound in loveless marriage-chains on the altar of monstrous social injustice" (235). Thompson's depiction of the New Woman as a decadent fraud, wanton and "irresponsible," evokes Mary Russo's construction of the female grotesque as the antithesis of western figurations of classical beauty. Drawing from Bakhtin's notion of the grotesque body within carnival—"the open, protruding, extended, secreting body, the body of becoming, process, and change"—Russo sees the female grotesque

Charles Dana Gibson, "We May Conjecture That Being a Bachelor the Hero Probably Imagines Himself the Latest Victim of Some Fair Entomologist." Illustration in *The Weaker Sex* (1903). Courtesy of the Library of Congress.

as "loaded with all of the connotations of fear and loathing associated with the biological processes of reproduction and aging" (219). Certainly, as some New Woman literature foregrounded an emerging female sexuality that violated the boundaries of marriage and rejected strictly heterosexual expressions, it inspired such fear and loathing. In Kate Chopin's *The Awakening* (1899), Edna Pontellier flirts with Robert Lebrun, has an affair with Alcée Arobin, leaves her husband, and finally embraces the power of her own sexuality in a symbolic union with the sea. Such depictions of unfettered sexuality prompted one reviewer to charge the novel with promoting "unholy imaginations and unclean desires" in the impressionable minds of young readers ("Books of the Week" 150).

Rather than trying to eliminate the threat that the image of the grotesque female body evokes, Gibson refigures that threat to reflect the evolving gendered and racialized anxieties in the new commodity culture. In what at first seems a curious contradiction, he draws the Gibson Girl as both a towering, potentially castrating figure and a weightless but alluring siren. When illustrated floating over chasms or tossed in waves, she seems unencumbered by the spiritual and moral determinacy deposited in Victorian white womanhood and hardly able to share in any of Christy's "Titanic labor" of carrying forward Anglo-Saxon civilization.

Such weightlessness suggested the danger of the Gibson Girl persona even as it indicated a liberation from the dictates of prescribed femininity. In "One of the Disadvantages of Being in Love with an Athletic Girl," a running Gibson Girl floats over a chasm as her lover waits helpless and astonished on the other side. Or in "Plenty of Good Fish in the Sea" (1902; *Social Ladder*), Gibson Girls are tossed and turned in a wave. In an image strikingly analogous to Edna Pontellier's final swim, Gibson's "Not the Sea Serpent, but Far More Dangerous" (1899; *Americans*) reiterated the threat that Edna's sea-sexuality posed to dominant culture's sexual mores. In this image, a Gibson Girl's head emerges from a vast expanse of ocean with an expression of blissful contentment. The Gibson Girl is "dangerous" here because of what Bram Dijkstra describes as the "antimaternal, luxuriantly auto-erotic implications of the theme of the weightless woman" (91). Narcissistically absorbed in her own sensual bliss, she seems unconcerned with finding a mate, let alone propagating the race. In some respects, like Wharton's Undine Spragg, whose fluctuating desires were akin to the undulations of the eponymous water nymph, the Gibson Girl's beauty threatened to mask moral vacuity. Was she, indeed, merely the embodiment of a "physical and moral life . . . suffocating in their ease, weightless in their lack of significance"? (Lears 45). The fetishization of her fractured form—only her head appears above water—merely foregrounds her essential lack and his. One must view her bliss, created by the sensual luxury of the swim and the acknowledgment of the gaze, from afar because the fetishized object is always out of reach.

At the same time, the success of Gibson's images lay in his ability to evoke dominant cultural anxieties associated with the liminal figure, then assuage them, only to evoke them yet again, a strategy characteristic of successful advertising. In images such as "Bygone Summers: A Frieze for an Old Gentleman's Room" (1902; *Social Ladder*) or "A Peach Crop" (1903; *Weaker Sex*), Gibson Girl heads are plentiful blossoms to be picked or fruit to be plucked by a delighted male viewer. As Dijkstra points out, positioning women in trees was a common variation on the anxieties of the weightless woman: "not merely symbolic of her desire to be 'fertilized' and of her urge for physical pleasure but also of her 'static' qualities, her physical, erotic self-sufficiency" (96). Without the "grounding" imagery of breasts and hips, however, her "erotic self-sufficiency" is diminished to make her consumption that much easier. The heads are at the point of harvest, fetishized products to be marketed and consumed. While the accessibility of her image, its very status as a mass-marketed commodity—Gibson Girl heads even appeared as an abstract wallpaper pattern—was at odds with her inviolability, such images removed much of the threat of the floating woman's sensual egoism or the statuesque woman's power to emasculate by restoring the primacy of patriarchal control.

Yet in this new culture dominated by "pecuniary values," such control was predicated less on biblical strictures or cultural mores and more on market-place success, which, given the fact that the country was still recovering from the financial panics of the early 1890s, made the role of the provider a necessarily anxious one. Maintaining a Gibson Girl image with the necessary clothing and jewelry could, quite easily, bankrupt her mate or her father. In his popular series *The Education of Mr. Pipp* (1899), for example, Gibson presents the forlorn, diminutive, socially awkward, and financially drained Mr. Pipp. A figure not unlike Mr. Spragg in *The Custom of the Country,* Mr. Pipp is dragged through Europe's clothiers and jewelers by his wife and two statuesque Gibson Girl daughters. The girls secure their corresponding Gibson Men, and the series ends with Mr. Pipp proudly holding his two grandchildren. At this point, his Gibson Girl daughters no longer gather around him vying for gifts or tower above him as they make their social debut; instead, all attention is fixed on the children. For the moment, paternalism and patrilineage replace consumerism, and Mr. Pipp, the caption tells us, "has learned that he has not lived in vain." By successfully maintaining his Gibson Girls until those maintenance costs may be covered by their husbands, Mr. Pipp is repaid in the form of his grandson, Mr. Hiram Pipp Willing, whose surname promises the next generation's dutiful acceptance of Gibson Girl development costs. At the same time, however, we are reminded that the bankruptcy process could continue; sitting on Mr. Pipp's other knee is his granddaughter, who may very well grow up to bankrupt yet another generation of American men.

In other words, by representing the male viewer/consumer's unrealized ideal, the Gibson Girl could evoke the very anxieties of inadequacy that purchasing her image was supposed to assuage. Viewing subjects could never be assured of gaining their love objects. The Gibson Girl may marry for money or title rather than love, and fetishizing her form would only make the possibility of her loss that much more terrifying. As these threats are continually reenacted and only partially alleviated by the male viewer's voyeuristic and fetishistic responses, they underscore the instability of subjectivity within the heterosexual marketplace in which the Gibson Girl is exchanged.

For women, their role in the new economy was even more vexing since their desire constituted both a threat and the foundation of the new consumer-based economy. Even as the Gibson Girl's sybaritic desires were continually emphasized, so too were implicit admonishments to control those desires with both the corset and the laws of decorum. Popular advice columns and advertisements likewise espoused the "rational" benefits of female self-management. Columnist Marie Gregoire, for example, makes a case for self-management in her defense of stays in the new bathing attire: "Bathing corsets are now made that are both rational and becoming. They are of canvas and have few bones; and, while not stiff enough or tight enough to impede the movements of the body muscles, do give some support to the figure and prevent the utter collapse and shapelessness that befalls many women when they discard stays entirely" (14). While dress reformers were proclaiming the ill effects of striving for the corseted "S"-shaped silhouette, a silhouette the Gibson Girl diligently maintained, they had only a minimal effect on an increasingly influential corset industry who benefited from the impracticality of making fashionable corsets at home (Banner 148). An advertisement for Redfern Corsets promises "perfection of shape," while the Rosalind Waist and Belt Adjuster offers further monitoring of that shape. The W.B. Erect Form Corset advertisement featured in a 1901 *Ladies' Home Journal* offers more definitive rewards for maintaining self-control (Weingarten 33). While two of the framing female figures seem to lose themselves in thoughts of romance as they wear the "French Shape" model, the larger figure in the center of the advertisement appears to wear her corset with personal pride—in semi-profile, her gaze cast ahead. The advertising copy proclaims, "It is a health corset. It is a surpassingly beautiful corset. It throws the shoulders back into a fine military poise." While the image of a soldier's "military poise" may evoke the desire of some new women for revolutionary change, it effectively co-opts that desire into the desire for managerial self-control.[9]

In advanced consumer capitalism, Robert Crawford maintains, an "unstable, agonistic" construction of personality is produced by the contradictory nature of contemporary economic logic. On the one hand, "producer-selves" must sublimate, delay, and repress desires for immediate gratification, thus cultivating the work ethic. In addition, I would argue, the producer ethic demands that one learn to exert better control over and manage others. On the other hand, as Crawford notes, "consumer-selves" best serve the capitalist economy by endlessly capitulating to their desires: by acting on impulse, indulging every whim (90). Because women are designated foremost as consumers, this tension is greatest for them; the producer self continually necessitates the regulation and suppression of the consumer self. Women's incentive to learn to manage and suppress these desires is the promise of power through indirect influence of the mates they attract.

The Gibson Girl was perhaps the first full embodiment of this tension in American advertising. With her self-control (corseted small waist and collared neck) and social control, in conjunction with her seemingly insatiable desire for goods, the Gibson Girl affirmed the values of the emerging corporate culture. Readers of those popular magazines in which Gibson's images appeared were often reminded of the importance of maintaining this tension. Consider the following punning exchange from a 1901 issue of *Life:*

> Isobel: How perfectly your frock fits, dear. I thought you college girls soared
>   above such trifles.
> Hypatia: Oh, No! We believe in the survival of the best fitted. (433)

Like Gibson, this anonymous writer assured readers that the New Woman as college girl maintained both her desire for consumer goods and the work ethic necessary for successful competition. The competitive ideal of the social Darwinist marketplace would be maintained even in a potentially subversive homosocial environment.

Gibson Girl status, then, required a contractual obligation. Only by performing the identity the Gibson Girl image implied could one reap the rewards her image promised. The successful marketing of the Gibson Girl and the products she endorsed was in great part due to the apparent ease with which it appeared one may fulfill that contract. Charles Dana Gibson's marriage to Irene Long- horne, a Virginian socialite and Gibson model, for example, was widely touted as the convergence of fantasy and reality. Several months before their marriage in November 1895, the *New York World* issued the caption, "The Face of Romance and the Face of Reality" next to an image of Gibson, Irene Longhorne, and the Gibson Girl. Advertisers for Eastman Kodak employed a free-spirited "Kodak girl" in 1902 to represent the image one might take with their product as well as the ease with which one may become the image photographed (Eastman). The Gibson Girl proved that one could become the image that one saw—an image of a desiring/desirable subject, expertly managing the desire she evokes. In an advertisement for Gibson Pyrography, a Gibson Girl type is shown creating a pyrographic Gibson Girl reproduction (Thayer and Chandler). And in *Life*'s "Contest of Beauty," a prize of $100 was offered to the person who "correctly" ranked twenty heads in order of their beauty. In numerous advertisements for new novels, the reader is offered a sum of money for choosing the best conception of the heroine from a series of female types. By scripting women as the judges of these contests, the advertisements discouraged the formation of a cooperative group consciousness among women, a consciousness arguably encouraged in women's colleges or in gender-segregated workplaces, and encouraged instead competition among women for that elusive position of most beautiful. Similarly, Gibson's "Rival Beauties" (1900; *Americans*) depicts two Gibson Girls feigning civility with one hand and dangling an axe with the other while their respective, and decidedly unattractive, suitors stand behind them, fearing the worst. Such advertisements highlight women's paradoxical position in consumer culture, where they are encouraged "to survey themselves as objects in relation to a male gaze, and . . . actively work to create themselves as objects in a consumer culture" (Lury 143). So even while Gibson frequently satirized female narcissism, he en- couraged that vanity since it fueled, to quote Thorstein Veblen, the "conspicu- ous consumption" necessary to achieve trophy status and thereby represent the "vicarious leisure" or wealth of the husband (83).

Advertisements and illustrations featuring black women often satirized their ambitions at becoming the more highly valued Gibson Girl. Edward Kemble's illustrations throughout the pages of *Life* caricatured black women performing a wide range of Gibson Girl activities—that is, golfing, flirting, bicycle riding, and shopping—to emphasize either their emasculating traits, as mammy figures; or their oversexed characteristics, as jezebels; or, more generally, their hopelessly imitative nature. On the October 5, 1899, cover of *Life*, for example, Kemble draws a black man gazing at a black woman in formal dress—as a parody of a classic Gibson Girl moment of romantic allure and feminine self-absorption. But here the woman is thin, her facial features grotesque, and clothes ill-fitting, while the man is short, pot-bellied, with similar grotesque features. The caption reminds readers of the joke—she will never be able to pass—even as it invokes the anxiety that some are passing. Likewise, an advertisement for F.P.C. Wax plays on the joke of the black Other as Gibson Girl. Here a smiling black mammy figure sees her reflection on the surface of an iron. Positioning the iron so close to her face while casting her in the role of domestic servant reminds readers of the ludicrousness of her attempt at Gibson Girl–like vanity.

·LIFE·

The Fat Lady on the Hill: MISTER WIMPLE DECLINES TO FINISH DE GAME WIF YOU. DAT LAST DRIVE OB YOURS HAB KNOCKED OUT ALL HIS FRONT TEEF, AND HE FEARS HE HAB SWALLOWED DE BALL.

Edward Kemble, "The Fat Lady on the Hill." Illustration in *Life* (July 13, 1899): 32. Courtesy of the Newberry Library.

Other advertisements featuring women of color tended to position them as part of an Orientalist aesthetic. In an advertisement for Turkish Trophies cigarettes, a dark-skinned woman lies in a harem, in costume, and casually propped on pillows (Anargyros). Her gaze is impassive, her expression open, her unmanaged body free for the taking. The cigarettes she advertises signify a social and sexual transgression that white women of the period are rarely associated with in advertising. Offering her as a "Trophy" is in fact a joke, a reminder of trophies more difficultly won, such as the Gibson Girl type advertised in a 1901 contest to choose the best conception of a fictional heroine: "The Prize on Sylvia's Head is $500" (Small, Maynard).

Nevertheless, this seemingly ubiquitous icon of "civilization" at the turn of the century, deployed to legitimate nativism at home and abroad, was co-opted by members of the black elite devoted to racial uplift. In periodicals like *The Voice of the Negro* and the *Colored American Magazine,* the "New Negro Woman" as Gibson Girl appeared as a rebuttal to all of the popular racist images of the mammies, lascivious wenches, and happy darkies seen so often in conjunction with the Gibson Girl images in *Life.* In "Rough Sketches: A Study of the Features of the New Negro Woman" (1904), John H. Adams Jr. depicts a series of black women as Gibson Girl types. In one caption he writes, "This beautiful eyed girl is the result of careful home training and steady schooling. There is an unusual promise of intelligence and character rising out of her strong individuality. A model girl, a college president's daughter ..." (323). While Adams's images privilege a Western, Anglo, and bourgeois conception of "beauty"—all of the "New Negro Women" are "well-dressed" and light skinned with European facial characteristics—they undermine the Gibson Girl's assurances of white racial supremacy by broadening the availability of the "womanhood" currency. The Gibson Girl trappings may be freely appropriated and transformed in order to argue for Gibson Girl privileges while also challenging Gibson Girl ideology.

The legitimacy as consumers that many white working women could embrace did not, however, extend to black women. Too often depicted as a parody of the white New Woman, the "New Negro Woman" as Gibson Girl had a much different relationship to her Gibson Man. Rather than threatening to bankrupt him with her lavish expenditures, the "New Negro Woman" was solely depicted as a noble icon worthy of esteem, self-sacrifice, and protection. Adams declares, "Look upon her, ye worlds! and, since there is none better, swear by her. If there is none purer, none nobler, which have stamped pre-eminence in the very countenance of man, woman and child, cast your glittering swords, and sheaths, and armor, at her untarnished feet and pledge the very life that you enjoy to the defense of her life" (325). The "New Negro Woman" should inspire the awe of Columbia and the reverence of the Steel-Engraving Lady while continually affirming her allegiance to her male counterpart.

As the Gibson Girl represents an exaltation of women's commodity status, her

S. Anargyros, "Turkish Trophies." Advertisement in *Life* (September 26, 1901). Courtesy of the University of Iowa.

image flaunts the very instability of her positions within the emerging corporate capitalist marketplace. Ascribed so much surplus value, she must continually find someone to fetishize her newly created form. While the Gibson Girl appeared to expire at thirty, married and financially secure—on the surface, a comforting end to the patriarchal narrative—the demands of the marketplace necessitate that she continue to want Gibson Girl status. By potentially refusing to take herself off the market, she may continue to search for better alternatives in mates and material conditions. Indeed, even as Gibson's images create a community of middle-class readers committed to the corporate-liberal ideals of upward mobility, commodity accumulation and discernment, self-management, and limited sociopolitical reforms, they remind those readers of how anxiety-ridden that role is for men and how truly perilous it is for women. Survival of the best fitted means that many of the insufficiently fitted may not survive. It seems significant, then, that at another turn of the century dominated by political and social insecurity, the Gibson Girl's image has reappeared—both figuratively, in the popularity of breast implants, Thigh Masters, and "tummy tucks," and literally, in the recent issue by Franklin Heirloom of an entire series of Gibson Girl dolls.

CHAPTER 2

Margaret Murray Washington, Pauline Hopkins, and the New Negro Woman

Now the fundamental agency under God in the regeneration, the re-
training of the race, as well as the ground work and starting point of
its progress upward, must be the *black woman*.
—Anna Julia Cooper, *A Voice from the South* (1892)

On April 3, 1901, Florence Ledyard Cross Kitchelt—socialist, suffragist, and settlement worker—described in her journal the appearance of Mr. and Mrs. Booker
T. Washington at New York City's Social Reform Club: "they both are especially
noted for their *common sense*. Mrs. Washington is lighter than he and has beautiful features, arched brows, blue (?) eyes, a Grecian nose, and a poise of the head
like a Gibson Girl. Her hands are white as mine and beautifully shaped. But her
hair is kinky" (84). While Kitchelt grants Margaret Murray Washington some
Gibson Girl status as she praises her "light skin," "Grecian nose," and "poise[d]
head," she ultimately denies Washington that status because of her "kinky hair."
Envisioning her with blue eyes and a Grecian nose while identifying with her
white and "beautifully shaped hands," Kitchelt "whitens" Washington in order
both to identify with her and to lend her greater credibility, that is, "common
sense." Educator, clubwoman, and essayist, Washington certainly worked to
claim Gibson Girl status for middle-class black women as it represented inviolable bourgeois womanhood. In 1895, she appears to have coined the term "New
Negro Woman" to describe black women who promoted the middle-class ideals
of home maintenance, etiquette, and "neatness of dress." Both Margaret Murray Washington's New Negro Woman and her husband's New Negro refuted
the proclamations by evolutionary theorists that condemned black Americans
to irrelevance or extinction in the modern age. Both Washingtons argued that
black Americans could present a more empowered and employable image of
themselves, especially in the New South, by publicly downplaying Jim Crow–
era abuses while personally committing themselves to racial uplift, what Kevin

Gaines defines as "an emphasis on self-help, racial solidarity, temperance, thrift, chastity, social purity, patriarchal authority, and the accumulation of wealth" (*Uplifting the Race* 2). Despite an ultimate deference to male authority, the "New Negro Woman" had the unique role of symbolic leader in this uplift mission, akin, in some respects, to Howard Chandler Christy's imperialistic vision of the American Girl as a marker of the nation's progress in carrying forward civilization. Indeed, Margaret Murray Washington's work suggests that as black women perform dominant middle-class identities—becoming New Negro Women—they not only inspire their mates to embrace a bourgeois production ethic, but they inspire white Americans to recognize their fitness for inclusion in such national rhetorics of progress.

By contrast, Pauline Hopkins's *Contending Forces* (1900) and her work in the *Colored American Magazine* (1900–1903) focus more on the hazards than on the possibilities of promulgating such images of black women. Hopkins begins three of her four long works of fiction with a description of the reification and commodification of black men and women as they are sold into slavery. The trauma of this event lingers and manifests itself again in the subsequent attempts of the antagonist to appropriate, manage, and ultimately rape the mulatta protagonist. While Hopkins, like Washington, stresses the importance of bourgeois respectability as a marker of "race progress," she also denounces the self-interested material and sexual consumption practices she sees promoted in the turn-of-the-century marketplace as well as in the rhetoric of the New Woman. Hopkins's fictional antagonists embrace and her protagonists reconfigure these solipsistic consumption practices. Because racist formulations of black material and sexual desire were increasingly used in the white press to justify Jim Crow legislation, disenfranchisement, and lynching, Hopkins dematerializes objects of desire and etherealizes sexual desire in a critique both of Jim Crow and modernity in general. At the same time, Hopkins seems well aware that critics of the New Woman associated her with a masculinity that signified de-evolution and savagery. Through a series of revisions of dominant New Woman types, Hopkins finally privileges a spiritual desire, not for new goods but for a "new era" of Pan-African communal identity and subsequent African American political empowerment, led, albeit indirectly, by African American women.

And yet the trajectory of Pauline Hopkins's career and the evolution of her political consciousness—especially the minefields she faced in claiming a prominent political voice for black women while resisting Booker T. Washington's public accommodationist policies—further complicate our understanding of her relationship to New Negro Woman ideology. While Hopkins never to my knowledge used the terms "New Woman" or "New Negro Woman" publicly, she would have been well aware both of the dangers of black women within the cultural elite claiming New Woman privileges and the possibilities of claiming New Negro Woman status. The dominant white version of the New Woman was repeatedly either censured or refigured in the black press of the period. The New Negro Woman, by contrast, was extolled and exemplified most prominently by Margaret Murray Washington, who often directly linked that figure to the optimistic uplift mission of the black women's club movement, a movement in which Hopkins held a leadership position. Both of the tropes of the New Woman and New Negro Woman inform Hopkins's work, and for most critics, even though they may not use these terms directly, the relative clarity of their imprint in Hopkins's work suggests the degree to which external pressures compelled her to limit her female protagonists' overt authority on race matters.

I argue, however, that Hopkins's rejection and refiguration of the New Woman/New Negro Woman was not simply a necessary appeasement to a patriarchal black literary elite but rather an attempt to refigure black femininity as a response not only to white racism but also to modern trends, racialized as white, that impeded racial justice. Indeed, Hopkins's criticism of the New Woman focused on the New Woman's association with disturbing modern forces—the "contending forces" of her first novel—which exacerbated intersex tension and precluded the kind of racial-justice epiphany whites needed. In her last novel, a sole female protagonist relies exclusively on indirect influence to help shape the race's future. Yet in both cases that female voice is made legitimate by a biological inheritance, directed by force of temperament and Christian imperative and imbued with slavery's legacy.

On the one hand, Hopkins's protagonists resemble the Washingtons' New Negroes. While working to subvert the popular racist ideology that the "new teaching" of Reconstruction politics led to the "new crime"—where savage black men or "New Negroes" rape genteel white women—Washington and Hopkins often employed a similar methodology, which only partially undermined the reasoning behind such conclusions. Hopkins's mulatta/o protagonists are physiognomically as well as spiritually and intellectually more advanced than either her Anglo-Saxon or Negro characters. While such a formulation undermined the prevailing view among evolutionary theorists that mulattoes were the degraded products of miscegenation, physically weaker than the average Negro and intellectually weaker than the average Anglo-Saxon, it remained within the logic of anatomical hierarchies, the cornerstone of popular social-scientific discourse. To use Nancy Stepan and Sander Gilman's term, Hopkins and especially Washington employed a strategy of "transvaluation" where one accepted "the terms set by the dominant discourse, but . . . change[d] the valuations attached to them" (91–92).

On the other hand, Hopkins's creation of mulatta/o protagonists as race leaders was essential to her Christian, monogenetic, "of one blood" ideal of racial origins, which could prove an even greater threat to the prevailing evolutionary arguments concerning the origins of man. Even though most theorists after Darwin maintained the likelihood of common racial origins, they imagined long periods of diverging parallel development with "one extremely ancient progenitor" (Haller 87). While both Hopkins and Washington stressed the importance of environmental factors in race progress, the Washingtons tacitly accepted the notion that slavery represented racial stasis. Denied the opportunity to compete as slaves, so the logic went, Negroes suffered an evolutionary setback from which they might never recover. Hopkins refuted this narrative by highlighting the accomplishments of slave revolt leaders in both her fiction and nonfiction. The Washingtons, however, chose to shift the terms of the debate. Rather than the model of slow evolutionary transformation, a narrative in which African Americans would always be by definition at a competitive disadvantage, they chose the logic of "performing" identity offered in consumer culture. Such a model suggests the promises and limitations of bourgeois individualism for African Americans at the turn of the century. The recipients of the Washingtons' uplift were, in the final analysis, responsible for their own development or lack thereof. Hopkins's "new era," by contrast, does not put the onus of change entirely on black Americans themselves but rather shifts it to white Americans, whose bigotry and materialism threaten not only their own redemption but also the very foundation of Western civilization.

Trying to fulfill an uplift mission in the heart of the Jim Crow South, the Washingtons had even greater constraints on their public rhetoric. In Hopkins's fiction, the South is the origin of primal sin and suffering and the place from which her heroines must escape. The crucial race leadership and surest signs of racial advancement—club work, black access to modern technologies (electricity, indoor plumbing), the swelling ranks of the black middle class—were, in her novels, distinctly northern phenomena. For Margaret Washington, the crucial race work was to be done in the South, which must be reimagined as the primary place of uplift and modernity, a place identified less with the degradations of slavery and more with the possibilities of reform. In an 1896 letter to Ednah Cheney, a frustrated Washington asserts that even though she did not belong to the "aggressive class" of female reformers, she wished that women such as Frances Willard, Ellen Henrotin, and Mary Dickinson[1] would "show a little less fear of their southern sisters" and speak out in support of colored women, thousands of whom "live a living death" (238): "The women who live north object to coming south to hold a meeting because of the travel. This is where work must be done for this is where the great mass of the colored women are" (238).

Pauline Hopkins was certainly aware of Margaret Murray Washington's work in the National Association of Colored Women's Clubs and at Tuskegee; Hopkins briefly mentions both in articles for the *Colored American*.[2] Both women, in fact, wrote for the *Colored American* at different times. Margaret Washington's articles appeared after the magazine was purchased by Booker T. Washington supporters John C. Freund and Fred R. Moore in 1904, shortly after Pauline Hopkins had been reportedly ousted by the magazine for an "attitude [that] was not conciliatory enough" to Washington's policies ("Colored Magazine in America" 33). Booker

T. Washington's influence in the magazine was evident soon after the *Colored American*'s inception when his own writing or laudatory profiles of his work regularly appeared. While publisher Robert Elliott and founding editor Walter Wallace claimed in the magazine's first issue that "No philanthrophical [*sic*], political, sectarian, or denominational clique, in any way influences directs or controls this management," they lent their support to Tuskegee and to Washington's accommodationist rhetoric ("Editorial" 60).[3] In a 1901 installment of her "Famous Men of the Negro Race" series, Hopkins praised Washington's "magnetic influence" more than his accomplishments, declaring, "When the happenings of the Twentieth Century have become matters of history, Dr. Washington's motives will be open to as many constructions and discussions as are those of Napoleon today, or of other men of extraordinary ability, whether for good or evil, who have had like phenomenal careers" (441).

Both Margaret Murray Washington and Pauline Hopkins knew the stakes to be won or lost in the contest over the trope of the New Negro at the turn of the century. Frequent discussions in the white press of the "New Negro Crime" helped to legitimate systematic disenfranchisement, Jim Crow laws, and mob violence by reiterating a narrative of emboldened black men eager to ravish helpless white women. According to popular novelist and essayist Thomas Nelson Page in the January 1904 issue of the *North American Review,* since the "new teaching" of social equality, "his passion, always his controlling force, is now, since the new teaching, for the white woman" (44). An unsigned editorial entitled "Some Fresh Suggestions about the New Negro Crime," published later that month in *Harper's Weekly,* echoed Page's argument: "the average negro does not believe in the chastity of women . . . his sexual desire, which always was a controlling force with him has become, since the new teaching of political and social equality, a desire for the white woman" (120–21).

As evils that white men should feel justified in doing everything in their power to prevent, miscegenation and its perpetrator, the "New Negro," found their greatest detractor in Thomas Dixon. In his best-selling novel *The Leopard's Spots* (1902), Dixon celebrated the end of Reconstruction and the reestablishment of Anglo-Saxon control, maintaining that the "exigency of war" threatened to transform the freed Negro "from a Chattel, to be bought and sold, into a possible Beast to be feared and guarded" (5). Dixon depicted this transformation to "Beast" and the realization of that most feared evil in his creation of the black villain and "new negro," Dick, who ultimately attacks the young, poor, white woman Flora Camp, whose sister had also been the victim of New Negro sexual depravity. Indeed, for Dixon, without the paternalism of slavery, the "new negro," or "real negro," showed his ineluctable evolutionary legacy. For many white evolutionary theorists, the political freedoms brought about by Reconstruction had created such an intellectual strain in Negroes that "primitive instincts [were] brought to the surface in manifestations of lust or 'bloodthirstiness, singly or combined'"

(Haller 53). After witnessing Dick's lynching at the hands of a frenzied white mob, the hero of the novel, Charlie Gaston, reassures himself that given the increased threat of miscegenation such mob action is inevitable: "Amalgamation simply meant Africanisation. The big nostrils, flat nose, massive jaw, protruding lip and kinky hair will register their animal marks over the proudest intellect and the rarest beauty of any other race. The rule that had no exception was that one drop of Negro blood makes a Negro" (386). To shore up the white supremacist ideology of the text, Dixon elides the class divisions between the poor white mob and the aristocratic Charlie Gaston, forging thereby, in Mason Stokes's words, a "white nation [that] is a homosocial nation" (154).

But essential to Dixon's white supremacist vision was a division between the New Woman and true woman. The true woman is essentially white and enables the transcendence of class divisions in favor of white racial solidarity. Indeed, since "one drop of Negro blood" is not always visually discernible, Dixon gives whiteness an essential spiritual component,[4] which the female protagonists embody. The initial romantic narratives of the poor white women, Anna and Flora Camp, narratives that are tragically halted when the women are assaulted by black villains, parallel the privileged true southern woman, the "One Woman" Sallie *Worth* (my emphasis), whom her suitor Charlie has "had enthroned in the holy of holies of his soul" (340). Any affront to white womanhood—*even* to poor white womanhood—is an assault on all white women, a unifying cause célèbre for white men that transcends sectional division and class conflict while reifying racial difference.

By contrast, the New Woman in the novel, Miss Susan Walker of Boston, "whose life and fortune was devoted to the education and elevation of the Negro race" (44), is less a woman than a "feminine bulldog" (45). Asserting that it "doesn't matter whether I am a woman or a man" (45), Walker promises to "prove" that the Negroes' "intellectual, moral and social capacity is equal to any white man's" (49). With her declaration that "I believe God made us of one blood," Dixon makes her commitment to social equality into one for miscegenation (49). She then appears at the end of the novel falling for the "scalawag" Allan McLeod, whose racial, religious, and romantic duplicity is shown repeatedly in the text. Despite the ministrations of the well-meaning Reverend and Mrs. Durham, McLeod shows an inexorable tendency toward degeneration as a product of a drunken Scotchman and a likely reprobate mother, a racial inheritance that Walker blithely ignores. Being duped by such a reprobate is one of the last signs on the slippery slope toward racial reversion. Backed as she is by Northern wealth, Dixon's New Woman promises a gender and racial indeterminacy that culminates in racial degeneration and social chaos, where sham and pretense erode the most fundamental pacts of public and private life.

The rhetoric of the "New Negro" and the "New Negro Woman" in the black press, however, worked generally to transvalue racist discussions of the "New

Negro Crime" in the white press and to put forth more "evolved" images of African Americans. And yet the focus of that figure would shift depending on the political perspective of its deployer. In the *Voice of the Negro,* one of the few periodicals to support Du Bois and denounce Washington's policies, John Henry Adams Jr. stresses the importance of transvaluing the term "New Negro": "most of the [white] newspapers and the evil men behind them, paint the new Negro out of the pigments of senseless antipathy, call him a brute and, fixing suspicion on him, seek to revert the cast of manhood into cowardly, cringing and wilful serfdom" ("New Negro Man" 450). For Adams, the real New Negro Man is "[t]all, erect, commanding, with a face as strong and expressive as Angelo's Moses and yet every whit as pleasing and handsome as Rueben's favorite model" (Adams, "New Negro Man" 447). Despite urban temptations and institutional racism, he succeeds both educationally and professionally.[5] Pictured throughout the article are representative images of men—the successful artist, dentist, government worker, race leader, teacher, and journalist—in poses of "studying, thinking, working" suggestive of the "new forces of the race" (450, 452).

The prevailing image of the New Negro in the Washington-controlled black press, however, was not one that emphasized success despite endemic white racism but rather one that suggested sudden transformation through force of will. In *A New Negro for a New Century* (1900), Booker T. Washington, N. B. Wood, and Fannie Barrier Williams offered an anthology of historical and biographical sketches concerning slavery, black involvement in military battles, and the black women's club movement. To counter the prevailing images of "mammies," "lascivious wenches," "coons," and "shiftless darkies" so popular in the white press, they presented a series of contemporary photo portraits (sixty-one in total) that served as a reiterative advertisement for the "New Negro." The photographs offer a parallel narrative that begins with the image of Booker T. Washington and the accommodationist policies he represents and ends with the image of Mrs. Booker T. Washington, emblematic of a black woman who "has come to join her talents, her virtues, her intelligence, her sacrifices and her love in the work of redeeming the unredeemed from stagnation, from cheapness and from narrowness" (426). Married to accommodationism, industrial education, and personal "progress" while signifying "virtue," "intelligence," and devotion to racial uplift, Mrs. Booker T. Washington becomes the epitome of race progress. Her image does not suggest the painful legacy of slavery, Jim Crow legislation, disenfranchisement, and lynching but a "new" future seemingly divorced from a "hated past." In the essay that follows a historical sketch of slavery in the New England colonies, the writer declares, "Let us smother all the wrongs we have endured. Let us forget the past" (140). As Henry Louis Gates Jr. argues, the painful history of racist oppression "is not only forgotten in *A New Negro,* it is buried beneath all of the faintly smiling bourgeois countenances of the New Negroes awaiting only the new century to escape the recollection of enslavement" (139).

Mrs. Booker T. Washington. Photograph in "Booker T. Washington, N. B.
Wood, and Fannie Barrier Williams," *A New Negro for a New Century* (Chicago: American Publishing House, 1900), 425. Author's collection.

The tropes of the New Negro, however, do not merely signify a hollow bourgeois self-transformation in an effort to avoid a painful historical legacy. The past
is virtually smothered in these narratives because that past was viewed by most
contemporary evolutionary theorists as a sign of a race doomed to irrelevance or
extinction in a competitive age. While definitions of race progress varied, many
believed as did Henry Bates and Frank Baker, editors of the *American Anthropologist* from 1891 to 1898, that "progress concerned only those races whose evolution
was unobstructed, whose cranial sutures were still 'plastic,' and whose brain

weight and prognathism evidenced a development away from quadrumanous features" (quoted in Haller 99). In fact in 1904, *Life* featured a simian Booker T. Washington figure standing with a Tuskegee newspaper under his arm.[6] Captioned "Life's Presidential Impossibilities II. A Dark Horse from Alabama," the image indicates how treacherous the logic of racial progress could be. Beginning the history of the race in a precolonized Africa or in an enslaved American context could potentially doom blacks to a noncompetitive starting position from which they could never catch up. Washington, Wood, and Williams redefine the competitive ground. In an era of shifting economic capital and bureaucratic meritocracies, evolutionary racial legacies are potentially less important than the job performed. Being unwilling or unable to claim an inherited authority may be irrelevant in the new corporate culture.

In discourse that reflects the centrality of racial uplift to the black women's club movement, a deference to patriarchy, and an anxiety over both the potential to evoke racist stereotypes and the status of the underclass, the rhetoric of the New Woman in the black press either refigured or rejected the dominant image of the New Woman in the white press. In an 1895 article for the reformist magazine *Lend a Hand,* Margaret Murray Washington offers what may have been the first use of the term "New Negro Woman" to define a woman whose primary concern is racial uplift within the home.[7] The "struggle for money, for power, for intellectual attainment" by black men and women may only begin, according to Washington, after they all have homes for themselves: "In the awful days gone by, the word 'home,' the word 'woman' was a mockery, so far as we are concerned; in fact, there was no home, there was no manhood. All were chattel, bought, used, and sold at the master's will" (255, 257). All relatively privileged women, according to Washington, should devote a considerable amount of time to teaching "the large class of negro women who have not had the same opportunity" (260) the art of "home-getting" and "home-making" (259). In rhetoric that recalls the work of "cult of domesticity" advocates Catherine Beecher and Harriet Beecher Stowe, Washington, like Fannie Barrier Williams, argued that because women and their homes reflect the moral status of a civilization, black women must be encouraged to create an ideal domestic space that reflects their race progress: "she will raise the standard of the home, and thus from the home will come stronger men to execute the nation's plan" (256). Only by following this strategy of racial uplift will there be fewer "thrusts at the immorality of the race," "lynchings of men and women," and broad recognition of the doctrine that "of one blood hath he made the nations of the earth" (260).[8]

And yet, most usages of the term "New Negro Woman" I found in the black press of the period emphasize the hazards as much as the potential of transvaluation. In the August 1900 issue of the *Colored American Magazine,* the editors offered a parody "under the auspices of the Young Men's Congressional Club" (the women's branch of which Hopkins was vice president). In the proceedings of a

mock divorce trial, the attorney accuses his client's spouse of being "or
hear '*New* Women,'" who "just because he didn't think as she *thunk*—
chasing him around de room wid a *red hot* poker" (Young Men's Cong
Club 144). The use of a parodic black vernacular suggests how problematic adopting the image of the independent white New Woman could be for black women.
As the parody evokes the mammy stereotype, it warns that a black version of
the New Woman could prompt the same derisive laughter from white audiences
that the mammy had for decades. For Professor and Mrs. J. W. Gibson in *Golden
Thoughts on Chastity and Procreation* (1904), a premarital advice book for black
readers, the real "new woman" was neither the "bold, heartless creature, willing to
assume men's apparel and rob them of their positions" nor "full of fads, neglect-
ing all her home duties, spending her time writing papers on woman's rights and
utterly distracting her husband" (171). She was "a womanly woman" devoted to
homemaking, who may have the "intellect . . . keen to catch the gist of public affairs" but "wise enough to know that she is 'the power behind the throne' rather
than 'a puppet on the throne'" (172). Writing for the *Colored American Magazine*
in 1904, Josephine T. Washington likewise reassured readers that the women gath-
ered for a Colored Women's Club meeting dressed "simply, many tastefully and
prettily, in womanly style, without any straining after mannish effects" (677). As
"new women," these club women were foremost concerned with "[t]he mission
of motherhood, how to improve the social life, how to help our boys and girls,
problems of Negro womanhood, the future Negro woman, character, a single
standard of morality, how to help the fallen, mother's meetings" (678).

Instead of the "selfish" attributes of the white "New Woman"—sexual freedom and individual accomplishment—the black expression of New Womanhood epitomized refinement, domestic accomplishment, and race progress. The
centrality of this variant of the New Woman to the uplift mission would be
most fully expressed in the *New Negro for a New Century* anthology. In *A New
Negro's* final essay, "The Club Movement among Colored Women of America,"
Fannie Barrier Williams claims that one of the worst legacies of the past is "the
degrading habit of regarding the negro race as an unclassified people" (379). An
outspoken activist in the Chicago women's club movement, Williams argues for
the importance of differentiating "'women's interests, children's interests, and
men's interests'" while insuring the status of "colored women, as mothers, as
home-makers, as the center and source of the social life of the race" (379). Like
promoters of the Gibson Girl, Williams illustrates different types—teachers, a
principal, nurse, dentist, stenographer—in order to create a market for new images. The article's numerous portraits of middle-class, professional black women,
who are all ostensibly members of the club movement, serve as advertisements
of racial "progress" while illustrating the membership growth of the organization (382). The emphasis Williams places on classification, however, serves to
distinguish between those who may organize and those who must be organized:

"Among colored women the club is the effort of the few competent in behalf of the many incompetent" (383).

Like the other essayists in *A New Negro for a New Century,* Williams's work rebutted the conclusions of popular ethnographic physiognomists whose work had gained legitimacy through anthropometric surveys conducted during the Civil War. As Martha Banta points out in *Imaging American Women,* many physiognomic texts assured Anglo-Saxon superiority through visual comparative analysis. Books such as Joseph Simms's *Physiognomy Illustrated; or, Nature's Revelations of Character: A Description of the Mental, Moral, and Volitive Dispositions of Mankind, as Manifested in the Human Form and Countenance* (1887) methodically classified and hierarchized characteristics of different races: "The ability to read with unfailing accuracy the characters of his neighbors, to put his finger on their foibles, and in fact to lay bare their weaknesses . . . puts into his hands a lever of the most powerful character" (23). While refuting such racist conclusions, Williams used a similar methodological approach. One can see in the photographic illustrations of women's distinguished countenances not only that they are leaders of the race but that they should be.

For Williams, as for most black women in the club movement, the primary goal of black women's clubs was to assist the black underclass while reeducating a misinformed and misguided white citizenry. The incentive of these clubs, Williams maintained, was to "help and protect some defenseless and tempted young woman; . . . aid some poor boy to complete a much-coveted education; . . . lengthen the short school term in some impoverished school district; . . . [and] instruct and interest deficient mothers in the difficulties of child training" ("Club Movement" 393). Williams recognized that the source of many of the virulent attacks against the character of black women stemmed from their perceived homelessness and consequent lack of Christian and maternal virtues. Homemaking, or the creation of "shrines of all the domestic virtues," was to be the principal objective of all club women's activities. Focusing less on the importance of material acquisition and more on monitoring behavior, ideal instructors involved themselves directly in children's home lives and espoused the virtues of "frugality and economy" ("Clubs and Their Location" 417). Efforts such as these, Williams argued, enabled members of the National Association of Colored Women's Clubs to perform their virtue to skeptical white women.

Williams accorded the highest status, "new woman" status, to the leaders within the black women's club movement. Educated and educator, refined and resourceful, each is "the real new woman in American life":

> This woman, as if by magic, has succeeded in lifting herself as completely from the stain and meanness of slavery as if a century had elapsed since the day of emancipation. This new woman, with the club behind her and the club service in her heart and mind, has come to the front in an opportune time. She is needed

to change the old idea of things implanted in the minds of the white race an
there sustained and hardened into a national habit by the debasing influenc⌐
of slavery estimates. ("Clubs and Their Location" 424–26)

Unlike the privileged white version of the New Woman, a New Woman who has
built upon and then evolved beyond her mother's position, what Carroll Smith-
Rosenberg calls the "new bourgeois matron" (245), this "real new woman" has
had to divorce herself from the "stain and meanness" of her past (Williams,
"Clubs and Their Location" 424). Exemplified by Mrs. Booker T. Washington,
whose image appears on the page opposite this passage, significantly larger than
the twenty other photographs that appeared earlier in the chapter, "the real new
woman" has succeeded "as if by magic" in "lifting" herself from the legacy of
painful struggle endured by previous generations (424).

As presented in *Voice of the Negro,* however, the New Negro Woman should
inspire racial protest against Jim Crow degradations as much as signify racial
progress to the nation. In his companion sketch to the New Negro Man, Adams
describes a New Negro Woman who, despite, and, in some sense, because of
the legacy of sexual violence her foremothers had to endure, may claim "true
womanhood" (326), a status that must be vigorously defended. He begins by
constructing a narrative between himself and a friend, Alford Emerson Clark,
who happened to see "two ladies, one white, one colored, engaged in a happy,
spirited conversation all the while unconscious, of the Southern social monster
which argues the inferiority of the Negro to the white folk" (323). The two men
debate which woman is better looking. Clark contends that the colored woman
is more attractive. Adams reasons that Clark's preference stems from the fact
that "[t]o the black man a white face means little or nothing. To the white man
it means his tradition, his civilization, his bond and recognition in the present
age, and his safe guard in the future. . . . He [Clark] saw in that colored woman
that which he could not see in the white woman so long as 'white' in America
stands for hope and black for despair" (323–24). Even as he celebrates the ability
of the New Negro Woman to signify civilization, Adams reminds his readers of
a potentially dangerous national disunity when the white woman as American
standard-bearer signifies only to the white population. The seven images inter-
spersed in the four-page narrative emphasize both the young women's "home
training" and the importance of "college training" (324). Rather than having as if
by "magic, . . . succeeded in lifting herself as completely from the stain and meanness of slavery," Adams's New Negro Woman is a testament to the wrongs done
the race in the past—"whom you have fettered with the chains of caste, whom
you have branded with the red iron of infamy, whom you have degraded with
the finger of your own lustful body" (324)—a testament that must be answered
in the future, but not directly, apparently, by the New Negro Woman herself. The
essay ends with the New Negro Woman as an icon in the domestic sphere. In the

essay's only full-length portrait, we see a Christy-girl-like Gussie, "an admirer of Fine Art, a performer on the violin and the piano, a sweet singer, a writer—mostly given to essays, a lover of good books, and a home making girl" (326).

Considering the nature of Jim Crow violence and disenfranchisement at the turn of the century, the urgency of these domestic injunctions is not surprising. In *Character Building: Being Addresses Delivered on Sunday Evenings to the Students of Tuskegee Institute,* Booker T. Washington reminds his audience that voting rights were being increasingly predicated on property ownership (57). It was through home ownership, maintenance, and improvement, he maintains, that one gained subjectivity. As critics such as Hazel Carby, Claudia Tate, Ann duCille, and Elizabeth Ammons have demonstrated, African American women writers of the period offered in their sentimental fiction a complementary domestic idealism. Tate argues, for example, that "[n]ineteenth-century black women's sentimental narratives symbolically represent the inalienable rights of black people as the consummated rights of families—thus their emphatic valorization of marriage and domestic idealism" ("Allegories" 126). And yet foregrounding the importance of bourgeois home production was employed at some cost. To avoid being the objects of consumption and persecution as well as to perform their own professional status, both Margaret Murray Washington and Pauline Hopkins advocate a bourgeois refinement dependent on a purchasing power available to only a small percentage of black women. Hoping to promote their "new negro women" by promising visual evidence of race progress, they necessarily relegate the majority of black women to the "old" school.

For the Washingtons, especially, the home was a source of anxiety because it both reflected and created an estimation of a modern self and had to be continually monitored. That monitoring was most important in those rooms in which Mary Russo's "grotesque" body—an unmanaged body potentially at odds with the "aspirations of bourgeois individualism" (219)—would be most evident, the bathroom and the dining room. In an address to the "Colored Women of Charleston" in 1898, Mrs. Washington claimed, "The average colored person dislikes water, and he won't keep himself clean. He bathes, if at all, once a week . . . He seldom uses a tooth brush. . . . . There is no excuse for this" ("Account" 467). Booker T. Washington made the acquisition of indoor plumbing—still a marker of modernity and affluence—and the act of bathing itself an assertion of allegiance to a Christian national ethic of progress: "As soon as possible every one of our houses should be provided with a bathroom, so that the body of every member of the family can be baptized every morning in clean, invigorating, fresh water" (61). The dining room, meanwhile, "should be the most attractive and most comfortable room in the house. It should be large and airy, a room in which plenty of sunlight can come" (61). Defined through segregation by their work during the day, Negroes should redefine themselves within their homes by literally and figuratively eliminating darkness and hence difference. By christening

"An admirer of Fine Art, a performer on the violin and the piano, a sweet singer, a writer—mostly given to essays, a lover of good books, and a home making girl, is Gussie." Illustration in John H. Adams Jr., "Rough Sketches: A Study of the Features of the New Negro Woman." *Voice of the Negro* (August 1904): 326. Courtesy of the Library of Congress.

themselves through daily baptisms and transforming their bodies from "grotesque" Other to classical self, they may claim a bourgeois subjectivity. Ideally, according to Washington, no one should be able to tell 'from the outside appearance, at least, whether the house is occupied by a white family or a black family" (60).[9] Within the home, meals were to be scheduled and possessions, especially those associated with cleanliness (dish cloth, broom, soap, and towels) were to be in their proper place: "[n]o matter how cheap your homes are, no matter how poverty-stricken you may be in regard to money, it is possible for each home to have its affairs properly systematized" (83).

In addition to household organization, both Washingtons sought to standardize their students' actions into a systematized work routine that challenged stereotypes of black inefficiency and profligacy while stressing their ability to manage new technologies associated with modernity.[10] In "How Electricity Is Taught at Tuskegee," the electrical engineering instructor at Tuskegee stresses how closely the school's dynamos need to be monitored and the centrality of that monitoring to their education: "the students learn more from this system of inspection and criticism than would be possible by any other means" (Pierce 672). With the introduction of telephone service, the school trained the "first colored 'hello girl' . . . in the world" (670). And in the Tenth Annual Report of the Tuskegee Woman's Club, of which Mrs. Booker T. Washington was president, a Dr. Kenney offered clubwomen in 1905 a lecture on the "Value of Electricity and Medical Science," a program apparently well received by club members ("Tenth Annual").[11]

By contrast, racist social critics such as Eleanor Tayleur saw black women's relation to modern culture as a parodic inversion of white middle-class norms. In an article entitled "The Negro Woman—Social and Moral Decadence," published in the January 30, 1904, issue of *Outlook,* Tayleur describes the precipitous downward path black women have fallen since slavery and Reconstruction. Tayleur maintains that as "she exists in the South to-day the negro woman is the Frankenstein product of civilization" (267). Because black women no longer have the close connection to white women they enjoyed under slavery, they revert to their naturally dissolute state: "In the peculiar code of ethics that governs the new negro woman any way of obtaining a livelihood is more honorable and respectable than working for it" (268). For Tayleur, the "new negro woman," always marked by her immutable racial characteristics, parodies the dominant white version of the New Woman: "she copies her independence in utter abandon of all restraints" (268). Tayleur sees the greatest evidence of the new negro woman's decadence in her home, especially as these homes have changed in an urban context: "In the cities the majority of negro women have no homes, but a room which they oftener than not share with strangers. The beds are unmade, the dishes unwashed, the floor unswept. Here children are born to be thrust out into the street as soon as possible" (267). Without private space, modern hygiene, or proper maternal care, Tayleur's new negro woman becomes a burden on an urban market economy demanding efficient management of self and others.

In "The Gain in the Life of Negro Women," which directly follows Tayleur's in the same issue, Margaret Washington refutes Tayleur's allegations by aligning black women only with what she sees as the safest elements of modernity. She begins by marshalling abundant statistical data demonstrating the number of black women receiving formal education, then celebrates this "superior class of negro women," and finally stresses the role black women's clubs have had in insuring that education is used at home.[12] Particularly noting the advanced sanitary conditions in these homes, Washington writes, "The majority of these club women have helped their husbands to purchase homes by their thrift and economy. Many of these residences are situated on prominent streets. They are well-designed, painted cottages of six and eight rooms, with bath and hot and cold water contrivances, well ventilated and constructed with an eye to sanitary arrangements. These homes are tastefully furnished" (273). Significantly, Washington does not invoke the term "New Negro Woman" and its associations with an unsettling independence but rather claims negro women abide by an "old-fashioned" helpmate ethic: "the negro women are unmodern in that they assume a share in working to pay for homes for their families" (273).

Yet in other discussions of club work, she creates a maternal position for herself where the underclass she has chosen to educate becomes childlike and therefore unaccountable. In 1901, she wrote a letter to Ednah Dow Littlehale Cheney—a prominent Boston women's rights advocate, Transcendentalist, and financial contributor to both Hampton and Tuskegee—thanking her for a financial contribution to the local women's club Washington sponsored. As Washington describes the efforts of this particular club in demonstrating sewing and gardening skills, she reminds Cheney of her distance from those she has chosen to teach: "you understand that these people are undeveloped children and one has to try the same art in helping teaching them" (11). Washington appeared to find her authority least assailable if, in describing the "least advanced" members of her race to prominent whites, she conceded to the prevailing anthropological opinion that the adult Negro was at the evolutionary level of the child Caucasian.

While both Washingtons may employ in the New Negro project "subversive repetitions," to use Judith Butler's term, of dominant racist texts, the fact that this discourse relies on the continued surveillance of the underclass and their own self-monitoring suggests the limitations of that paradigm. In negotiating the difficult terrain of trying to win the support of white moderates nationally and the tolerance if not support of southern whites locally, both Washingtons adopt a public voice that displaces anger over the convict lease system, Jim Crow legislation, lynch law, and popular racist ideology onto the black underclass. In educating this underclass, they continually return to the home and the body as sources of anxiety. Since racist theorists like Tayleur and Dixon create for themselves an intrusive gaze that always finds evidence of physical immorality and excess, the domestic image-making terrain becomes nearly impossible to navigate. Margaret Murray Washington can only promise her readers that screens are used in crowded rooms to ensure privacy, that cleanliness and order have become domestic ideals, and that furnishings are tastefully selected. Booker T. Washington can only promise diurnal baptisms and airy dining rooms. Together they can only assure white readers that their students can manage new technologies. In order to legitimize their vision of the New Negro, they must disembody themselves while embodying the black underclass, an underclass always in need of improvement.

Even though Pauline Hopkins was likewise committed to many of the bourgeois aspects of uplift ideology, she exhibited much more ambivalence toward the undergirding patriarchal ideology of the New Negro and the individualist modern materialist ethic of the New Woman. As a professional writer who was single, African American, female, and increasingly anti-Washington, she faced mounting pressure to defer to male members of the black elite with whom she worked. According to William Stanley Braithwaite, a literary critic, poet, anthologist, and contributor to the *Colored American,* Hopkins felt she deserved more authority over the affairs of the magazine than she was granted. In a retrospective sketch of the magazine's history, Braithwaite criticized Hopkins for thinking too highly of her own literary capabilities: "As a novelist Miss Hopkins regarded herself as a national figure, in the company of Charles W. Chesnutt and Paul Lawrence Dunbar and as such felt free to impose her views and opinions upon her associates in the conduct of both the book and magazine publications" (25). Hopkins apparently had little faith in the aesthetic judgment of founding editor Walter Wallace and "resented bitterly" white publisher Robert Elliott's "veiled authority" (25). Her own frustration at not being taken seriously is evident in a letter she wrote to black nationalist John E. Bruce on April 6, 1906. Despite having argued for the union of the "Negro with labor for a number of years . . . being only a woman [I] have received very small notice."[13]

Yet like Margaret Murray Washington, Hopkins would find the black women's club movement an invaluable outlet for exercising her authority on race matters even as she drew more on Christian rhetoric in her vision of progressive Negro womanhood. She was vice president of the Women's Auxiliary to the Young Men's Congressional Club and a member of the Woman's Era Club of Boston,[14] to which she read portions of her first novel, *Contending Forces* (1900). In the June 1900 issue of the *Colored American,* Hopkins describes her editorial position on the objectives of women's clubs: "We believe it to be the club women's task to 'little by little turn the desire of the world from things of the flesh to things of the spirit. She must make the world want to do things that raise it higher and higher'" ("Women's Department" 121). Hopkins envisions "new avenues of work and an outlet for thoughts that breathe" for those middle-class black women committed to work "in the name of God and humanity" (122).

According to Hopkins, black women's potential for spiritual leadership would be threatened by their commitment to issues beyond the domestic sphere, a position that reflects not simply a more conservative political stance but also an understandable reluctance to engage in larger political movements characterized in part by their commitment to white supremacy. She expressed a more conservative position on women's suffrage than that of many of the contemporaries she profiled, such as poet and novelist Frances Harper, journalist Ida B. Wells-Barnett, Woman's Era club founder Josephine Ruffin, and Margaret Murray Washington, who supported full female suffrage although she claimed, "Personally woman suffrage has never kept me awake at night" (Crogman 195). Hopkins advocated limited suffrage on issues concerning a woman's personal and property rights, children, and public schools but rejected full suffrage, in part because she feared that black women's moral authority, an authority continually attacked in popular racist texts, would be compromised by the vagaries of political life: "Physically, women are not fitted for the politician's life; morally, we should deplore seeing woman fall from her honorable position as wife and mother to that of the common ward heeler hustling for the crumbs meted out to the 'faithful' of of [sic] any party in the way of appointments to office" ("Women's Department" 122). Hopkins also reminds her readers that full suffrage for all women would mean that white women would have the further opportunity to oppress black women: "If we are not the 'moral lepers' that the white woman of Georgia accuses us of being, then we ought to hesitate before we affiliate too happily in any project that will give them greater power than they now possess to crush the weak and helpless" ("Women's Department" 122). As Paula Giddings has pointed out, the National American Women's Suffrage Association (NAWSA) strategy of expediency in the late nineteenth century fueled the ambivalence many black women felt towards the idea of politically aligning themselves with white women (124). Hopkins was certainly aware of NAWSA's arguments that suffrage for white women would bolster, rather than undermine, the power of white voters afraid of African American and immigrant domination.

Hopkins's position reflects her concern that sex solidarity might prevent the racial solidarity needed for communal uplift, a concern that reoccurs in her fiction. In *Contending Forces*, Hopkins at first encourages her readers to see her mulatta protagonist, Sappho Clark, within a white New Woman paradigm. In response to Dora's effusiveness over the beauty of their new boarder, her brother Will retorts with a typical New Woman parody, the mannish spinster: "I'll bet you a new pair of Easter gloves that she's a rank old maid with false teeth, bald head, hair on her upper lip" (96). Hopkins then, in a startling move, evokes the reverse stereotype in the name she gives her protagonist. "Sappho Clark" connotes an intellectual exceptionalness that will never be fully understood, a story that can only be known in fragments and potentially a same-sex desire that can never be fully spoken.[15] Sappho's work as a stenographer, a profession that, as Mary Helen Washington notes, is "one of the first nonnurturing professions black women have in fiction" (80) and one that Hopkins herself held off and on during her lifetime, gives Sappho a financial independence and storytelling legitimacy—it is through her that stories are accurately told and recorded—that supports her uplift mission in the community. But her profession is also one that engendered a good deal of popular anxiety at the turn of the century since it could require intimate contact between women and men in the private space of the office. As mulattas, Hopkins's characters are doubly vulnerable, a fact that the tragic history of Hopkins's other stenographer, Elise Bradford in *Hagar's Daughter,* bears out. Given Sappho's history, which we do not learn until later, her removal from the heterosocial workplace to a space dominated by black women's collective uplift mission is imperative. Written upon by a white racist culture, Sappho must expose that narrative to rewrite her own story as well as to serve her community—through church meetings, hospital visits, and Mrs. Willis's sewing circle—all made possible by that women's organization but also through Dora's support. Even though Dora "did not, as a rule, care much for girl friendships, holding that a close intimacy between two of the same sex was more than likely to end disastrously for one or the other . . . Sappho Clark seemed to fill a long-felt want in her life" (97–98). One might even, as Siobhan Somerville does, read Dora's relationship with Sappho as jeopardizing the heterosexual romance narratives of the text (151). And yet the physically and morally idealized Sappho seems to offer the most concentrated commitment to the race only after she marries the Du Boisian race leader Will Smith. Instead of searching for personal independence or homosocial allegiance, she defers to patriarchy and racial solidarity. "My wife, my life," the last lines read, "O, we will walk this world / Yoked in all exercise of noble end. . . . Lay thy sweet hands in mine and trust to me" (402).

And yet Sappho's racial history as religious history offers a reverse narrative trajectory, one from enslavement to liberation, from woman silenced to woman voiced. It is a narrative development epitomized by the illustrations, which begin with the frontispiece of a brutalized Grace Montfort—prone, bloody, and half-naked, flanked by white slave catchers with whips—and end with the "blinding" power of Sappho as risen Christ, tall, richly dressed, with child newly acknowledged, facing the bedazzled Will Smith. The moment when Sappho's full history is revealed—her rape by her father's half brother, imprisonment in a brothel, and separation from her child by that rape—does not point to the incommensurability of cultural transmission and New Woman content, as Sean McCann argues (793), but rather to the refiguration of the dominant New Woman script. It is because Sappho is marked by "lack of virtue" and *"illegitimacy"* (149) as the victim and product of a white man's rape that she must be refigured as the (white) Sappho of transgressive desire and intellectual accomplishment and refigured yet again as true/new woman.

What Hopkins does in this novel is not simply present us with a heroine who, as many critics have argued, challenges dominant racial and gendered stereotypes, but rather expose the burden and inevitable contradictions of an overdetermined bourgeois black female identity at the turn of the century. Sappho is a "dooced purty 'ooman.... havin' black blud" (64), "rank old maid" (96), tragic mulatta, New Woman artist, potentially dangerous siren, race leader, duteous wife—"markers," to use Hortense Spiller's words in a broader sense, "so loaded with mythical prepossession that there is no easy way for the agents buried beneath them to come clean" (203). As these markers are rewritten and denaturalized, the agent who engenders them does become "clean." As a critique of the (white) New Woman who challenges convention and the sexual double standard but has none of the history of sexual appropriation and violence with which to contend, Sappho is crucified and reborn, the real true/new woman. She is the black female Christ who, having suffered the crucifixion, is now risen, not simply subservient companion to the race leader Will Smith, but moral leader to a nation desperately needing redemption.

The development of Mrs. Willis's character likewise is a double voiced one dependent on both the dominant New Woman and New Negro Woman scripts and on the threat of degeneration her mixed-race status presents. The "brilliant widow of a bright Negro politician" (143), Mrs. Willis is "[s]hrewd in business matters," "well-read and thoroughly conversant with all current topics" (144–45). Upon being widowed, she decides that her best financial opportunity is to take up "the great cause of the evolution of true womanhood in the work of the 'Woman Question' as embodied in marriage and suffrage" (146). The topic she brings to the Sewing-Circle club meeting—"[t]he place which the virtuous woman occupies in upbuilding a race" (148)—is the central issue of the novel, and Mrs. Willis works to define it by reclaiming virtue for mulattoes.

Hopkins achieves this reclamation by locating the potential for virtue in a Lamarckian evolutionary narrative modified by Christian ethics. First she establishes not just the ubiquity of the mulatto but a mulatto made up in part by the "best" white blood: "the mighty unexpected results of the law of evolution, seem to point to a different solution of the Negro question than any worked out by the most fertile brain of the highly cultured Caucasian.... [W]e do not allow for the infusion of white blood, which became pretty generally distributed in the inferior black race during the existence of slavery. Some of this blood, too, was the best in the country" (87). Mrs. Willis then assures her audience that "the native African woman is impregnable in her virtue" (149). And when Sappho asks "do you think that God will hold us responsible for the *illegitimacy* with which our race has been obliged, as it were, to flood the world?," Mrs. Willis responds in a way that shifts that evolutionary paradigm to a Christian one based on free will: "we shall not be held responsible for wrongs which we have *unconsciously* committed, or which we have committed under *compulsion*. We are virtuous or non-virtuous only when we have a *choice* under temptation.... The sin and its punishment lies with the person *consciously* false to his *knowledge* of right" (149–50).

At the same time, the primary threat to that virtue is characterized as a defining feature of a race seemingly safely ensconced at the top of the evolutionary ladder.

Mrs. Willis, for whom "a strain of white blood had filtered through the African stream" (145), initially conceived her uplift mission out of "selfishness": "The advancement of the colored woman should be the new problem in the woman question that should float her upon its tide into the prosperity she desired." Her efforts to establish women's clubs "bore glorious fruit" (147). What is striking here is that Mrs. Willis's "selfishness" is both the consequence of and potential offered by her white blood, which, without the mitigating effects of the more virtuous black blood, becomes pure selfishness. In *Hagar's Daughter,* the dangerous—because selfish—New Woman mulatta figure is Aurelia Madison, the cigarette smoking, gambling, and scheming female antagonist who desperately tries to ensnare hero Cuthbert Sumner into a marriage. Indeed, Hopkins's commitment to African American women's personal advancement was tempered by concerns that as club women they not become like Selma White, the social-climbing New Woman heroine in Robert Grant's best-selling novel *Unleavened Bread* (1900): "There are, unhappily, many Selima [*sic*] Whites among us: but is this all? Is there nothing behind the outward veneer of fuss, feathers, fine dress, and posing for public admiration?" ("Women's Department" 121).

So when Luke Sawyer speaks to the American Colored League at the climax of *Contending Forces,* he is defining a white financial rapaciousness that easily turns to sexual predatoriness. Spencerian in nature, these essentially masculinized "white" forces are most destructive to the Negro:

> "I want to tell the gentlemen who have spoken here tonight that conservatism, lack of brotherly affiliation, lack of energy for the right and the power of the almighty dollar which deadens men's hearts to the sufferings of their brothers, and makes them feel that if only *they* can rise to the top of the ladder may God help the hindmost man, are the forces which are ruining the Negro in this country. It is killing him off by the thousands, destroying his self-respect, and degrading him to the level of the brute. *These are the contending forces that are dooming this race to despair!*" (255–56)

Miscegenation is ultimately, then, the evolutionary possibility brought about when that "strain of white blood" is left not to degenerate into its base qualities of greed and selfishness—"the hoarding of giant sums of money by trusts and combinations" (87)—but is directed for the common good. The new woman, as represented by Mrs. Willis, embodies that threat and possibility. Liable to be selfish because of her white strain, she is moved to uplift as a black woman committed to club work—her gender and vocation neutralize the racialized threat of her ambition.

The novel, however, also features a parallel plot that showcases the limitations for the dominant New Negro Woman and (white) New Woman paradigm for those black women not in the cultural elite. Although treated comically throughout the narrative, Mrs. Davis is made a vital part of the uplift mission in a way that emphasizes the importance of bridging class differences among blacks to create coalitions. She raises money for the church and demonstrates her largesse by offering her prize money to the women with whom she had been most fiercely competing. And yet as a woman over fifty who is pursuing a much younger man and who speaks in a black dialect, Mrs. Davis is presented as an unseemly, albeit likeable, parallel to the more serious romantic heroines: "Mr. Jeemes he held to it thet 'ooman's all right to ejecate herself even to be a minister, fer no man could be suferior to 'ooman, 'cause she was his *rib*. An' ever sence that I kin' o' thought what a shame it was fer a man to be minus one o' his ribs all along o' 'ooman, untell I made up my mind thet ef Jeemes wanted me he *could have back his lost rib*" (366). When Mr. James takes Mrs. Davis out bicycle riding, she wears her "new pale blue bicycle suit with a pink shirtwaist an' a white sailer hat an' tan-colored shoes an' gloves" (367), a color pastiche that parodies mannish dress reform. They end up crashing: "We got along all right untell we was a-comin' down a hill. Mr. Jeemes was a-coastin', an' the tail o' that linen duster o'hisn was a-sailin' out behin' like a flag floppin' in an east wind. The fust thing I knowed he was a-stickin' fast head fust into a pile o'sand and where they was makin' mortar to build a cellar, an' me on top o'him! . . . Jeemes is purty black, but he was a white man when he got out o'thet san' heap. As fer me, I tore my gloves, los' my hat, an' busted a new pair o'corsets right off me" (367). The passage bears citing in some length because it predicts a comic gender and racial confusion when a black woman and man adopt a dominant white New Woman activity. Together they look like "a couple o'jay birds stuffed," and when James turns white, it is a minstrel reversal. While white new women can claim the physical freedom of the bicycle ride, as we shall see in Cather's "Tommy, the Unsentimental," for a black woman that bicycle ride, especially down a hill, is dangerous because it is associated with a sexual licentiousness that black women must continually refute. Bicycle riding, and to some extent, the rhetoric of gender equality—"fer no man could be suferior to 'ooman, 'cause she was his rib"—becomes, then, emblematic of a white New Woman's self-indulgence, since neither the pursuit of gender equality nor bicycle riding are communally imperative in an era when the primal sin of slavery has reemerged in the vigilantism of lynch law.

Hopkins's second novel, *Hagar's Daughter*, would revisit New Woman character types presented in her first novel but with a growing indictment of New Woman "freedoms" as they reflect a dangerous modernity, racialized as white. The independent, "fair and pale" stenographer in *Hagar's Daughter*, Elise Bradford, proves to be in a much more vulnerable position working in the white community. While both Bradford and Sappho suffered sexual exploitation by white men, bore a secret child as a result of that predation, and now defy their status as victims in part through white-collar employment, Bradford is finally murdered by her white employer/seducer. The "loyal" friend Dora in *Contending* becomes the disloyal quadroon Aurelia Madison, whose masculine social vices

"EVERYBODY WAS A-LOOKIN' AN' A-GAPPIN' AT US."

R. Emmett Owen, "Everybody Was A-Lookin' and A-Gappin at Us." Illustration in Pauline Hopkins, *Contending Forces* (1900). Courtesy of the Library of Congress.

of smoking, drinking, vamping, and gambling signify a debauched, coded white modernity. Saddled with a wife who "has a fad on temperance," the conniving General Benson relishes Aurelia: "It's a relief to be with a woman who can join a man in a social glass, have a cigar with him, or hold her own in winning or losing a game with no Sunday-school nonsense about her" (77–78). Even more strikingly, Aurelia is associated with the blinding light of the modern Gibson Girl as siren. She uses her power to men's detriment (129); she "bewildered" (115), "dazzl[ed]" (235); her "beauty blinds men" (194). For Hopkins, this Gibson Girl–like sexual power and claim to mannish privilege signifies a reversion to savagery. When confronting her love interest, Sumner, for the last time, Aurelia "listened to him with the watchfulness of a tiger, who sees the hunter approaching, her strong, active brain was on the alert, but now her savage nature broke forth" (237). At the same time, in a reversal of the logic that defined the mannish New Woman in Dixon's *The Leopard's Spots,* Aurelia's gender transgressions are in large part a consequence of racial prejudice: "Beautiful almost beyond description, many of them educated and refined . . . they refuse to mate themselves with the ignorant of their own race. Socially, they are not recognized by whites . . . honorably, they cannot procure sufficient means to gratify their luxurious tastes . . . debauched whitemen are ever ready to take advantage of their destitution (159).

By contrast, the gender transgressions of the black characters, Venus and Jewel Bowen, are sanctioned because they are disinterested. Venus cross-dresses to rescue Jewel Bowen, thereby becoming a hero, and Jewel early on is the "Western Girl," who comfortably wields a revolver. In Hopkins's work, the West, as we see in her next novel, *Winona,* represents freedom from race prejudice—"The free air of the land of the prairies was not polluted by the foul breath of slavery" (288)—and therefore a site more open to gender and racial transgression. Jewel is a "Western girl with all the independence that the term implies" (118). In *Winona* too, Hopkins turns away from the urban New Woman to the western girl, who cross-dresses and rescues her love interest, a man who is nearly crucified for his abolitionism.

Hopkins offers a complex renegotiation of the New Woman/New Negro Woman script, struggling at first to find safer ground on which to write that script while later in her last novel rejecting that script all together. As Hopkins's work focuses on the principal characters' renunciation of racism—internalized and externalized—she moves into a narrative terrain where the trope of the (white) New Woman is too racially incendiary and the trope of the Washington New Negro Woman is too accommodationist. By comparison with her earlier work, the vision of Negro womanhood Hopkins offers in her last novel seems a step back to a silenced tragic mulatta deferring to male authority. And yet, while Hopkins diminishes the role of a female network defining and supporting the New Negro Woman, she grants her greater authority to lead the race in a pan-African new era.

Indeed, in Pauline Hopkins's last long work of fiction, *Of One Blood* (1903), the heroine, Dianthe Lusk, seems to be a submissive, tragic mulatta in love with one man and at the mercy of another—what Jennie Kassanoff decries as a "passive object of exchange" ("Fate" 176). Unlike her earlier novels *Contending Forces* (1900) or *Hagar's Daughter* (1901), *Of One Blood* offers a female protagonist who directs little of the action and seems to fade from the narrative as the important race work is enacted. Claudia Tate and Kevin Gaines have also speculated about the significance of Hopkins's apparent decentering of her female protagonists in her later magazine fiction. As Hopkins's serial novels "abandon the woman-centered discourse of female development," according to Tate, they signal the "dissolution of the 'heroine's text' of black female authority as an effective pedagogical strategy for stimulating social reform during the early years of the twentieth century" (*Domestic* 208). Similarly, Gaines argues that the relatively small role given to the female protagonist in *Of One Blood* reflects the ways in which the author herself was compelled to defer to male authority within the black elite. Adopting patriarchal family norms, Gaines notes, was one way to garner "credibility" in a racist culture ("Black" 434).

While I agree that Dianthe's overt passivity is evidence of the extent to which Hopkins felt herself marginalized within the turn-of-the-century patriarchal black uplift movement, the significance of Dianthe's indirect influence has not been fully recognized. Like her mother and grandmother, Dianthe Lusk embodies a spiritual authority that serves as the foundation for the male protagonist's race work. Hopkins gives her, significantly, the name of John Brown's first wife, a woman known for her "earnest piety" that apparently "inspired [Brown] to be more righteous himself" (Oates 16).[16] For Hopkins, who had heralded Brown's militant antislavery tactics in her previous novel, *Winona* (1902), Brown signified a zealous, revolutionary, white commitment to black liberation while his wife signified the spiritual earnestness fostering that militancy.[17] Similarly, the character Dianthe refuses to take advantage of her skin-color privilege—though a mulatta, she is "[f]air as the fairest woman in the hall" and could and does, albeit unwittingly, pass as white—while offering spiritual inspiration to and justification for her husband's/brother's race struggle. In her characterization of Dianthe, in particular, Hopkins relies on the New Thought and social purity movements of her day, which advocated the power of mind over matter. As Beryl Satter notes, for social purity activists, "While the mind of competitive man was warped by his raging desires, 'advanced' woman lacked destructive desire. Instead, woman's 'mental force' was fueled by her 'heart force'—understood not as irrational emotion, but as high-minded love and spiritual morality" (Satter 12). Dianthe is that "rational, pure, and deeply moral" New Woman who would "help redeem a race and a nation now threatened with moral dissolution" (Satter 12).

At the same time, however, Dianthe represents both the legacy of imperialist conquest—within the context of U.S. slavery and the colonialization of Africa—

and the promise of a "new era" of pan-African identity politics. A palimpsest of sorts, she, more than her brothers, must uncover her history, which is also the history of her mother and generations of black women who have suffered sexual exploitation at the hands of white masters, before that "new era" may begin.

It is through the coded "Go Down, Moses" spiritual that Dianthe acts as a conjurer, offering a kind of "communal summons" for liberation while we as readers realize the conspiratorial nature of that summons.[18] A struggling student of medicine and mysticism, Reuel Briggs meets Dianthe as she performs with the Fisk Jubilee Singers. He becomes entranced with this "willowy figure of exquisite mould" who sings "Go down, Moses" with a voice inspired with "the divine fire": "All the horror, the degradation from which a race had been delivered were in the pleading strains of the singer's voice" (*Of One Blood* 453–54). Hopkins embeds the history of Moses within the representation of Reuel (Reuel is the name of Moses's father-in-law in the Old Testament),[19] making Dianthe's summons that much more powerful. Even the Machiavellian Aubrey Livingston, who turns out, like Reuel, to be Dianthe's brother, acknowledges that "she had the glory of heaven in her voice, and in her face the fatal beauty of man's terrible sins" (488).

When she mysteriously falls into a death-like trance after a train accident, Briggs uses his expertise in "volatile magnetism" to awaken her and they subsequently fall in love. Her recovery incomplete, Reuel is persuaded to have her pass as white while staying at the home of the wealthy white Vances. It is there that she would unconsciously sing the same spiritual she had sung earlier but now in union with a "weird contralto, veiled as it were, rising and falling upon every wave of the great soprano" (502). As Cynthia Schrager points out, this double voicedness reflects the "reemergence of her African American identity from 'behind the veil'" while linking her to her mother, Mira, and the history of black women in slavery (Schrager 192). Near the end of the novel Dianthe sings "Go down, Moses" once again, this time to Aubrey after she has discovered, from her grandmother, Aunt Hannah, the whole terrible truth of their incestuous marriage caused by the legacy of slavery (*Of One Blood* 609). The spiritual with its imperative lyrics, "Go down Moses, way down in Egypt's land, Tell ol' Pharaoh, let my people go," links the liberation of African Americans with Ethiopians while serving to remind Aubrey of his role in exploiting both.

In addition to Reuel, Dianthe's mother, Mira, is also conjured into the race struggle because it is Mira who can voice more directly the violent consequences of slavery's legacy and imperialist conquest. Like Dianthe, Mira was also subject to mesmeric trances, although Mira's were characterized by a dramatic prescience that both forecasts and shapes the subsequent events. A sexual victim and puppet of her white master, Aubrey Livingston Sr., Mira was frequently placed in a trance state by her master and called upon to perform mind reading for the amusement of his guests. On one occasion, she foretells the devastation of the Civil War with a vividness that suggests that a John Brown-like, revolutionary, Old Testament justice is finally at hand: "All the women will be widows and the men shall sleep in early graves. They come from the north, from the east, from the west, they sweep to the gulf through a trail of blood. Your houses shall burn, your fields be laid waste, and a downtrodden race shall rule in your land. For you, captain, a prison cell and pauper's grave" (487).[20] She claims a biblical authority for her revelations—when she appears to Dianthe, she underscores the twelfth chapter of Luke: "For there is nothing covered that shall not be revealed" (506)—that not only unveils the full horror of slavery but its continuing legacy during Jim Crow (the tragedy of the novel could have been averted had not race prejudice necessitated Reuel's passing and his African expedition). And, finally, she uncovers the greed of imperialist conquest. Appearing in a vision to Reuel, who had just been hailed as king of the lost Ethiopian city of Telassar, she leads him to his friend Charlie Vance and the treacherous servant Jim Titus, who both, in effect, have been punished for trying to abscond with the African city's wealth.

As Kevin Gaines argues, Hopkins's position on imperialism—as evidenced by her 1905 *Colored American* series, "The Dark Races of the Twentieth Century"—was an ambivalent one. Despite, for example, her denunciation of Belgian imperialist atrocities in the Congo, "her evangelical piety prevented her from questioning the missionary component of imperialist ideology—the idea that the light of Christianity, civilization, and commerce would rescue so-called heathen peoples from barbarism" ("Black" 447). So when Reuel is offered the throne as King Ergamenes, he makes it a precondition that the Ethiopians exchange their spiritual beliefs for Christianity. Without hesitation, the prime minister, Ai, agrees to do so: "O Ergamenes, your belief shall be ours; we have no will but yours. Deign to teach your subjects" (563). Reuel's restoration also suggests a return to patriarchy; he marries Queen Candace, who has been waiting for the coming of Ergamenes to inaugurate a dynasty of kings. Yet Hopkins criticizes the imperialist mission more than Gaines acknowledges because that conquest is so closely paralleled with a legacy of American racism that condones the domestic imperialist conquest of black women by white men.

Indeed, Dr. Aubrey Livingston's sexual exploitation of Dianthe parallels the conquest of Ethiopia he helps to orchestrate. While he develops an overwhelming carnal desire for Dianthe, he subsequently works to do away with Reuel Briggs and his fiancée Molly Vance. Reveling in luxury, desire, and leisure—"Shades of my fathers, forbid that I should ever have to work!" (447)—Livingston displays the very social and moral decadence Tayleur accused black women of exhibiting. Livingston's carnal desire, as opposed to Briggs's ethereal one, reverses the racist paradigm that black men want to rape white women (Livingston at this point in the novel is read as white) while reminding readers of white men's rapes of black women during slavery. His name and profession also evoke the medical missionary Dr. David Livingstone, whose work in Africa was followed by an era of European exploitation. Aubrey is the one who, having effectively derailed Reuel's

U.S. job offers by telling prospective employers of his racial identity, presents the expedition to him with the hope that Reuel will go and leave Dianthe subject to his own advances. Aubrey also presumably enlists Charlie Vance and Jim Titus for the expedition, both of whom are more interested in the pecuniary rather than the intellectual rewards of the venture.

As Wilson J. Moses points out in *The Golden Age of Black Nationalism 1850–1925*, this journey to Africa reveals the extent to which Hopkins was influenced by the goals of pan-Africanism and more specifically, I would add, by "Ethiopianism," where Africa rises in fortune and influence as the West declines (159, 200). This western decline is represented not only by the satyric Livingston and evil Jim Titus, whom Livingston enlists to kill Reuel,[21] but also by the crassly commercial aspects of the expedition. Traveler Charlie Vance, for example, views the African expedition as a kind of P. T. Barnum Orientalist adventure easily made profitable. Inspired by the caravan before him, Vance imagines ways of marketing such a scene: "Arabs, camels, stray lions, panthers, scorpions, serpents, explorers, etc., with a few remarks by yours truly, to the accompaniment of the band—always the band you know, would make an interesting show—a sort of combination of Barnum and Kiralfy . . . There's money in it" (514). For Vance, social worth is determined only by the promise of future material prosperity: "Here [on the island of Meroe] there was no future. No railroads, no churches, no saloons, no schoolhouses to echo the voices of merry children, no promise of the life that produces within the range of his vision. Nothing but the monotony of past centuries dead and forgotten save by a few learned savans [*sic*]" (526).

Vance's undiscriminating vision of modernity—a vision that includes technological advance, established religion, and social vices—once again demonstrates Hopkins's racialized critique of modern progress, which Briggs will come to reject. Indeed, when he began the expedition, Briggs too had "dreamed of fame and fortune he would carry home to lay at a little woman's feet" (516), but then he learns what nearly destroyed the glorious Ethiopian kingdom to which he is heir. While materially wealthy—silken robes, tinted glass, golden statues, and jeweled crowns—Telassar is but a remnant of a once much greater civilization, virtually destroyed by its crass hedonism: "Stiff-necked, haughty, no conscience but that of intellect, awed not by God's laws, worshipping Mammon, sensual, unbelieving, God has punished us" (558). As Ai explains to Briggs, the people of Telassar have managed to retain their commitment to the "One Supreme Being" or "Ego" (562). The Ego must "wean the body from gross desires and raise it to the highest condition of human existence" to be finally united with the Creator (562). Rather than simply working to "Africanize prevailing notions of Western civilization" (Gaines, "Black" 445–46), Hopkins again rejects the modern "pecuniary values" at the heart of that Western civilization.

Returning again late to the narrative as an embodiment of such a critique, Dianthe will use her knowledge to guide, albeit indirectly, Reuel's work as a race leader. She discovers from Aunt Hannah, "the most noted 'voodoo' doctor or witch in the country" (603), that she, Livingston, and Briggs are in fact siblings and that Aunt Hannah is their grandmother; all bear the mark of the lotus lily signifying their royal lineage. The veiled racial caste system, rather than innate racial characteristics, has created the ensuing tragedy. Enraged, Dianthe tries to poison Livingston, who catches her in the act and forces her to drink the poison instead—"Drink! deeper yet! Pledge me to the last drop" (610)—a scene parallel to Reuel's earnest injunction that Candace drink to seal their marriage covenant (571). As Thomas Otten notes, while the latter is the cup of pan-African unity, the former is the poison of "One-drop laws and the politics of racial identity they bespeak. Aubrey's domination of Dianthe is based on a racial purity he turns out not to possess and on the failure to recognize the origins he and Dianthe share" (250).

Dianthe's death, however, is not her erasure. With a triumphant orchestral flourish and thousand-voiced chant, she is offered "the welcome of ancient Ethiopia to her dying daughter of the royal line" (615), and with Reuel holding her in his arms, she "stamped there all the story of her guilt and remorse" (616). Both stories then become necessarily entwined in the pan-African future. Queen Candace, who bears a resemblance to Dianthe "so striking that it was painful" (568) and who also possesses a "magic influence" over Reuel, is the regenerated, pan-African Dianthe (570). Dianthe's "death," then, could be read as the New Thought protective measure of claiming stillness as a means of rejecting the imperative to "mirror man's desire" (Satter 124). As the reincarnated Queen Candace, Dianthe has escaped her sexual exploitation to become a pan-African leader, still exerting the power of New Thought control.

The legacy of slavery and the threat of modern capitalist imperialist expansion—both of which are written on the body of Dianthe Lusk—demonstrate the hazards of what otherwise appears a celebratory "of one blood" universalist ideology. On the one hand, Hopkins constructs the utopic Telassar as a testament to the possibility of interracial harmony when Western civilization's Ethiopian roots are fully realized. After being drugged and led into the recesses of the secret community, Briggs awakens to find himself in a Great Pyramid where he sees "dark-visaged" strangers who "ranged in complexion from a creamy tint to purest ebony" (*Of One Blood* 545). On the other hand, however, Hopkins's insertion of Livingston into the protagonist's family reminds readers both of the hazards of colonial missions abroad and the paradox of an "of one blood" ideal in Jim Crow America. Dianthe's only escape from Livingston's conquest and appropriation is her quite literal etherealization. And when Reuel returns to Telassar, he returns, significantly, with Old Aunt Hannah, in effect insuring that the scientific positivism of Western culture—"There he spends his days in teaching his people all that he has learned in years of contact with modern culture"—will continue to be tempered by the "shadows of great sins [that] darken his life" (621). These shadows signify his "serious apprehension" over "the advance of mighty nations penetrating the dark, mysterious forests of his native land" (621).

While both Pauline Hopkins and Margaret Murray Washington subversively redeploy the dominant rhetoric of the New Woman and the Gibson Girl, as well as other more vehement forms of popular "new" racist rhetoric, in order to construct and market an image of black women as bourgeois subjects, they do so with strikingly different acknowledgments of the costs involved. As Margaret Murray Washington publicly advocates a New Negro Woman grounded in the domestic middle-class ideals of uplift ideology, she also reminds her readers that such ideals also mean a continual monitoring of self and surveillance of the black underclass. Pauline Hopkins, by contrast, begins her novelistic career with a refiguring of the dominant New Woman/New Negro Woman to showcase a potentially radical black female involvement in race matters only to reject those paradigms as unrealizable and flawed. In her last long work of fiction, Hopkins presents a New Woman who covertly conjures and indirectly directs and who serves as a vehicle through which modern forces revitalize rather than corrupt. It was this pure New Woman—not the treacherous Aubrey Livingston nor even the New Thought scientist, Old Testament Reuel—who would lead the race in the new era. As true New Women, only Dianthe and Candace have the spirited authority to inspire and unite the race in a pure, rational, selfless quest toward an end to racial prejudice and a beginning of renewed pan-African race pride.

CHAPTER 3

Incorporating the New Woman
in Edith Wharton's *The Custom*
of the Country

> "Why, Tom, I can learn as well as you, and a good deal better, for I
> like business, and you don't."
> . . .
> "It seems to me that it is something like women's smoking: it isn't
> wicked, but it isn't the custom of the country."
> —Sarah Orne Jewett, "Tom's Husband" (1884)

Written during the course of Wharton's break with her husband Teddy, her affair with Morton Fullerton, the sale of her beloved home, growing tension with
her long-time publisher, Scribner's, and just after the financial crash of 1907,
The Custom of the Country (1913) reflects Wharton's own marital, domestic, and
financial anxiety.[1] A crisis of managerial control is at the heart of many of these
anxieties—how would she manage Teddy, her sexual transgressions, her career,
and her growing wealth. Wharton's self-described "great American Novel" illustrates the consequences of not developing managerial tactics in a rapidly incorporating American culture, a culture that "promulgated its message of unity through subordination" (Trachtenberg 213). Throughout *The Custom of the
Country,* Wharton validates a shift from entrepreneurial to managerial values
that reflects her own concerns as well as progressive reformers' demands to regulate a vicissitudinous Wall Street and unfettered corporate power. Attentive to
contemporary debates in social science, Wharton creates a "cultural dialogics"
of evolutionary discourse to legitimate this shift.[2] Wharton validates the management of the protagonist and New Woman, Undine Spragg, as she charts her
movement from a proprietary capitalist with tendencies toward degeneracy into
a corporate employee, tractable though not entirely subdued. By marking this
transition in racial, economic, national, evolutionary, social, technological, and,
most strikingly, gendered terms, Wharton cautions that the New Woman—as
white, lower-middle-class American; as new money, new technology, and new
ethic—promises to unmoor the nation if not the world.

With her relentless appetite and status as simultaneously person, pro
abstract "force," Undine is subject to the valuations of a fluctuating ma
As essentially the owner-manager of her own enterprise, Undine sells herself
but is compelled to be a "price-taker" rather than a "price-maker," whose price
is determined by the men she attracts.[3] By contrast, her first and last husband,
Elmer Moffatt, represents the "corporate reorganization of industry" and the
social tensions such a reorganization brings.[4] While Moffatt does not form a
corporation per se, he is a major stockholder in other corporate ventures and
engages in a series of corporate behaviors: forming coalitions with investors to
purchase companies while working to maximize the profit of his fellow investors,
delegating the management of those companies in which he invests, and representing ideals of efficiency and time management.[5] At the same time, the way in
which he wields corporate power—especially his involvement in the "natural"
monopolies of railroads and public utilities—would have provoked fears of unregulated trusts (Sklar, *Corporate Reconstruction* 184). A shadowy but persistent
presence in the novel, the Ararat Trust investigation is eventually derailed, and
at the height of Moffatt's success, he and Rolliver "got the whole town in their
control" (*Custom of the Country* 537). As Martin Sklar notes, "the trust question
and the antitrust debates were in essence about the passage of American capitalism from the competitive to the corporate stage of its development" (*Corporate
Reconstruction* 2). The irony in *The Custom of the Country* is that rather than
demonstrating a nostalgia for the proprietary capitalist era of small-producer
competitive capitalism, and the American ideals of free enterprise and individual
initiative that era represents, Wharton satirizes both pecuniary and corporate
ethics, deriding Undine's and Moffatt's rapaciousness even as she offers a tacit
endorsement of the former's sheer force and the latter's corporate savvy.

But it is Wharton's tacit endorsement of Moffatt's "corporate personality" that
critics have failed to acknowledge. Even as Wharton satirizes his unscrupulous
deal making and voracious collecting, she fundamentally endorses the corporate
managerial skills that he exerts, in large part because the New Woman as Undine
represents an even more dangerous primitive element of American capitalism.
For Wharton, Undine is not, as Claire Preston argues, the "inexorable wave of
the future" but a wave from the past symbolizing ultimately the atavistic nature
of a modern American culture crashing though the ramparts of old New York,
old Europe, and beyond. Moffatt, similar in force but different in texture, promises to direct, and therefore mitigate, the wholly destructive nature of Undine's
unalloyed wave energy.

That the icon of unregulated, dangerous energy is Undine Spragg suggests not
merely Wharton's own anxiety about the feminization of larger cultural anxieties
over an unregulated marketplace and American power more generally but also
her anxiety about the New Woman as a sexually and socially transgressive figure.
I argue that Undine is Wharton's most developed New Woman figure. In her
fiction prior to World War I, Wharton represents her New Woman protagonists

both as social reformers and as Gibson Girl types, but it is in the latter incarnation that they provoke the most anxiety and need for containment and therefore gradually take center stage in her fiction. As characters whose powerful, wavelike desires threaten to destroy even the most venerable of social traditions, they defy easy categorization. Their social ambitions create a kind of moral indecipherability that frustrates the anthropologist's reading. In Wharton's novella *Sanctuary* (1903), the antagonist Clemence Verney is "patently of the 'new school'" because her ambition overrides any commitment to traditional moral precepts; her "feverish activities and broad-cast judgments, [her] ... very versatility made her hard to define" (84). Even though Gerty Farish and Carrie Fisher in *The House of Mirth* (1905) are typical New Woman types in their commitment to progressive causes such as working girls' clubs and municipal reform, they both appear relatively harmless: the former a dowdy old New York philanthropic idealist and the latter a voluble leisure-class reform hobbyist, who for the economic titan Gus Trenor "was simply a mental habit corresponding to the physical titillations of the cigarette or the cock-tail" (67). By contrast, the New Woman Bertha Dorset, whose "restless pliability" is reflected in her shameless social maneuverings and sexual exploits, ruins Lily Bart (21). In *The Fruit of the Tree* (1907), Justine Brent is "so free and flexible in all her motions that she seemed akin to the swaying reeds and curving brambles which caught at her as she passed," a flexibility that when extended to the ethical arena suggests a disconcerting ability to reconcile selfless corporate idealism with a conceivably selfish act of euthanasia (300). The "awfully modern," sexually experienced Sophy Viner in *The Reef* (1912) is potentially even more threatening to established social orders because her questionable moral judgment may be traced to general shifts in American racial inheritance. Seeing her unexpectedly on the docks before his departure to France, the ambassador George Darrow struggles to classify this "fluid type": "She was clearly an American, but with the loose native quality strained through a closer woof of manners: the composite product of an enquiring and adaptable race. All this, however, did not help him to fit a name to her, for just such instances were perpetually pouring through the London Embassy, and the etched and angular American was becoming rarer than the fluid type" (14).

Undine, of course, is the most fluid of types as her name denotes: a water sprite and wave motion. She is at once new species, new product, new technology, new money, new morality, and New Woman, an emblem of American prosperity and ingenuity along with inexorable moral degeneration.[6] Vibrant and empty—a product of her nouveau riche father's ambition and her mother's dullness—Undine is a tremulous new species liable to revert if left to her own resources. The novel's "ad-hoc sociologist," Charles Bowen, may try to locate her as "a monstrously perfect result of the system" of American marriage, but she remains remarkably insubstantial, both product and process, never quite created. Named after a "hair-waver father put on the market the week she was born" and evoking the eponymous water nymph, Undine is at home in the crude suffusion of electric light: "[h]er black brows, her reddish-tawny hair and the pure red and white of her complexion defied the searching decomposing radiance: she might have been some fabled creature whose home was in a beam of light" (80, 21). Like Gibson's "Another Moth," she seems to act as an incandescent filament radiating a deadly attractive radiance. With her "sensitiveness to new impressions combined with her obvious lack of any sense of relative values," Undine relishes the Nouveau Luxe, a garish resort devoted to the shallow and fleeting entertainments demanded by the nouveau riche. Feeling trapped by one of the illustrious marriages she finagles and unhampered by the old New York ideals that sabotaged Lily Bart's marital machinations, Undine deftly obtains one divorce and then another while acting as a false signifier of both gentility and maternity. She, in fact, loathes maternity unless her child—an unfortunate consequence of her second marriage—may be used as a successful prop or pawn.

Wharton provides ample evidence that she loathes the "new ethic"—quick marriages, easy divorces, avarice, and imitation—and yet she does not wholeheartedly reject it. Most Wharton scholars agree that in *The Custom of the Country,* Wharton offered her most explicit indictment of the "capitalist-patriarchal America" that worked to create the rapacious Undine (Donovan 71). Indeed,

Charles Dana Gibson, "Another Moth." Illustration in *Life* (January 9, 1902): 30–31. Courtesy of the Newberry Library.

Ann MacComb notes, "The divorce industry must have seemed par-galling to Wharton because [of] its reputation for encouraging 'rotary marriage' along the lines of the period's pervasive 'rotary consumerism'" (767). Yet Wharton also continually and emphatically reminds readers of Undine's vitality. As her name suggests, Undine undulates, rising and falling like the stocks on Wall Street, riding the waves, so to speak, and coming up on top. In this respect, I agree with Cynthia Griffen Wolff, who has argued that Wharton never condemns Undine's energy as such: "Only 'free-floating' energy is monstrous. Energy that has become divorced from human concerns is vitiated; energy that has been contaminated with insatiable hungers is emotionally distorting" (244). Suffering only periodic bouts of carefully orchestrated "nervousness," Undine thrives in this marketplace of potentiality. Certainly, the excitement of that motion—the rapid dynamics of Undine's moral descent in conjunction with her financial ascent—sold Wharton's novel.

Undine's character, in fact, both reiterates and contradicts the dominant narrative of the waning Gibson Girl she resembles. Her inviability and force suggest the power of an American nation arguably superior to Europe technologically and economically. Like the Gibson Girl's elaborate but enticingly loose coiffure, the vitality of Undine's red hair suggests the unpredictable motion of her desires. In love with her own image, Undine too has an insatiable desire for both material goods and social prominence, desires that threaten to bankrupt her father as well as her mates. Yet Wharton's construction of Undine evokes the Gibson Girl image only to exacerbate the cultural fears she embodies and in turn undermine the values on which the status of her image depends. When Undine marries the French nobleman Raymond de Chelles, she makes the frequently satirized Gibson Girl mistake of marrying for title rather than for love, thereby shirking her responsibility in nation building, that is, inspiring American men and propagating the race. Charles Dana Gibson assured readers that the Gibson Girl's vanity and material desires did not eviscerate American men—quite the contrary. With his chiseled, clean-shaven, square jaw, the Gibson man met the Gibson Girl's challenge with earnest adoration. The implicit and sometimes explicit endings of his pictorial narratives showcased matrimony and maternity, effectively undermining the social threat the Gibson Girl's social transgressions inspired. As an icon of bourgeois white womanhood, she promises to alleviate Rooseveltian fears of race suicide by having a large family. Undine, by contrast, offers few assurances of the desirability, let alone the fertility, of American native-born white women. With only one child and no desire for others, with atavistic desires continually resurfacing, and with an indeterminate racial heritage—certainly not the "etched and angular American" type—Undine is, at best, a dubious asset to racial progress. Threatening the progenitorship of her morally and intellectually more "advanced" husbands, Undine represents a new species, destined to be short lived.

If in the Gibson Girl narrative marriage promises to manage the threat of un-

controlled female sexual and consumer desire, then Undine's perpetual speculating and sudden devaluations remind readers of their own insecurity in an
economy increasingly subject to a volatile Wall Street. When Wharton began her
"great American novel," the country was still recovering from the crash of 1907.
With the collapse of the overextended Knickerbocker Trust Company—which
Wharton considered to be the cause of *The Fruit of the Tree*'s disappointing
sales[7]—came a slew of other trust and commercial failures. By late November of
1907, forty leading stocks were selling on average $52 a share below their 1906 peaks
and approximately one worker in six was unemployed (Wyckoff 47; H. Smith
463). Even though J. P. Morgan rallied other bankers and restored confidence,
calls for greater regulation of corporate power grew in frequency. Progressives,
Senator Robert La Follette, for example, charged that the panic was instigated by
wealthy interests who wanted both to smother business rivals and to prove that
prior efforts to regulate corporations had only destabilized the economy (Thelan
62–64). Despite the fact that Roosevelt had worked with Morgan to quell the
panic, he had already been engaged in a crusade to curb corporate excesses and
publicly declared that "certain malefactors of great wealth" had accelerated the
1907 crisis "in order to discredit the policies of government" (Mowry 218–20).

Weakened by endogamy and outmoded social codes, Undine's two old-mon-
ied husbands suffer from the exigencies of Wall Street natural selection as soon
as they marry her, while the up-and-coming Elmer Moffatt, by contrast, learns to
speculate successfully. He embodies what Walter Benn Michaels has characterized
as the "corporate personality" at the turn of the century. It was the corporation's
ability to act as an intangible person, intangible in its insatiability for wealth and
person-like in its power to act, that made it a source of cultural anxiety: "[t]o
writers like James 'Cyclone' Davis and Henry D. Lloyd, it was this combination of
personhood and intangibility that conferred upon corporations 'unprecedented'
powers—above all, the 'power to act as persons, as in the commission of crimes,
with exemption from punishment as persons'" ("Corporate Fiction" 194). Shrewd,
seemingly straightforward, and occasionally compassionate, Moffatt survives and
eventually triumphs because of his unquenchable desire for wealth, his ability
to forge alliances based on mutual self-interest rather than on previous friendships, and his ability to evade legal entanglements. With his "immense nebulous
schemes for the enlargement and development of any business he happened to
be employed," he looms "huge and portentous as some monster released from
a magician's bottle" (553, 468). By the end of the novel, nothing seems out of his
reach: "[h]e leaned back in his chair with an air of placid power, as if he were so
sure of getting what he wanted that there was no longer any use in hurrying, huge
as his vistas had become" (538). And seeming to have emerged from nowhere,
he defies categorization or explanation: "whenever any attempt was made to focus his hard sharp personality some guardian divinity seemed to throw a veil of
mystery over him" (216, 457). Although his business dealings are nearly always

unethical, he consistently avoids legal repercussions. While working as a private secretary for Harmon B. Driscoll, who is trying to forge railroad and public utility monopolies—"Now they've got all the street railroads in their pocket they want the water-supply too" (130)—he offers insider information and then uses that information later to blackmail Driscoll for his silence, effectively both using and then derailing the Ararat Trust Investigation to his own advantage. He offers Ralph a stake in a complicated real estate deal that "seemed all right while [Moffatt] talked of it . . . but vaguely wrong when he thought it over afterward" (259). He advises Undine to extort money for her child from the Marvells and then later offers Ralph the option of obtaining that money by entering into a monopoly utility scheme. When Ralph does not immediately recoup the money he has invested with Moffatt, Moffatt has only to blame the vicissitudes of the market.[8]

Yet despite stressing his unethical corporate behavior, Wharton also seems to condone other characteristics integral to his corporate success. Moffatt's "precision of conduct," "jovial cunning," and shrewd business affiliations, without regard to nepotism or personal grudge, give him a managerial leg up over Undine. Despite his voracious appetite for wealth, he exerts the self- and interpersonal control necessary for managerial success. He keeps to his appointment times— "[u]nder all his incalculableness there had always been a hard foundation of reliability" (249)—and controls his anger. In a conversation with an accusatory and desperate Marvell, he "spoke with extreme deliberation, separating his syllables like a machine cutting something into even lengths" (463). Even though Undine had deserted him in their first marriage, he approaches her affably, thereby smoothing the way for her to agree to his business proposition. As a fellow ex-husband of Undine's, Ralph would seem to be a rival, but Moffatt foregoes jealousy in favor of capitalizing on a business opportunity, which eventually, albeit too late, yields Marvell the payoff Moffatt had assured. And by shifting his allegiance from Driscoll to Rolliver, he disregards past business animus—"never had the time to nurse old scores" (535)—to make the business connections necessary to prosper. While Undine shows a similar impersonalism in her success, her assent depends less on vying for strategic alliances than on taking advantage of ready opportunities and leaves more human devastation in its wake—an ex-husband driven to suicide and a child lost and fatherless. During the shift from entrepreneurial to managerial capitalism, "increasingly enfeebled appeals [were made] to dog-eat-dog social Darwinism: It was cooperation that now made firms, economies, and nations fit to survive" (Sklar, *Corporate Reconstruction* 11).[9]

Unlike Ralph Marvell or Raymond de Chelles, who purchase Undine solely for their own personal viewing pleasure thereby evincing an old-era proprietary ethic, Moffatt puts Undine to work both to display his own wealth and to procure more of it. Moffatt does not simply acquire Undine to be the latest object in his "collection of 'unmatched specimens,'" as MacComb argues (782), but rather channels her energy to service his corporate interests. In fact, by the end of the novel, Undine has lost some of her singular attractiveness to justify solely an aesthetic interest on Moffatt's part: "you're not the beauty you were," Moffatt offhandedly remarks (568). And later we are told Undine "felt under his cool eye, no more compelling than a woman of wax in a show-case" (574). Undine becomes increasingly aware of his detachment, his ability to prioritize his affairs in such a way that personal ties have relatively little importance compared to business imperative: "If the call were that of business—of any of the great perilous affairs he handled like a snake-charmer spinning the deadly reptiles about his head—she knew she would drop from his life like a loosened leaf" (563). Throughout the novel, he capitalizes on her connections. In exchange for his silence about their first marriage, he asks Undine to promise a future introduction to a member of her new set (115), a debt he later collects as a meeting with Marvell that results in a lucrative business deal. She gives him access to the Duke's Ingres and other inaccessible galleries including de Chelles's, helping him, albeit indirectly, to secure de Chelles's coveted tapestries. But, most importantly, her rapacious desire "to have the best" matches his own: "[h]ere was some one who spoke her language, who knew her meanings, who understood instinctively all the deep-seated wants for which her acquired vocabulary had no terms" (536). In conjunction with his own, her desires, coupled with her connections and heightened social perceptions, promise to help him secure his desires provided he respects her currency in the marketplace, which he steadfastly does. Indeed, as MacComb notes, by keeping Undine's previous marriage to him a secret and by devising the plan to, in effect, mortgage her son, Moffatt "manages his interest in her like a stock investment" (782). Yet without his ability to control the market, to, in effect, set the price, Undine will always be dependent on him, to be in effect employed and managed by him.

In tandem with the rhetoric of incorporation, Wharton invokes a complex array of evolutionary theories, which fascinated her throughout much of her career and directly shaped her understanding of white women's social positioning. She had long been interested in the works of Darwin and Thomas Henry Huxley, Herbert Spencer, and Jean Baptiste de Lamarck, among others (Benstock 62). In her autobiography, *A Backward Glance*, she eulogized her longtime friend Egerton Winthrop, who introduced her to the "wonder-world of nineteenth century science. He it was who gave me Wallace's 'Darwin and Darwinism,' and 'The Origin of Species,' and made known to me Huxley, Herbert Spencer, Romanes, Haeckel, Westermarck, and the various popular exponents of the great evolutionary movement" (94). In her short-story collection *The Descent of Man* (1904), Wharton had offered a critique of the ways in which women figure in the dominant Darwinian narrative. The title story of the collection follows the ethical descent of a Professor Linyard, who compromises his scientific standing for the financial rewards of producing popular pseudo-scientific sentimental essays, essays relished by his primarily female reading audience. On the one hand, the story seems to confirm what Marysue Schriber has observed as Wharton's fear that the feminization of American culture was bringing about its intellectual and moral decline. Wharton, Schriber maintains, adopts Darwin's arguments concerning the intellectual and moral inferiority of women, who do not have to compete in natural or sexual selection (36–37). Such an argument would seem to be strengthened by Wharton's unfavorable depiction of "sheltered" American women some fifteen years later in *French Ways and Their Meaning* (1919): "It is because American women are each other's only audience, and to a great extent each other's only companions, that they seem compared to women who play an intellectual and social part in the lives of men, like children in a baby-school. They are 'developing their individuality,' but developing it in the void, without the checks, the stimulus, and the discipline that comes of contact with the stronger masculine individuality" (102–3). On the other hand, Schriber neglects to consider that Linyard creates his own ideal female companion and consumer of his ideas. His imaginary female confidante, a woman who has "to the utmost this quality of adaptability," always listens to and encourages him (*Collected* 347). By satirizing the ease with which Linyard rationalizes his own moral descent—a descent made manifest in his creation and cultivation of female companions who only reflect rather than contradict his ideas—Wharton challenged Darwin's assumptions of innate feminine frivolity. That frivolity now appears as an ameliorative social strategy rather than an inviolable biological fact.

During the course of writing *The Custom of the Country*, Wharton was also directly influenced by contemporary challenges to Darwinian theory. Sailing back from Europe to the United States in May 1908, she read Vernon L. Kellogg's *Darwinism To-day* (1907) and Robert Heath Lock's *The Recent Progress in the Study of Variation, Heredity, and Evolution* (1906).[10] Kellogg argued that while Darwin's theories of natural selection may explain the continuous changes of evolution, they did not sufficiently explain the formation of new species (73). While recognizing the challenge that DeVries's mutation theories posed to natural selection arguments, Kellogg eventually embraced an essentially Lamarckian perspective in which the transmission of acquired characteristics was primarily responsible for new species formation (382–83). Lock, on the other hand, used the arguments of the Mendelians and Mutationists to herald Francis Galton's eugenic vision. Using Mendel's gene theories, Lock argued that variations in behavior are ultimately the result of inherited good or bad genes, the presence of which could be easily deduced by observing behavior. At the end of his study, Lock warns that "[p]romiscuous breeding has produced a weakness of character that is too timid to face the full stringency of a thoroughly competitive struggle for existence, and too lazy and petty to organize the commonwealth co-operatively. Being cowards, we defeat natural selection under cover of philanthropy; being sluggards, we neglect artificial section under cover of delicacy and morality" (289).[11]

While lending itself to eugenic arguments, Mendelian gene theory did work to dismantle some of the sexual and racial stereotyping forwarded in Darwinian narratives. As Cynthia Eagle Russett notes, Mendelian genetics undermined recapitulation theory, where one could supposedly see evolutionary development in the growth of the fetus into the adult. Recapitulation theory had often been used to promote race and sex hierarchies, a vision in which women had ceased their evolutionary development somewhere between a child and man. Adherents of Lamarck, who argued that all characteristics acquired during the lifetime of each parent were transmissible to the child, were also challenged by the renewed attention given to Mendelian theories. As Russett points out, such attacks undermined Darwin's arguments about the inheritance of mental capabilities according to sex (Russett, *Sexual Science* 157–59). In *The Origin of Species*, Darwin maintained that in the struggle for survival and in the efforts to attract a mate, male intelligence developed further, an increase that was passed to male offspring alone (73). If women were now viewed as able to acquire mental traits from their fathers as well as their mothers, any assurances of male intellectual superiority were put into question. Discrediting the Lamarckian notion that acquired characteristics could be inherited, however, also undermined arguments in favor of women's higher education: "Neo-Darwinism thus taught an ambivalent lesson. While it dispelled the notion that men and women were evolving in different directions, it also denied the hope of a shortcut to enhance feminine braininess through educating the maternal stock" (Russett, *Sexual Science* 160).

In *The Custom of the Country*, Wharton appears ambivalent about the hereditary logic of both Darwinian and eugenic arguments. On the one hand, Wharton's construction of Undine seemed to legitimate Darwin's claims of some innate female behavioral characteristics. Undine's intuitiveness, imitativeness, and vanity are all characteristics that Darwin saw as the hereditary legacies conferred on women. In *The Descent of Man*, he maintained, "Women are everywhere conscious of the value of their beauty; and when they have the means, they take more delight in decorating themselves with all sorts of ornaments than do men" (2:371–72). On the other hand, Undine also represents the very struggle for existence that, in Darwin's view, prompted evolutionary development. Quickly recovering from her "nervous attacks," Undine as sheer energy fuels the five-hundred-plus pages of this novel. Undine does not merely adopt Darwin's ethic of survival of the fittest in the marriage marketplace, she is the very "eternal flux of Nature" that prompts evolution (Kellogg 374). As her undulating desires represent the fluctuations of Wall Street, electrical waves, changing fashions, and social rules, they compel natural selection to occur.

Wharton demonstrates a similar ambivalence toward eugenic theories. By creating characters such as Undine, Marvell, and de Chelles who are ultimately products of their genetic legacy, Wharton validates race-bound laws of inheritance. Yet the fact that Undine "derive[s] her overflowing activity" from her father could be a hereditary possibility made logical by Mendelians, a sign of environmentally produced degeneracy to Lamarckians—her "masculine" energy exacerbated by a frenetic American culture—or, according to Darwinists, an atavistic throwback to a more savage age. And arguably Undine's "worst" quality, her rending of traditional family structures, is genetically untraceable. According to Darwin's vision of a moral hierarchy, Undine appears stuck on the lowest rung of the moral ladder since the "higher [moral rules] are founded on the social instincts, and relate to the welfare of others. They are supported by the approbation of our fellow-men and by reason. The lower rules, though some of them when implying self-sacrifice hardly deserve to be called lower, relate chiefly to self, and owe their origin to public opinion, when matured by experience and cultivated; for they are not practiced by rude tribes" (*Descent* 1:100). Undine's father and Ralph Marvell, by contrast, appear to have cultivated the "higher moral rules" that their relative failure on Wall Street only confirms. Mr. Spragg's moral vision, a vision "murky" in business matters but loosely based on a system of "personal obligation," is resolutely clear in his "private rule of conduct," which, like Marvell's, depends on traditional patriarchal notions of family structure (260, 239). The fact that these two characters from different social strata share an inability to compete and a roughly similar personal code of conduct—that is, a code of self-sacrifice in maintaining female dependents—undermines a eugenic reading. In addition, Wharton gives the successful Elmer Moffatt virtually no ancestral history besides suggesting that he is from modest means and outside the centers of power. His rise to fortune as well as his ethical plummets are genetically untraceable, which again suggests the limits of a eugenic reading of the text.

In Wharton's fiction of this period, then, incorporation supersedes evolution as the rhetoric of social control. In *The Fruit of the Tree* (1907), the novel that immediately preceded Wharton's first sketches of *The Custom of the Country,* Wharton celebrates the corporate vision of her new woman and new man protagonists. A financially and critically unsuccessful novel, *The Fruit of the Tree* takes on labor reform, euthanasia, and the woman question in addition to corporate restructuring. The novel begins by describing the efforts of the idealistic John Amherst to reform the debilitating labor conditions at the local cotton mills where he is assistant manager. Longing to create systemic change in the hierarchical relations between owners and workers, Amherst initially appears to offer a direct indictment of the corporate system: "The disappearance of the old familiar contact between master and man seemed to him one of the great wrongs of the new industrial situation. That the breach must be farther widened by the ultimate substitution of the stock-company for the individual employer—a fact obvious to any student of economic tendencies—presented to Amherst's mind one of the most painful problems in the scheme of social readjustment" (48). Amherst disavows the corporate system, however, only as it acts as a family proprietary enterprise—the owner of the mills only visits his property occasionally—siphoning rather than reinvesting the wealth. Amherst's plans for the mills' recuperation, in fact, directly employ corporate restructuring methods. Hoping to hire according to merit rather than nepotism, to create recreation facilities and incentives for employee advancement, and above all to maintain an efficient base of operations, Amherst longs to implement his corporate ideals.[12]

Despite its ambivalent treatment, the efficiency ethic is, arguably, the hero of the novel. It was Amherst's love of the machine, both its finely tuned system and its awesome power, that compelled him to forego his leisure-class opportunities and enter into mill management:

> ... the monstrous energies of the mills. It was not only the sense of power that thrilled him—he felt a beauty in the ordered activity of the whole intricate organism, in the rhythm of dancing bobbins and revolving cards, the swift continuous outpour of doublers and ribbonlaps, the steady ripple of the long ply-frames, the terrible gnashing play of the looms—all these varying subordinate motions, gathered up into the throb of the great engines which fed the giant's arteries, and were in turn ruled by the invisible action of quick thought and obedient hands, always produced in Amherst a responsive rush of life. (56–57)

As the machine and its hierarchy of interlocking parts are anthropomorphized, so the bodies that run those machines become objectified, and virtually invisible as a part of the larger social machine. With the humanizing influence of corporate reforms, the monstrous energy would be kept in check and the workforce would gain visibility.

Amherst's opportunity to implement his reforms comes when the absentee owner of the mill dies and his widow comes to inspect her property. Hoping to spur a social consciousness in the Gibson Girl–like Bessy Westmore by showing her firsthand the misery on which her luxurious lifestyle depends, Amherst takes her on a tour of the mills. While he derives pleasure in the carefully managed energy of the machines, Bessy hears unrelenting noise—"the interminable ranks of meaningless machines" (59). Unable to connect a worker's suffering with the systemic conditions at the mill and unable to sustain attention beyond her own immediate situation, Bessy, not unlike Lily Bart, expresses only a fleeting empathy with the individual workers' misfortunes. Similarly, while she does not reflect an Undine-like social Darwinist struggle, she is nonetheless an analogous parasite on the proprietary capitalist male members of her family enterprise.[13]

By contrast, the sober reflections of the sometime nurse Justine Brent reveal her profound sympathy with Amherst's efforts. Brent, in fact, seems to be the moral focus for much of the book (one of Wharton's working titles for the novel was, in fact, "Justine Brent"), and her renunciations are invariably selfless. While Justine, like Undine, is characterized as having limitless energy, that energy is tied to an unthreatening natural world. Her selflessness, community idealism, and capacity for regeneration are in direct inverse proportion to Undine's self-absorption, selfishness, and tendency to reversion. Like Amherst, Justine always reinvests her earnings from the company back into the company.

Yet Justine too must be managed. When she euthanizes the injured Bessy, who for some time has been unhappily married to Amherst, her actions suggest a moral independence too easily read as self-serving and therefore needing containment. Narrowly escaping murder charges, Justine is exiled from the family. Amherst meanwhile realizes their reformist vision of the mills when he inherits Bessy's fortune:

> Westmore prospered under the new rule. The seeds of life they had sown there were springing up in a promising growth of bodily health and mental activity, and above all in a dawning social consciousness. The mill-hands were beginning to understand the meaning of their work, in its relation to their own lives and to the larger economy. And outwardly, also, the new growth was showing itself in the humanized aspect of the place. Amherst's young maples were tall enough now to cast a shade on the grass-bordered streets; and the well-kept turf, the bright cottage gardens, the new central group of library, hospital and club-house, gave to the mill-village the hopeful air of a "rising" residential suburb. (621)

Justine's energy, reflected in the passage's organic metaphors, is now subsumed by Amherst's larger managerial vision. With Bessy's death and Justine's banishment, those unsettling elements of the new morality are quelled and corporate restructuring flourishes.[14]

Likewise, in *The Custom of the Country,* Wharton transforms the threat of the New Woman as sexual aggressor and social parasite into the threat of an unalloyed proprietary capitalist running the show. And once again, it is the monstrous energy kept in check that the corporate capitalist signifies. Compared to Undine's male fictional contemporaries whose sexual desires mirror their desires for capital—for example, Frank Cowperwood in Dreiser's *The Financier*—her desires are markedly asexual. Preferring to capitalize on the desire she elicits, Undine essentially disembodies herself in her relationships with men. On her honeymoon with Marvell, she "had never shown any repugnance to his tenderness, but such response as it evoked was remote and Ariel-like, suggesting, from the first, not so much of the recoil of ignorance as the coolness of the element from which she took her name" (152). By crafting Undine's relationships as a series of Wall Street maneuvers, Wharton gives her a businesslike detachment in their cultivation. When the "primitive" "Invader" Peter Van Degan offers her a substantial loan and then expects repayment in sexual favors, Undine carefully manages her disgust: "It was easy enough to rebuff him, the easier as his physical proximity always roused in her a vague instinct of resistance; but it was hard so to temper the rebuff with promise that the game of suspense should still delude him. He put it to her at last, standing squarely before her, his batrachian sallowness unpleasantly flushed, and primitive man looking out of the eyes from which a frock-coated gentleman usually pined at her" (230–31). This detachment not only gives Undine the power of sexual choice—thereby refuting Darwin's premise in his discussion of human sexual selection—but also enables her to recover quickly from rebuffs and vie for ever better marital options. Untethered to abiding moral and religious precepts while rapidly adjusting her opinions and self in hopes of material gain, Undine represents an earlier generation's feverish quest for acquisition. Undine's desexualized, pragmatic attachments suggest the pecuniary nature of all relationships within proprietary capitalism. While Moffatt displays a similar pragmatism in his business relationships, he also shows a capacity for human warmth, especially in his relationship with Paul, that Undine is unable to muster.

Yet Wharton both promises and warns her reader that Undine's ambition carries with it her eventual demise. While Undine has also inherited her mother's dullness—both women share a sharply limited range of intellectual energy, preferring the sycophantic ministerings of manicurist Mrs. Heeny in moments of emotional distress—Undine shares none of her mother's "proper" maternal concern necessary to carry on the race. Indeed, to apply Alison Berg's reading to a different Wharton protagonist, Undine is "dysgenic" not for her promiscuity but for her lack of maternal concern (76), which explains why, in part, Undine's ruthlessness is satirized more emphatically than Moffatt's. But maternal investment in Wharton's work signifies more than Berg's analysis suggests. In much of Wharton's fiction, maternal devotion is a moral saving grace since it demands selflessness and connection—mother love, according to Darwin, was the highest form of love—in a self-absorbed consumer culture. In Wharton's "The Mission of Jane" (*The Descent of Man,* 1904), for instance, the smug husband Lethbury suddenly realizes that his parochially girlish wife has suffered her maternal longings to remain unassuaged: "Maternity was no doubt the supreme function of primitive woman, the one end to which her whole organism tended; but the law of increasing complexity had operated in both sexes, and he had not seriously supposed that, outside the world of Christmas fiction and anecdotic art, such truisms had any special hold on the feminine imagination. Now he saw that the arts in question were kept alive by the vitality of the sentiments they appealed to" (*Collected Short Stories* 368). The "mission" of their adopted child, Jane, is to fulfill that "supreme function" and eventually unite the estranged couple. By the same token, in *The House of Mirth* (1905), Lily Bart's drug-induced imaginary embrace of Nettie Struther's baby at the end of the novel is depicted as a kind of primeval return to a "natural" state. As she succumbs to the drug overdose, Lily is finally able to escape the alienation of her relentlessly commodified life: "the tender pressure of its body . . . still close to hers: the recovered warmth flowed through her once more, she yielded to it, sank into it, and slept" (251). Undine, by contrast, cries bitterly at the news of her pregnancy, uses her son as leverage in an act of extortion, and adamantly refuses at one point to have any more, declaring to husband Raymond de Chelles, "you'd better leave it to your brother to perpetuate the race" (503). Such "unnatural" behavior suggests the extent to which Undine is subject to reversion. While her desire to imitate old New York society and the French aristocracy represents a significant break from the stolid provincialism of her parents, her evolutionary hold as a new species appears tenuous. A fluke of nature, she is liable to revert to an earlier and more primitive form if she ceases movement. Like all of the other New Woman figures in this novel, gallivanting about Europe and the waterholes of the Northeast, Undine is effectively committing "race suicide."

Her young son, Paul, offers no redemption and no promise of eventual family cohesion. With the inherited disposition of his father, Paul wanders lost and confused about the great Moffatt house at the end of the novel, uncomforted by Mrs. Heeny's vision of experience as a series of acquisition coups. After Mrs. Heeny reads to Paul the newspaper clippings describing Undine's speedy divorce and remarriage to Moffatt, a description punctuated by a "dazzling" account of Undine's wedding gifts, "one fact alone stood out for him—that she had said things that weren't true of his French father" (586). Maintaining this moral vision in the midst of the enormous wealth, power, and ethical morass Moffatt promises him would likely lead to the same nerve depletion that ruined his father.

The novel's ad hoc "sociologist," Charles Bowen, by contrast, views Undine as merely a product of that enterprise. Much of the scholarly work concerning this novel has, in my view, inordinately privileged the comments of Bowen—Wolff, for example, claims him as "our most reliable guide" (238)—even though he fails to see Undine in her multiple roles as proprietary capitalist, commodity, and dynamic of exchange. Forbearing to condemn immediately Undine's relentlessly self-interested behavior, Bowen reads her actions anthropologically. He defends Undine as an unfortunate product of the American marriage system after she misses her son's birthday party at the home of her in-laws: "How much does he let her share in the real business of life? How much does he rely on her judgment and help in the conduct of serious affairs? . . . It's normal for a man to work hard for a woman—what's abnormal is his not caring to tell her anything about it" (206). His prescription for such doomed relationships is a return to the chivalric code of the medieval romance: "Why does the European woman interest herself so much more in what the men are doing? Because she's so important to them that they make it worth her while! She's not a parenthesis, as she is here . . . The answer's obvious, isn't it? The emotional centre of gravity's not the same in the two hemispheres. In the effete societies it's love, in our new one it's business" (207). According to Bowen, caring for women in "the old barbarous possessive way" is what the "poor deluded dears" really want (207–8).

Bowen's argument contradicts that of the foremost leisure-class sociologist of the period, Thorstein Veblen, according to whom such sentiment was the impetus for the desire for freedom and purpose characteristic of "the New-Woman movement" (358–60). For Veblen, the New Woman, one of those from the "less manageable body of modern women," originates from the "well-to-do classes" (356–57). Her "undue reversion to the impulse of self-expression and workmanship" logically follows from the ineffable ennui that leisure culture and conspicuous consumption inevitably provoke: "She is petted, and is permitted, or even required, to consume largely and conspicuously—vicariously for her husband or other natural guardian. She is exempted, or debarred, from vulgarly useful employment—in order to perform leisure vicariously for the good repute of her natural (pecuniary) guardian" (356, 358). In Veblen's paradigm, Undine's "invidious" self-expression and workmanship disbar her from the ranks of the New Woman even as they signify Wharton's misgivings about New Woman energy untempered by Old Money values.

Bowen's arguments are also contradicted, as Ellen Dupree points out, by Undine's experience with Raymond de Chelles ("Jamming"). When Undine is forcibly domesticated in the Marquis de Chelles's castle, she reverts to an even earlier stage of evolutionary development; "barbarous possessiveness" only seems to compel Undine to adopt yet a different form of primitive behavior. Feeling the quite literal isolation of life at the castle where she is surrounded by a moat, and watching her beauty diminish, "Odd atavisms woke in her, and she began to pore over patent medicine advertisements, to send stamped envelopes to beauty doctors and professors of physical development, and to brood on the advantage of consulting faith-healers, mind-readers and their kindred adepts" (521–22). This tendency to reversion reminds readers that simply including Undine in more of the decision making would in no way "cure" her inherited behavior.[15] Her essentially imitative qualities, her inability to readily adapt to trying circumstances, suggest none of the imaginative skills necessary to survive long term. As Vernon Kellogg writes, "Selection will inexorably bar the forward movement, will certainly extinguish the direction of any orthogenetic process . . . which is not fit, that is, not adaptive" (374).

Ironically, Undine's second and third husbands suffer from similarly self-sabotaging inherited tendencies, which reflect their fundamental inability to compete in a marketplace driven by Wall Street fluctuations personified by Undine. Sheltered from workplace struggles too long, Ralph Marvell is unable to cope with the business world into which Undine's expenditures thrust him. He can only rely on the business dealings of Elmer Moffatt, imagining none of his own. The stultifying if ennobling old New York rituals and ideals to which Marvell had clung, and which are his evolutionary legacy, ultimately become irrelevant in the face of the "chaos of indiscriminate appetites" that characterize "modern" society: "Ralph sometimes called his mother and grandfather the Aborigines, and likened them to those vanishing denizens of the American continent doomed to rapid extinction with the advance of the invading race. He was fond of describing

Washington Square as the 'Reservation,' and of prophesying that before long its inhabitants would be exhibited at ethnological shows, pathetically engaged in the exercise of their primitive industries" (73–74). While steadfast in adhering to his dictum of an overarching moral vision for business and domestic life, Marvell feels the evisceration of his limited nerve force in the face of Undine's mutability, her "modern" sensibility. Ill-equipped both morally and intellectually to deal with the crass, cutthroat, and occasionally exhilarating business maneuvers of Wall Street, Marvell's brief foray into speculation culminates in his realization that "[h]e seemed to be stumbling about in his inherited prejudices like a modern man in mediæval armour" (469). When Undine eventually tires of his inability to secure enough money for her increasingly extravagant purchases and sues for divorce, Marvell refuses to risk scandal by contesting the terms. Realizing he has lost custody of his child, Marvell sees "that the weakness was innate in him. He had been eloquent enough, in his free youth, against the conventions of his class; yet when the moment came to show his contempt for them they had mysteriously mastered him, deflecting his course like some hidden hereditary failing" (437).

While Undine's third husband, Raymond de Chelles, and the French aristocracy he represents are seemingly more robust, under the test of her inherited nature they too appear on the verge of collapse:

> If Raymond de Chelles had been English he would have been a mere fox-hunting animal, with appetites but without tastes; but in his lighter Gallic clay the wholesome territorial savour, the inherited passion for sport and agriculture, were blent with an openness to finer sensations, a sense of the come-and-go of ideas, under which one felt the tight hold of two or three inherited notions, religious, political, and domestic, in total contradiction to his surface attitude. That the inherited notions would in the end prevail, everything in his appearance declared, from the distinguished slant of his nose to the narrow forehead under his thinning hair; he was the kind of man who would inevitably "revert" when he married. (275–76)

The fact that de Chelles has inherited acquired characteristics that a study of his physiognomy clearly reveals demonstrates Wharton's dialogic play of both Lamarckian and Mendelian principles. Within the domesticated setting of marriage, de Chelles, like Undine, reverts to the behavior of his ancestors. Too long domesticated and cultivated, a victim of artificial selection like Marvell, de Chelles contains within him the seeds of his own more immediate destruction. As Lock warns, "The modifications which occur under cultivation are in most cases decidedly weakly as compared with the original forms, as every gardener knows to his cost. They are only enabled to survive to a recognizable stage, because cultivation consists in the removal of competition" (35). Unable to cope with the new ethic, he eventually succumbs both to Undine's pressures and to his brother Hubert's, whose enormous gambling debts force him to sell his priceless family tapestries.

While Raymond seems destined to have no heirs, the philandering Hubert, married to the nouveau riche American Looty Arlington, immediately begets a child.

The tension in Undine's final marriage—the fact that Elmer Moffatt must produce money in order to consume Undine, while Undine must produce (maintain, imitate) herself in order to consume Moffatt's goods—is what fuels this relationship and ultimately acts as a metaphor for the larger market economy. The socially parasitic Popple and Undine's final husband, Moffatt, literally bulge with their acquisitive desire, be it of social glitterati or rare objects d'art. While Moffatt visually displays all the signs of his social limitations—he is "thick yet compact, with a round head set on a neck in which, at the first chance, prosperity would be likely to develop a red crease"—his stout form suggests a marketplace resilience (108). And if his inability to imitate fully the social value of those objects that he has acquired makes him ugly, it also grants him independence.

Wharton herself had made a less profitable alliance in her own marriage, one that she regretted, and must have identified at least somewhat with her voracious protagonist; she not only gave Undine her own nickname, "Puss," but also expressed a similar devotion to ceaseless energy in her personal correspondence. For Wharton, such fervent energy was necessary to cope with the demands of her neurasthenic husband and to succeed in the new industrial age. Feeling both coerced and compelled to remain with Teddy during his frequent bouts of nervousness, Wharton's relationship with her husband was often a "strain" that either distracted her from or drove her to her work (*Letters* 215). Fearing Teddy's imminent departure from a Swiss sanitarium in June 1910, Wharton writes to her sometimes capricious lover, Morton Fullerton, "You don't know what it is to say to myself, as I do, that my work is, must be, my only refuge, my only raison d'être, & then, as soon as I feel my wings, to be struck down again like this!" (*Letters* 220). Like Undine, Wharton was frustrated with her husband's inept business maneuvers and seemingly frivolous complaints about her expenditures. In a 1912 letter to "Minnie," Mary Cadwalader Jones, Wharton writes in a voice that sounds like Undine's complaints of Marvell: "the assumption that Teddy is a homeless martyr, victimized by my frivolous tastes for an effete society, is a voluntary one, a deliberate part pris to relieve his family of any responsibility. They know his real condition & the impossibility of living with him, & have told people so, who have told me. Luckily all my friends understand."[16] Wharton usually wrote daily, socialized often, and traveled frequently, prompting Henry James to dub her life a "whirligig" (Benstock 270). Fearing inclusion in one of her hectic motor trips throughout Europe, James compared her in the summer of 1912 to a raptor who "rode the whirlwind" and "played with the storm" (quoted in Benstock 261).

At the same time, Wharton must have found inspiration for Marvell, as a frustrated writer dealing with a spouse's seemingly petulant demands, in her own relationship with her husband. While fighting with Teddy for control of her financial estate in 1910, Wharton urges him to be reasonable, reminds him of his poor business decisions, announces her own financial success, and placates him with an expensive gift:

> what you call "having to be a passenger for the rest of your days"—that is, not be-ing able to manage my money affairs & decide about household matters—would make you dissatisfied & unhappy, [sic] whatever plan of life we tried to carry out together I can do nothing to alter these conditions, which are the result of your nervous breakdown, nor can I help the fact that your having lost a part of your fortune weighs with you more than the fact that, when you came back last year, I was ready to overlook everything you had done, & to receive you as if nothing had happened.
> ... I am so flush now, thanks to my "sage economics," that I should like to of-fer you a small open car, like the kind you have always said you would prefer for such a trip.[17]

Fearing an indefinite tenure in his "passenger" status, Teddy, like Undine, hopes to gain control by allocating family resources; Wharton, like Marvell, struggles to assuage unreasonable discontent.

Just as the sale of the Mount, a sale that excited Teddy and depressed Edith, epitomized Wharton's uncertain domestic position, objects in *The Custom of the Country* are continually wrenched away from their origins.[18] Marvell's sapphires, the Archduchess's pearls, and the Count's tapestries—all wrenched away from their original owners—signify an Old World logic of rightful family inheritance necessarily rewritten to create new social meanings for their new owners. Mar-vell is distraught less because of his wife's lies about resetting the family jewels and more because of the thought "that she had been unconscious of the wound she inflicted in destroying the identity of the jewels" (214). Moffatt seems un-perturbed that his collections of rare objects are a jumble of different aesthetic styles, provenances, and histories. Even Undine's wedding gift—"a necklace and tiara of pigeon-blood rubies belonging to Queen Marie Antoinette"—evokes the violence of new money wrenching the long-held prizes of the old. The final scene, in fact, is one of continual misrecognition. The acquisition of objects, husbands, and home are the "new" means of ordering experience and prove to be mere secondhand reports to be picked up out of a basket at will.

And yet if the red hair and rubies evoke a bloody wrenching of goods from old Europe, they also signify the precariousness of Undine's position within the new economy. Like the notoriously callous and extravagant Antoinette, Undine appears destined for overthrow. Moffatt's end-of-novel redness, by contrast, signifies both predatory success and corporate restraint. "[L]ooking stouter and redder than ever" (592), the "billionaire Railroad King" wears in his buttonhole "the red rib-bon bestowed on him for waiving his claim to a Velasquez that was wanted for the Louvre" (592). Now so wealthy as to be immune to the vicissitudes of the market,

Moffatt can afford a benevolent gesture, but the red ribbon and the red rubies create a more resonant tie between corporate restraint and proprietary ruthlessness. By harnessing that proprietary intractable force, Moffatt both guards against and profits from it. So, in the final scene, Undine has arranged a dinner party sure to have as much business as social opportunity. The guest list—including the Shallums, the Chauncey Ellings, Walsingham Popple, even Peter Van Degan—are her connections, not his, an assemblage of glitterati parasitic but useful. Despite her misgivings about Moffatt's boorishness, despite now wanting to be an ambassadress, Undine works well for him, and so confident is Moffatt in his power he can provoke her discontent good-humoredly.

A rare but transplanted art object herself, Undine reminds readers of the consequences of such removals. At once an exhilarating and threatening conduit for the reader's pleasure, Undine reminds her audience that shopping not only means being shopped for, but ultimately means engaging in "possession rituals" that prove transparent and ineffectual.[19] Even as Undine seeks to own objects and construct a self that reflects her changing social identities, the performative capacity of those goods fails her. Undine looks "vainly for the originals" among Mabel's set and is besieged by fakes in Aaronson the riding instructor. Disappointed early in the novel at the Fairford dinner because the fireplace logs are real and the meat is discernible—"she thought it dull of Mrs. Fairford not to have picked up something newer"—Undine remains addicted to novel experiences and is never able to master a cohesive and convincingly old-moneyed interior. As "an exact copy of the Pitti Palace," Undine and Moffatt's home is filled with other families' ancestral portraits and heirlooms, a home rather like their favorite hotel Nouveau Luxe, with its "incorrigible habit of imitating the imitation" (273). Wharton's novel may likewise promise readers that all "valuable" objects and the vast array of privileged experiences they represent are available for purchase, but it also reminds them that these objects will never completely mesh with their decor. In Scribner's advertisement for *The Custom of the Country,* Wharton herself appears in lavish dress, gaze cast down at a book, both the epitome of the genteel reader whom readers might become as they identify with Wharton's satiric voice and share in her panoptic investigation—"the entire fabric of 'society' is unrolled and spread out for view"—and the genteel presence they will never become (Charles Scribner's Sons).

As Undine represents both a trajectory toward social and economic "reversion," she is both a threat that needs to be controlled and one whose control suggests yet a new threat. The violence of Moffat's acquisition and the primitiveness of his imitation in the text remind readers that the new ethic of incorporation carries with it not merely vestiges of the old proprietary capitalism but also new threats of monopolistic power. President Roosevelt depended on J. P. Morgan, who had met his antitrust efforts with such arrogance in 1902, to bail out the financial markets in 1907. Similarly, Moffatt's rapid accumulation of wealth in conjunction with his ability to control Apex and Undine suggests both the danger of monopolistic control and the threat of pecuniary capitalism.

By satirizing the problem, Wharton also implies a solution, one increasingly debated before the presidential election of 1912. The tension in the novel evokes that between Theodore Roosevelt's New Nationalism, coined in a 1910 speech, and Woodrow Wilson's New Freedom, not coined until 1912 but implicit in his campaign rhetoric leading up to the election (John Cooper 174). In his speech summarizing the "New Nationalist" political philosophy, Roosevelt argued, "Combinations in industry are the result of an imperative economic law which cannot be repealed by political legislation. The effort at prohibiting all combina-tion has substantially failed. The way out lies, not in attempting to prevent such combinations, but in completely controlling them in the interest of the public welfare" (Harbaugh 323). Indeed, for Roosevelt the "biggest corporations had for the most part achieved their stature through efficient competition, . . . large corporations were here to stay, and . . . present economic conditions represented progress." The key for Roosevelt, then, was "conduct not size," and the best solution was to concentrate not on promoting competition but on supervising corporations, protecting public interests, and alleviating vast wealth disparities (Cooper 212; Hawley 7–8). Wilson's New Freedom held, by contrast, that trusts emerged because they enjoyed special privileges and because they used unfair practices to crush rivals. The answer was legislation to promote more efficient free competition (Hawley 7). Wilson believed that "comparatively few of the biggest corporations had achieved their stature through efficient competition, that those corporations were not necessarily here to stay, and that present condi-tions did not always represent progress over the past" (Cooper 212–13). For Wil-son, the answer was not laissez-faire but using government power to insure that the market would be open to new competitors (213). Throughout the course of the novel, Wharton offers a tacit endorsement of the New Nationalism because Moffatt's "combinations," although in need of supervision, are naturalized and legitimated in a way that Undine's ruthless free competition is not. With his ap-parently inexhaustible wealth, marketplace assurance, and deal-making savvy, Moffatt promises a better-managed corporate entity, even as his burgeoning waistline and priceless collections, not to mention his marketplace maneuvers, signify the threat of monopolistic power. At once affable, corrupt, vulgar, vora-cious, inevitable, and efficient, Moffatt is the face of the new Wall Street titans and needs to be managed rather than undone.

At the same time, by creating Undine as a proprietary-capitalist personality bested at her own game, Wharton ultimately emphasizes the shift in patriarchal tactics from the old entrepreneurial to the new managerial corporate culture. Yet considering the fates of other privileged New Woman protagonists, Undine appears a successful if shallow New Woman heroine. Neither dead, outcast, im-poverished, insane, nor subject to any fleeting desires for moral uplift, Undine has reached the marital jackpot. Characterized by an inexhaustible desire that could inspire and enervate, however, Undine represents an outmoded proprietary ethic, which her susceptibility to reversion suggests. As an unregulated, proprietary personality, Undine carries with her a volatility that disrupts many long-established marriage markets. Having signed the marriage contract, Undine becomes essentially an employee. She helped Moffatt acquire de Chelles's tapestries, and she will continue to help him increase and display his capital. Her young son Paul similarly moves from exploitable asset under Undine's care to future business partner under Moffatt's. Wharton's New Woman, then, may seem new, may feel new to those suffering from her exigencies, but is not really new at all. It is the danger of that misrecognition that Wharton calls upon her readers to heed.

CHAPTER 4

Sui Sin Far and the Wisdom of the New

"With her quaint manners and old-fashioned mode of life, she carries our minds back to times almost as ancient as the earth we live on. She is a bit of olden Oriental coloring amidst our modern Western lights and shades; and though her years be few, she is yet a relic of antiquity" (59). So Sui Seen Far begins "The Chinese Woman in America" (1897), with a gesture that both confirms the Chinese woman's status as exotic ethnic Other and popular sociological arguments that found the Chinese burdened by "a race character that looked almost wholly to the past and gained little from present experiences" (Haller 150).[1] The photographs that accompanied the essay would reinforce this perspective. In one, a Chinese bride appears, and in the other two, Chinese mothers are seated with their children; in both photographs the women wear traditional Chinese dress, their expressions remote. With "sensibilities as acute as a child's," Sui Seen Far's Chinese women embody a popular turn-of-the-century Orientalism ("Chinese Woman" 60). Devoted to husband, children, and "pretty things" while hoping to return to China one day, the Chinese woman is a refuge from the demands of an exacting American workplace.

Yet even as Sui Seen Far appeals to readers' fascination with Oriental exoticism, she Americanizes the Chinese woman by associating her with a most familiar type, the American New Woman. Immediately after the introduction I quoted, she notes that a "Chinese woman in a remote age invented the divided skirt, so it is not a 'New Woman' invention" (59). And while devoted exclusively to her husband and with "[n]o question of 'women's rights' perplex[ing] her," she is what "the Chinese call young married females, 'New Women.'" (64). By assuring readers of her vanity, propensity to gossip—"when they are met together, there is such a clattering of tongues one would almost think they were American women" (62)—commitment to acquiring beautiful objects, and middle-class status, Sui Seen Far constructs the Chinese woman in America as a version of the most popular conception of the New Woman, the Gibson Girl. At the same time, however, she critiques that American type for developing a public, potentially divisive vanity: "The ordinary American dresses for the eyes of her friends and enemies—particularly the latter—and derives small pleasure from her prettiest

Pierce, "Chinese Mothers in California." Illustration in Sui Seen Far, "The Chinese Woman in America." *Land of Sunshine* (January 1897): 63. Courtesy of the University of Iowa.

things unless they are seen by others" (64). In a move that refutes the popular conception of the Chinese woman as prostitute, Sui Seen Far notes that the Chinese woman dresses for herself alone, thereby eschewing the corruptive potential of the male and female gaze alike. With her commitment to her family, the Chinese New Woman, then, promises none of the social divisiveness of her American counterpart. She is both quaint exotic and contested trope, culturally familiar and a sign of cultural critique.

A year earlier, however, in Walter Blackburn Harte's Kansas City journal the *Lotus,* Sui Seen Far had promoted a version of the Chinese New Woman more closely associated with social transgression and resistance to patriarchy. "The Story of Iso" depicts a rebellious Chinese daughter who criticizes male privilege, and after speaking to a mysterious "red-headed stranger," she rejects ancestor worship and arranged marriages (118). "[E]verlastingly disgraced" in China, she is taken across the sea by the "red-headed people." Hearing the story of Iso, the narrator's cousin declares, "She who is called in China 'The woman who talks too much' is called by us '[t]he new woman'" (119).

I begin with these two early pieces of Sui Seen Far's work because they suggest the complexities and contradictions of her deployment of the New Woman trope. The popular tropes the rhetoric of the "New" generated in her work—namely the "New God," the new Chinese woman, and the New China—are crucial sites for her engagement precisely because they linked gendered, class, and ethnic citizenship less to biological difference and more to commercial performance. Her stories and essays continually expose those contradictions of an American culture that promoted Horatio Alger myths of upward mobility while reifying class, race, and gender distinctions that thwart the realization of those narratives. By constructing performative rather than racialized criteria for citizenship, she writes Chinese Americans into the history of the nation by making their anxieties—be it of workplace demands, parental responsibilities, consumer pressures, or new gender roles—akin to those of her white readers. And yet, Sui Seen Far's attempt to deploy the already overdetermined figure of the New Woman was necessarily co-opted by editors hoping to capitalize on the commercial potential of an exotic regionalist aesthetic and complicated further by her own complicity in that marketing process. Despite and in some sense because of marketplace demands, Sui Sin Far evokes the dominant trope of the New Woman to represent a host of cultural anxieties Chinese culture may help to mitigate, in effect suggesting that a bicultural identity offers a much safer alternative to American social life.

Paradoxically, then, these texts construct the Chinese as both already new and enticingly old. As works of regionalism or local color fiction, both works highlight the effects of modern cultural incursions on traditional Chinese life, but rather than showing that culture adapting to outside influence, they suggest its cultural intransigence, in effect constituting it, to use Richard Brodhead's words, "as a self-contained form belonging to the past rather than an interactive force still adapting in the present" (Brodhead 121). Safely ensconced in the past, Chinese culture can be more easily appropriated to be enjoyed by white "tourists," a dynamic that Brodhead sees as an essential trait of regionalism: "The paradox of this genre is that it purports to value a culture for being intactly other at the very time that it is offering outsiders the chance to inhabit it and enjoy its special 'life'" (133).

Despite their ideological differences, both texts highlight Sui Seen Far's status as an insider informant, offering white readers an exotic Other to appropriate and consume. Published in *The Land of Sunshine: An Illustrated Monthly of Southern California,* "The Chinese Woman" at first seems a departure from the magazine's principal goal: to promote southern California real estate with content that was "exclusively Western in text, unswervingly American in spirit" (Bingham 57). Yet editor Charles Lummis's interest in ethnics as the basis for local color pieces—in this case Chinese, Indians, or Mexican Americans (Bingham 164)—encouraged authors to act as cultural mediators, what James Clifford describes as "informants." As her pseudonym suggests, Sui Seen Far has privileged access into this reclusive community, for having "seen far," she may tell "you" how to become acquainted with the exotic "her," the "Chinese woman":[2] "She lives among us, but is as isolated as if she and the few Chinese relations who may happen to live near were the only human beings in the world" (59). "The Story of Iso" is likewise crafted to emphasize Sui Seen Far's "insider" knowledge of the Chinese countryside, omens, and worship rituals.

It was not until some ten years later in the progressive, nationally syndicated *Independent* that Sui Sin Far would explicitly complicate her status as informant by acknowledging the difficulty she had in gaining access to that Other that was also, in some respects, herself. As daughter of an English father and Chinese mother, the English-born Edith Maude Eaton grew up speaking English, knew little Chinese, and was not always accepted by the Chinese community to which she tried to gain access. Indeed, when a San Francisco newspaper hired her to obtain subscriptions in Chinatown, she admitted that "save for a few phrases, I am unacquainted with my mother tongue. How, then, can I expect these people to accept me as their own countrywoman? The Americanized Chinamen actually laugh in my face when I tell them that I am of their race" ("Leaves" 131).

The ideological complexity of Sui Seen Far's voice and project suggest the complexities of cultural hybridization, what Lisa Lowe describes as "the uneven process through which immigrant communities encounter the violences of the U.S. state, and the capital imperatives served by the United States and by the Asian states from which they come, and the process through which they survive those violences by living, inventing, and reproducing different cultural alternatives" (82).[3] Writing during a period of Chinese exclusion acts, unwritten segregation policies, anti-Chinese riots throughout the Northwest and West, the prevailing "Yellow Peril" rhetoric in the press, and the rising popularity of an Orientalist aesthetic, Edith Maude Eaton/Sui Seen Far/Sui Sin Far works to make the Chinese presence in the U.S. legitimate by subverting, and occasionally reproducing, both these and other discriminatory discursive practices she encounters.

As feminist critics Amy Ling, Annette White-Parks, Elizabeth Ammons, Kate McCullough, and Patricia Chu have demonstrated, Edith Eaton's work explores both the conflicts and possibilities of her border positions during this period of intense sinophobia. Kate McCullough, for example, has cautioned readers and critics to complicate our understanding of Sui Sin Far's state, ethnic, gendered, but particularly national border crossings: "in representations of Chinese-American communities and the characters who constitute them, Sui Sin Far reveals and challenges the ways the American cultural imagination depends, as Geoffrey Bennington puts it above, on the 'other nation,' embodied by the figure of the Chinese, in order to naturalize national binary oppositions such as citizen/immigrant, American/foreigner, insider/outsider, and white/Chinese" (228). By denaturalizing these binary oppositions, Sui Sin Far recognizes the extent to which in the late nineteenth and early twentieth century, "blood determines both personal identity and cultural location" (McCullough 228). Patricia Chu examines the ways in which Eaton anticipated the concerns of contemporary Asian American writers when she both struggles "to transform the connotations of 'American' to include those of Asian descent; and . . . to create imaginatively the elusive subjectivities of the immigrant generation" (122). Yet Eaton's work, Chu argues, also anticipates an alternate tradition in which Asian American women writers challenge a "division of labor (in which men adapt and wives are asked to both maintain the old ways and absorb the men's ambivalence about these ways) and replicate it in their own representations of Asian and immigrant women as wives and mothers. . . . *Mrs. Spring Fragrance* also challenges the stereotype of the Asian woman as intrinsically less adaptable than her male counterpart by depicting women who are culturally more adept at assimilation than their husbands yet true to their home culture" (127–28).

I would like to suggest, however, that we complicate even further our understanding of "dominant" and "resistant" voices both within and surrounding Sui Sin Far's work by highlighting those moments of ideological contradiction in the presentation of her voice to a predominantly white reading audience. Her writing during the period of 1888 to 1913, when the bulk of her literary work was originally published, suggests a cultural identity in process and in conflict. "Partly inherited, partly modified, as well as partly invented," Sui Sin Far's cultural identity emerges in relation to dominant discourses that subordinate it as Other even as these discourses enable new points of resistance.[4] We must read that cultural identity reflected in her work in its shifting contexts—inherited Chinese and English traditions, modified by Canadian, Jamaican, and American experiences, and the partly invented self of Wing Sing, Fire Fly, Sui Seen Far/Sui Sin Far (water fragrant flower or narcissus)[5]—as we note the shifting axes of power that shaped its construction and reception.[6] Even though Annette White-Parks's concept of "tricksterism" as the ability to resist prevailing racist ideologies while appealing to a wide audience ("We Wear the Mask" 16) is helpful in understanding Sui Sin Far's cross-cultural literary strategizing, it does not fully account for those shifting axes of power within her publishing venues, which she may or may not have anticipated. Under intense pressure to sell her work, she undoubtedly either crafted her short fiction and essays to appeal to the editorial goals of each magazine or allowed her work to be framed with those goals in mind. At the same time, the position each magazine developed toward such issues as Sino-American relations following the Boxer rebellion, the feasibility of American investments in China, travelogues of the "exotic" Orient, and the emergence of the Chinese and American New Woman influenced the ways in which her work would be framed. While such discourses often undermined the political protest elements of Sui Sin Far's work, they could lead to ideological fissures that would support the subversive elements in her fiction. In other words, while recognizing the cultural hybridity of her voice, I want to emphasize the ideological contradictions inherent in the conception and context of her work, especially in relationship to the rhetoric of the New Woman.

On the one hand, Sui Sin Far's work confirms popular anxieties about the pressures to succeed in a new American culture and new social roles for women. While she heralds the traditional Chinese values of filial duty and communal consciousness, she questions the "new" American ethic of individual advancement and sexual freedom. Rather than depicting the social structures of the largely homosocial environments in turn-of-the-century Chinatowns,[7] she most often invokes a markedly middle-class, American, heterosocial domestic space and a safely ethnic urban space, one easily navigated by white tourists. Such a revision of the Chinese community within the United States countered arguments about Chinatowns as threatening dens of vice and Chinese women as prostitutes liable to corrupt white men. Within her fictionalized domestic space, the "old" Chinese traditions become a refuge from the anxieties of the "new" social and economic demands of American culture.

On the other hand, allegiances to traditional religious beliefs or cultural practices in Sui Sin Far's work rarely threaten a western-style, corporate-capitalist market system. Those Chinese-identified Chinese American characters who are unwilling to claim the "new" competitive ethic of American culture appear in Eaton's fiction as essentially "old school." Because racist sociologists claimed that the Chinese had inherited an unwillingness, rather than an inability, to assimilate, Sui Sin Far, I argue, crafts American-identified Chinese American male characters who successfully compete within the American marketplace and thereby assure readers that Americanization is both possible and preferable. While she may criticize aspects of the "new" American culture and New Woman that thwart the formation of politically necessary alliances between Chinese American men and women, she readily accepts the western influence necessary in the formation of a "New China" and the "New Chinese" overseas.

Sui Sin Far's attitude toward the Chinese New Woman is necessarily a vexed one because each word in the phrase is at the center of a contested sociopolitical debate. While she links the Chinese American woman with the term New Woman, she does so uneasily, acutely aware, like Hopkins, that the trope carries with it connotations of intersex tension and increasingly racialized sexual transgression even as it represents a personal freedom counter to popular stereotypes of Chinese women's inherent docility. Rather than spearheading specific reforms, Sui Sin Far's Chinese American female protagonists act as cultural interpreters who offer readings of American culture that are most validated if they demonstrate bicultural influence. Likewise, Sui Sin Far cautions against heralding the accomplishments of the dominant version of the white New Woman as suffragist and social reformer lest her triumph mask class oppression or lead to marital discord. Unless her position is moderated by a Chinese or Chinese-like influence, the New Woman is generally more a sign of social decay than social advance.

Stories such as "The Gamblers," which Sui Sin Far wrote for the February 1896 issue of the newly founded journal the *Fly Leaf*, foreground the host of ideological contradictions around the rhetoric of the "new." Edited by her brother-in-law, Walter Blackburn Harte, the short-lived *Fly Leaf* declared itself on its cover as "A Pamphlet Periodical of the New—the New Man, New Woman, New Ideas, Whimsies and Things" and targeted young, progressive readers.[8] In many respects, her story seemed to reiterate derogatory stereotypes central to the "yellow peril" rhetoric of the period. Threatening Western civilization, patriotism, and white economic dominance, the yellow peril was viewed as a racial hazard from a biologically and morally inferior race (W. Wu 1). Indeed, in his study of the history of "Orientalism," Edward Said notes:

> Along with all other peoples variously designated as backward, degenerate, uncivilized, and retarded, the Orientals were viewed in a framework constructed out of biological determinism and moral-political admonishment. The Oriental was linked thus to elements in Western society (delinquents, the insane, women, the poor) having in common an identity best described as lamentably alien. Orientals were rarely seen or looked at; they were seen through, analyzed not as citizens, or even people, but as problems to be solved or confined or—as the colonial powers openly coveted their territory—taken over. (207)

With this combination of "biological determinism and moral-political admonishment," a litany of arguments was continually expounded against the Chinese: they constituted a threat to Republican and Christian institutions, they displaced white laborers by working and living more cheaply, they were unable or unwilling to assimilate, and they constituted a threat to public morality by fostering prostitution and general vice (Lee 115–18; Haller 150). The fear that the Chinese might gain a military strength like the Japanese and threaten Anglo-Saxon world domination was not uncommon. In a 1904 article for the *Living Age,* O. Eltzbacher writes, "Therefore the deduction that China would imitate Japan, that a victorious Japan would soon convert the latent danger of the yellow peril into an actual danger by reforming China and then contending with the white races for the dominion of the world, seems very plausible" (223). From 1850 to 1940, such yellow peril rhetoric was, as William F. Wu notes, the prevailing theme in American fiction about Chinese Americans. Stereotypes of Chinese Americans included inscrutability, excitability, stupidity, and craftiness, in addition to a variety of occupational stereotypes—including "tong killers, heartless husbands, female slaves, and torturers, as well as loyal domestic servants and successful merchants" (4).

Using motifs that are uncharacteristic of the body of her work in general, Sui Seen Far creates in "The Gamblers" gambling, opium-addicted, and murderous Chinese characters—images reinforced by illustrations of fiendish-looking villains alongside the text. Within the context of the magazine, however, the delinquent and excitable Chinese American protagonists are framed as suffering from a more general modern American susceptibility to unwise nervous expenditure. Rather than the Chinese presence being a threat to the American (Eaton does not, significantly, include American characters in her story of Chinese vice), the former and the latter share a similar outside "new" threat, intrinsic to neither but culturally imposed on both.

The story begins with a description of Ah Lin who shows all the signs of having embraced the "New God," money; his limited nerve force has almost completely dissipated: "he shambled on indifferently, slowly and heavily, apparently totally unconscious of physical discomfort" (14). Upon entering the gambling house, he envies the "peace and a foretaste of oblivion" the opium smokers have found (15). His "small well-shaped hands [that] did not look as if they were accustomed to manual labor" suggest Ah Lin's susceptibility, as a one-time member of a professional class, to the disastrous consequences of embracing the "New God" (14). After he and fellow player Hom Lock "bowed themselves before the image—the Chinaman's gambling god," Ah Lin loses his meager resources while Hom Lock wins big (15). A fight ensues until finally the gambling god "calmly looked down upon two dead men" (18). Sui Seen Far's byline is printed directly underneath this last line suggesting her privileged perspective. She has "seen far" into the folly of these all "too American" Chinese men.

"The Gamblers" is framed by two stories that also warn of the consequences of being lured by such false gods. In the previous issue of the *Fly Leaf,* L. Lemmah satirized this "New God" as "a being of an infinite indifference to syndicates (*sin*-di-cates!), deals (in which lurks the de'il!), coal oil monopolies (whence comes endowments that throttle free speech on social questions), sugar trusts (that capture Congress), and the ways of a man with a mind—or, what is quite as wonderful—the ways of a new maid with an old man" (22). "The Gamblers" is followed by Percival Pollard's "One Failure to Forget" in which a group of friends gather to discuss various strategies for ensuring blissful forgetfulness; work, drink, and women are all suggested. One year later the central protagonist, Farlough, appears looking "healthier and stronger" and finds that while his friends have chosen the two more debauched options, "my work is such a pleasure to me that the past has been atoned for long ago, and none of my memories are tainted by regrets" (24). Within this context, then, Sui Seen Far's story suggests less the endemic vice of Chinatown and more the general susceptibility, a susceptibility shared by privileged white "brain-workers," to the lure of the "New God"—easy money, hedonistic pleasure, and consequent nervous dissipation.

Sui Sin Far's autobiographical essays would reiterate this critique of the "new" American values while legitimating her own status as a writer. In "Leaves from the Mental Portfolio of an Eurasian," which Sui Sin Far published in the *Independent* in January 1909, she evoked both Whitman's *Leaves of Grass* and Fanny Fern's *Fern Leaves from Fanny's Port-Folio* (1853). Indeed, her title suggests both Sui Sin Far's desire to evoke the democratic ideals of this "great American" poet as well as the sympathy for economic exigencies that popular sentimental women writers foregrounded to justify their own status as writers. Struggling to survive alone, facing threats to her virtue, racist taunts, and imminent poverty while remaining committed to claiming her Chinese-Anglo identity, Sui Sin Far aligns her own experience with that of many nineteenth-century sentimental heroines.[9] While giving her voice literary authority through association, her title also suggests why her narratives were necessarily short and episodic. To counter arguments that the Chinese were insensible and brutish, Sui Sin Far feminizes her Chinese ancestry, from which, she claims, her acute sensitivity is derived: "I have come from a race on my mother's side which is said to be the most stolid and insensible to feeling of all races, yet I look back over the years and see myself so keenly alive to every shade of sorrow and suffering that it is almost a pain to live" (127). Throughout this essay, Sui Sin Far implies that both her Chinese ancestry and her "attacks of nervous sickness" have made her keenly attuned to emotional and physical nuances: "At eighteen years of age what troubles me is not that I am what I am, but that others are ignorant of my superiority. I am small, but my feelings are big—and great is my vanity" (128). She explains her travels across the country as being motivated by the advice of a doctor "who declares that I will never regain my strength in the East" (130). As Tom Lutz has argued, neurasthenia was considered evidence of "the highest levels of civilization," a disease available only to the most refined and affecting only the most "advanced" races (6). Like her more established contemporaries Edith Wharton and Charlotte Perkins Gilman, Eaton claims for herself and Chinese Americans susceptibility to this privileged disease.

While a necessarily peripatetic lifestyle, ever-present financial pressures, and poor health prevented her from developing close, long-standing relationships with any literary community, Sui Sin Far suggests that her cultural, familial, and ethnic displacement combined with her physical frailty gave her essential artistic capabilities, not the least of which was a spiritual foundation in a material age.[10] In "Sui Sin Far, the Half Chinese Writer, Tells of Her Career," she assumes a commitment to developing the essential ethereality of the sentimental heroine. Speaking reverently of an early mentor, Mrs. Darling, Sui Sin Far writes, "She also inspired me with the belief that the spirit is more than the body, a belief which helped me through many hours of childish despondency, for my sisters were all much heavier and more muscular than I" (6). She travels north from Jamaica to "cure" her malarial fever and moves westward again on the advice of a physician, declaring herself "immune to material things" when absorbed in her work. By suggesting that Sui Sin Far creates herself as both "nervous" writer and sentimental heroine, I certainly do not mean to belittle the reality of her personal and professional struggles, but rather to suggest that she presented those struggles to the progressive audience of the *Independent* and the literary-minded readers of the *Boston Globe* in such a way as to receive a sympathetic hearing.

Sui Sin Far's one volume of collected works, *Mrs. Spring Fragrance* (1912), again suggests the complexity of both her hybrid voice and cultural positioning. The rich red cover is embossed with the title in a gold, orientalized typeface and a green, white, and gold image of Chinese water lilies and dragonflies in the midst of a full gold moon. In the bottom right-hand corner appear four Chinese characters, which approximately translate as "signed by Sui Sin Far" (White-Parks, *Sui Sin Far* 197). Along the spine of the book, one water lily appears under "Mrs. Spring Fragrance by Sui Sin Far," suggesting the ways in which the author, like the central protagonist for which the collection is named, is a key element of this stylized "Oriental" aesthetic. Translated literally, "Sui Sin Far" means "water fragrant flower" or narcissus, a Chinese lily (Ling 41). The pages of the book further encourage this aestheticism of character and event. While encountering Sui Sin Far's stories of cultural conflict, racism, and social alienation, the reader is continually reminded of this exoticizing aesthetic.

Advertising for *Mrs. Spring Fragrance* reinforced both this exoticizing aesthetic and evolutionary theories that situated the Chinese as essentially still childlike in their evolutionary development. The publisher's announcement in the *New York Times Book Review*, which also foregrounds the orientalized typescript and Chinese characters, reads, "Quaint, lovable characters are the Chinese who appear in these unusual and exquisite stories of our Western Coast—stories that will open an entirely new world to many readers" ("Publisher's Announcement"). The copy emphasizes the children's stories that occupy the latter half of the volume, an emphasis that would have confirmed the notion that the Chinese had stagnated in their evolutionary development (Haller 151–52): "Our understanding and sympathy are awakened by the joys and sorrows of Little Me, Pau Tsu, Tie Co., and the Prize China Baby, while their misdeeds and misfortunes become of absorbing interest. Altogether they make as desirable reading as the title suggests" (Publisher's Announcement").

Reviews of *Mrs. Spring Fragrance,* though mixed, emphasized the thrust of Sui Sin Far's social commentary even as they perpetuated stereotypes of a population unable or unwilling to assimilate. Even as the reviewer for the *Boston Globe* noted Sui Sin Far's efforts to create Chinese characters with whom white people could identify, the reviewer also asserted that the Chinese were more sensitive than whites: "The tales are told with a sympathy that strikes straight to one's heart; to say they are convincing is weak praise, and they show the Chinese with feelings absolutely indistinguishable from those of white people—only the Chinese seem to have more delicate sensibilities, and more acute methods of handling their problems" (as quoted in White-Parks, *Sui Sin Far* 201). In her autobiographical essay for the *Boston Globe* published a month earlier, Sui Sin Far had asserted her claim to those "more delicate sensibilities," in what I argue was an effort to give herself some of the same privilege accorded to white brain workers suffering with neurasthenia while disavowing stereotypes of the insensible Chinese. Within the context of the review, however, the idiosyncratic nature of her sensitivity becomes a more generalized racial trait that serves to differentiate the Chinese population from the white. Despite reservations concerning much of Sui Sin Far's work, a reviewer for the *New York Times Book Review* nonetheless praises those stories in which Sui Sin Far offered "far and deep" insight into "the character of an Americanized Chinese . . . into the lives, thoughts and emotions of the Chinese women who refuse to be anything but intensely Chinese, and into the characters of the half-breed children" ("A New Note" 405). By declaring the near "superhuman" undertaking of Sui Sin Far's project while highlighting her portrayal of "Chinese women who refuse to be anything but intensely Chinese," this reviewer is less sanguine about differences between whites and Chinese, instead suggesting the inscrutability of a potentially unassimilable, ethnically Other population.

Those stories that I will examine from the collection all demonstrate the conflict between the performative nature of those "new" identities offered within American culture, the hegemonic discourses of their respective contexts, and the special role of women as negotiating these discourses. A sequel to the first story, "Mrs. Spring Fragrance," "The Inferior Woman" begins with Mrs. Spring Fragrance's declaration that she is going to write "a book about Americans for her Chinese women friends. The American people were so interesting and mysterious" (22).[11] Ingeniously reversing the trajectory of the "inscrutability" designation, Mrs. Spring Fragrance establishes herself in the role of an interpreter of American culture. Adopting the American dress and attitude—at one point her husband teases her, "You are no Chinese woman . . . You are an American"—she is able to traverse easily the cultural boundaries in her integrated, middle-class community. Her markers of difference, her name as well as her pink parasol and fan—both in fashion in 1912—become "charming" idiosyncrasies, thereby diminishing the threat her cultural analysis might pose to white readers. Although he is not positioned as a cultural interpreter, Mr. Spring Fragrance's identity is also cast most strongly in American terms:

> As a boy he had come to the shores of America, worked his way up, and by dint of painstaking study after working hours acquired the Western language and Western business ideas. He had made money, saved money, and sent money home. The years had flown, his business had grown. Through his efforts trade between his native town and the port city in which he lived had greatly increased. A school in Canton was being builded [*sic*] in part with funds furnished by him, and a railway syndicate, for the purpose of constructing a line of railway from the big city of Canton to his own native town, was under process of formation, with the name of Spring Fragrance at its head. (31–32)

By stressing Mr. Spring Fragrance's commitment to Chinese industrial development, Sui Sin Far both promises the Chinese American's potential for upward mobility and forecasts China's continuing commitment to western-style expansion. In response to her husband's irritation at not being recognized for his accomplishments, Mrs. Spring Fragrance quotes Confutze, whose pragmatism supports the newly developing American managerial business ethic: "Be not concerned that men do not know you; be only concerned that you do not know them" (32). Her response suggests both her fundamental involvement in her husband's struggles and her ability to effectively interpret those struggles through a bicultural lens.

The central action of the story involves Mrs. Spring Fragrance's quest to "understand" the class-based objections of her friend Mrs. Carson to the marriage of her son, Sam Carson, to Alice Winthrop, the "inferior woman." On the advice of her husband as to the best means of researching this issue for her book, Mrs. Spring Fragrance visits "the superior woman," Miss Evebrook, the privileged suffrage advocate whom Mrs. Carson would prefer marry her son. While eavesdropping outside of Miss Evebrook's window, Mrs. Spring Fragrance hears her surprising defense of the inferior woman:

> It is women such as Alice Winthrop who, in spite of every drawback, have raised themselves to the level of those who have had every advantage, who are the pride and glory of America. There are thousands of them, all over this land: women who have been of service to others all their years and who have graduated from the university of life with honor. Women such as I, who are called the Superior Women of America, are after all nothing but schoolgirls in comparison. (35–36)

The parallel narrative between Mr. Spring Fragrance and Alice Winthrop—both suffering unwarranted prejudice—demonstrates Sui Sin Far's desire to broaden the activist commitment of her progressive reading audience. In a move that at once affirms her own position as a single woman writer, her struggle for financial security, and her reliance on male mentors, Sui Sin Far presents positive images of both Miss Evebrook's and Alice Winthrop's contrary life choices. Miss Evebrook has settled on ten years of freedom, "ten years in which to love, live, suffer, see the world, and learn about men (not schoolboys) before I choose one" (37). In response to Miss Evebrook's request that Alice speak at a meeting about the "suppression and oppression of women by men," Alice refuses, maintaining, "As a woman I look back over my years spent amongst business and professional men, and see myself, as I was at first, an impressionable, ignorant little girl, born a Bohemian, easy to lead and easy to win, but borne aloft and morally supported by the goodness of my brother men, the men amongst whom I worked" (38). While harmony is ultimately restored and the "inferior woman" is accepted by her mother-in-law to be, Mrs. Spring Fragrance's final words in this edition of the story affirm the class advantages enjoyed by the "superior woman": "Ah, the Superior Woman! Radiantly beautiful, and gifted with the divine right of learning! I love well the Inferior Woman; but, O Great Man, when we have a daughter, may Heaven ordain that she walk in the groove of the Superior Woman" (47).

When "The Inferior Woman" originally appeared in the progressive *Hampton's Magazine* in May 1910, the last sentence of the story bestows the final accolade upon the working-class Alice Winthrop. Mrs. Spring Fragrance declares, "I love well the 'Superior Woman,' but O Great Man, when we have a daughter, may heaven ordain that she walk in the groove of the 'Inferior Woman!'" (731). Such a change suggests the extent to which Sui Sin Far or her editor shaped her fiction according to its venue. Published in New York City, *Hampton's Magazine* was known for its muckraking and support of progressive causes like the rights of working women. The ending in the McClurg volume appeals to an audience whose alliances are more closely connected to the middle class.

In "The Story of One White Woman Who Married a Chinese," Sui Sin Far would reiterate many of the same objections to dominant New Woman identity she offered in "The Inferior Woman," but this time Chinese culture becomes a necessary anodyne for the social disruption New Woman ideology represents. The main character's husband Jim, "an omnivorous reader of socialistic and new-thought literature," has made women's suffrage "one of his particular hobbies" (112). He grows to reject his traditional family-oriented wife and the arguments she makes in favor of "ordinary working women": "Once I told him that I did not admire clever business women, as I had usually found them, and so had other girls of my acquaintance, not nearly so kind-hearted, generous, and helpful as the humble drudges of the world—the ordinary working women" (112–13). Her vision of Miss Moran, the New Woman collaborator on her husband's book, is couched in the anti–New Woman rhetoric of the time: cold, antimaternal, "broad-shouldered, masculine-featured, and, as it seemed to me heartless" (116).[12] Associated with divorce, infidelity, and enervating stenographic labor, the last of which Edith Eaton herself often performed, the new represents all that the narrator must flee. When she divorces her husband and is on the brink of suicide, Liu Kanghi rescues her and subsequently becomes her husband, a domestic arrangement that would have seemed to most readers dangerously exotic. In Albert Beck Wenzell's "The American Girl who Marries an Oriental" (1896), a modestly bedecked Gibson Girl figure bursts in on her sarong-wearing husband who carries a saber apparently to command his half-naked harem. Sui Sin Far's character wears American clothes, has hair cut short, and appears "a good-looking young man": a direct counter to such stereotypes because Liu has been energized but not overwhelmed by the marketplace ethic of desire and the new. With Liu as intermediary, the narrator is able to embrace the Chinese community. When she suffers a bout of "nervous prostration," that Chinese community offers a rest cure. By providing employment that she can perform while caring for her child, Liu made them "both independent, not only of others but of himself," a somewhat startling New Woman conclusion given what at first may seem a less autonomous domestic arrangement (131).

The story of their relationship is continued in "Her Chinese Husband," where the protagonist relates more anecdotes about Liu Kanghi's ability to bridge new and old: "He told me one day that he thought the stories in the Bible were more like Chinese than American stories, and added: 'If you had not told me what you have about it, I should say that it was composed by the Chinese'" (133). A member of both the "Reform Club, and the Chinese Board of Trade," Liu Kanghi appears evenly modulated. James Carson, on the other hand, is depicted as having overspent his limited nerve force by too great an investment in the new and profligate behavior—an "ardent lover" who "reproached me with being cold, unfeeling, a marble statue, and so forth" (134). Yet Sui Sin Far does not unequivocally embrace the old ethic, either. The old, in fact, destroys Liu Kanghi. He is shot at the end of the story by Chinese fearful of the cultural change he represents.

Such an ambivalent vision of the effects of new social mores and the New Woman belies the extent to which the American popular press endorsed Chinese women's changing roles following the success of Sun Yat-sen's revolution in October 1911. In "The New Woman in China and Japan," Adachi Kinnosuke writes, "The Chinese revolution has already done many remarkable things. Setting up a republic in the ancient home of autocracy is not the most amazing of its performances. What is more significant, especially in the eyes of the future East, and more surprising and, withal, thoroughly natural, is this: It has staged the New Woman of the New East,—staged her dramatically" (71).

The editor of this two-article series proclaims, "In Japan and China women are attending the universities, entering into business and professions, and already taking an active part in public life" (71). Kinnosuke's "Representative 'New Women' of China" includes Sue Yi Yat, "A Chinese girl, born in America, who has entered a military school in China"; Dr. Mary Stone (Shi Ma-Li-A), "A successful physician who in a single year has treated nearly 16,000 patients"; and

Albert Beck Wenzell, "The American girl who marries an Oriental must be prepared for real changes in her home life." Illustration in *Life* (January 30, 1896): 78–79.

Dr. Kin, "[w]ho for twenty years has been engaged in reorganizing the hospital system of China" (73). Two months after Sui Sin Far published her last known essay, "Chinese Workmen in America" (July 1913) in the *Independent,* the Rev. Charles Bone published "The Awakening of the Women of China" where he hails "propaganda against footbinding," "the introduction of female education," and the "sudden outburst of feminine activity in the sphere of politics" (668–69).[13]

In "The Wisdom of the New," then, it seems odd that Sui Sin Far foregrounds the difficulty, if not the impossibility, of a Chinese-identified, Chinese American woman adopting "new" American cultural and commercial values. Part 1 of the story takes place in China and begins with a conversation between Old Li Wang, "the peddler, who had lived in the land beyond the sea," and Wou Sankwei, the young only son of the deceased town magistrate. Li Wang entertains his young listener with tales of the American marketplace: "about the winning and the los-ing, and the stories of the losing were even more fascinating than the stories of the winning. 'Yes, that was life,' he would conclude. 'Life, life'" (48). While Sui Sin Far constructs American culture as an essentially thriving maker of men, she constructs the Chinese family as an impediment to any such self-reliance. As the precious only son, Sankwei is "waited upon hand and foot" by his mother and sister with nothing to do "but sleep, dream, and occasionally get into mischief" (48). When Sankwei hears the story of Ching Kee, yet another sojourner back from the "land beyond the sea," and how he "accumulated a small fortune," Wou's own living situation pales in comparison: "'Tis a hard life over there,' said he [Ching Kee], 'but 'tis worth while. At least one can be a man, and can work at what work comes his way without losing face.' Then he laughed at Wou Sankwei's flabby muscles, at his soft, dark eyes, and plump, white hands" (49). Fearing his future as a "woman man" in China, Sankwei ventures to America. For Sui Sin Far, then, America offers an activity cure to a tradition-bound Chi-nese middle class that has become increasingly effete and neurasthenic.[14] Such a strategy also works both to refute the racist trope of the Chinese immigrant as indefatigable peasant laborer and to sell a vision of America, and specifically the West Coast, as a still-viable frontier, where money may be won or lost according to one's commitment to hard work and creative enterprise. Yet Sui Sin Far also constructs China as amenable to western-style change. In response to her son's request for a blessing and promise to return to China, Wou's mother questions whether or not "the signs of the times were that the son of a cobbler, returned from America with the foreign language, could easier command a position of consequence than the son of a school-teacher unacquainted with any tongue but that of his motherland?" (50). On condition that she may choose a wife for her son before he leaves, Wou's mother grants her blessing.

Part 2 opens with Wou Sankwei "busily entering figures in a long yellow book" as the junior partner and bookkeeper of San Francisco's Leung Tang Wou and

Co., a position that would seem to promise a return to his "flabby muscles" and "plump white hands" but instead attests to his commitment to upward mobility. While Wou may use a Chinese counting machine and eat at a local Chinese restaurant, his work ethic is definitively American: "Self-improvement had been his object and ambition, even more than the acquirement of a fortune" (51). By defining the Americanization process through the adoption of American business practices, rather than through the maintenance of an American heterosocial domestic space, Sui Sin Far suggests that the Americanization process is much easier for single men, an important argument considering the vast preponderance of single Chinese men in the United States at the turn of the century.

Having saved enough money to bring his wife and son to America, he announces his plans to his American benefactor, Mrs. Dean, and her niece, Adah Charlton. Lamenting the fact that Wou's new wife is illiterate—"It is the Chinese custom to educate only the boys. At least it has been so in the past"—while praising Wou as one who is "as up to date as any young American," these women articulate the tension that Sui Sin Far explores, that of the conflict between traditional Chinese cultural practices and those necessary to "succeed" in the American marketplace (53). Contrary to Amy Ling and Annette White-Parks's reading, however, this tension, I argue, is not resolved through the expulsion of Pau Lin, Wou Sankwei's wife, from the narrative. Sui Sin Far's construction of China remains the site of change.

Part 3 of the story is written from the perspective of Pau Lin and begins with her arrival from China. Tired from her long voyage and from nursing her sick child, Pau Lin, overcome by a "feminine desire to make herself fair to see in the eyes of her husband . . . arrayed herself in a heavily embroidered purple costume, whitened her forehead and cheeks with powder, and tinted her lips with carmine" (54). Like Sui Sin Far's vision of the Chinese American woman in 1897, this construction of Chinese femininity signals her similarity to and difference from the Gibson Girl type; she may be intrinsically vain but not to enhance her competitive position in the marriage market. While Pau Lin's voice seems to be safely confined to inconsequential domestic matters, Wou is indulgent. The central site of contention proves to be Adah Charlton's sketches of their child for a book on Chinese children that she is illustrating, suggesting Sui Sin Far's own unease with the "quaint" Orientalized images of Asian children marketed to white audiences. When Pau Lin's second child dies, one of Adah's images of Yen falls out of her husband's pocket, fueling yet more jealousy. Pau Lin exclaims, "Sooner would I, O heart of my heart, that the light of thine eyes were also quenched, than that thou shouldst be contaminated with the wisdom of the new" (68). By casting Pau Lin's critique of Americanization in terms of female jealousy, Sui Sin Far undermines her legitimate concerns. She gives Adah Charlton the opportunity of definitively interpreting Pau Lin's actions: "I did not realize this before you told me that she was jealous. I only wish I had. Now, for all her ignorance, I can see that the poor little thing became more of an American in that one half hour on the steamer than Wou Sankwei, for all your pride in him, has become in seven years" (70).

While Sankwei is criticized for not consulting his wife in the Americanization process, declaring that he would make no effort to Americanize her because "The time for learning with her is over" (58), Pau Lin's rejection of Americanization is continually reiterated. When Pau Lin corporally punishes their son for speaking "the language of the white woman" and Wou Sankwei chastises her, she commiserates with the other Chinese wives of merchants. When she describes an immigrant experience antithetical to that presented in the introduction—a hard-working Chinese man is fleeced by an unscrupulous white con man—her friend, Lae Choo, responds by warning of a Chinese reprisal for those who too readily adopt American values. "'The new religion—what trouble it brings!' exclaimed Lae Choo. 'My man received word yestereve that the good old mother of Chee Ping—he who was baptized a Christian at the last baptizing in the Mission around the corner—had her head secretly severed from her body by the steadfast people of the village, as soon as the news reached there'" (61). Evoking the anti-Western sentiment aroused during the Boxer rebellion, this vision of America's new religion of greedy acquisition and mission-served Christianity would seem to contradict earlier optimism about the possibilities for Westernization in China. Pau Lin and Lae Choo, then, act as both critics and informers, testifying to what those who advocate reform in China might be up against while criticizing the arrogance of the American civilizing mission.

Pau Lin's vision of Chinatown suggests similar anxieties about the Americanization process:

> Streaming along the street was a motley throng made up of all nationalities. The sing-song voices of girls whom respectable merchants' wives shudder to name, were calling to one another from high balconies up shadowy alleys. A fat barber was laughing hilariously at a drunken white man who had fallen into a gutter . . . A Chinese dressed in the latest American style and a very blonde woman, laughing immoderately, were entering a Chinese restaurant together. Above all the hubbub of voices was heard the clang of electric cars and the jarring of heavy wheels over cobblestones. (62)

The pernicious, chaotic atmosphere encapsulates Pau Lin's rejection of the American new—new immigrants, interethnic mixing, social vices, and technologies. Pau Lin's vision of Chinatown is subsequently transformed, however, by Mrs. Dean's interpretive descriptions of Chinese religious practices during the Harvest Moon Festival. What to Pau Lin was chaotic threat becomes to ethnic mediator Mrs. Dean cultural enrichment. She tells her companion, Adah Charlton, "the Chinese mind requires two religions. Even the most commonplace Chinese has yearnings for something above everyday life. Therefore, he combines with his Confucian-ism, Buddhism—or, in this country, Christianity" (76). Practical in business matters but spiritually minded, the Chinese have the fundamental qualities of "ideal" Americans. When the two women by chance meet Yen with Lee Tong Hay, Mrs. Dean proclaims, "He can turn himself into a German, a Scotchman, an Irishman, or an American, with the greatest ease, and is as natural in each character as he is as a Chinaman" (75–76). Lee's performance of other more accepted ethnicities reminds readers of the performative possibilities of American citizenship and, in conjunction with assurances that Chinese American religious practices are both pragmatic and spiritual, the easy assimilability of Asian Americans. Indeed, by stressing that Chinatown is a performance for white tourists, Sui Sin Far redefines the "pleasure" of Chinatown; rather than being enthralled by the spectacle of "exotic" events, spectators should enjoy the consciously performed cultural pluralism of the participants; potentially threatening ethnic difference becomes benign urban cosmopolitanism. At the same time, however, Sui Sin Far's construction of Chinatown challenges notions of what Richard Brodhead has described as a "vacation mentality" within women's regionalist literature, where the region's Old World traditions offer an escape from the anxieties of modern life, namely "foreign" immigration, class tensions, and contemporary industrial production (146–47). Pau Lin's vision of Chinatown as threat is not subsumed by Mrs. Dean's vision of a safer cultural pluralism, nor is that pluralism divorced from nativist anxieties about the dissolution of ethnic difference. Indeed, because of Sui Sin Far's emphasis on Chinatown as a place of cultural flux, its status as a vacation destination, where one may recoup energies taxed in a modern world, is decidedly in question.

The fate of Pau Lin confirms the difficulty of finding refuge from the dis-ease of modern life in the community of an ethnic Other. Ultimately, Pau Lin's fears of her husband's interest in an American New Woman and her growing estrangement from her son brought about by Americanization prove overwhelming, and Pau Lin kills her child, declaring, "He is saved, . . . from the Wisdom of the New" (84). By refusing to compete with Adah for her husband's attentions and by refusing her own son's entry into the market economy, Pau Lin effectively rejects the American mother and wife's role in the market economy, that of the maker of competitive little men. Immediately after their son's death, Wou Sankwei decides to return to China. In a letter to Adah Charlton, he explains his departure by declaring that his wife's "health requires a change," implying that Pau Lin is in need of a rest cure (84). While "The Wisdom of the New" suggests the potential consequences of familial estrangement that an embrace of the "new" American ethic necessarily entails, the story also promises readers that those who do not "successfully" assimilate will leave. Contrary to Annette White-Parks's argument, this return to China does not heal "the cultural gap and their marriage" (222) but merely foregrounds the consequences of such a gap. The return to China represents a retreat, and as Lae Choo's warning about the "new religion" reminds us, a retreat not without the specter of further conflict.

Eaton, herself, was deeply invested in organized efforts for western reform in China, popularly described in calls for a "New China." In 1903 she hailed the Los Angeles arrival of Chinese Reform Party spokesperson Leung Ki Chu, whom she described as "the hero of thousands of the most enlightened Chinese people" ("Leung"). Imagining the cries of his distant wife, Sui Sin Far writes,

> Oh, China! Unhappy country! What would I not sacrifice to see thee uphold thyself among the nations? Far bitterer than death it is to know that thou who wert more glorious than all now liest as low as the lowest, while the feet of those whom thou didst despise rest insolently upon thy limbs. . . . And now, the empire, which is the oldest under the heavens, is falling and other nations stand ready to smite the nation that first smote itself. . . . The government, being foolish and correct, has lost the hearts of the people. Who shall restore them. ("Reform Party" 26)

In Sui Sin Far's "The Story of Wah," published almost six years later in *The Westerner,* Wah is a leading member of the Chinese Reform Party who rejects the importation of opium and hails western business practices. Three months after the publication of the story, Sui Sin Far again hailed the efforts of the Chinese Reform Party: "The Chinese of the Reform Party in America are acutely conscious, and have been, for many years, of the necessity of a new way of living for the Chinese—and not only a new way of living—a new way of thinking. . . . nothing causes their eyes to glisten more than to know that China is encouraging educational and industrial reforms, while those of them who have become Christians look forward with bright faith to China's religious reformation" ("Reform" 26).

The reform movement in China was developed by Chinese nationalists after China's humiliating military defeat by Japan in 1895.[15] Led by K'ang Yu-wei, the Reform Party believed that to relieve the national crisis, China had to transform its government practices toward a western model, beginning with instituting a constitutional monarchy (Chong 16). The efforts of the reform movement in China, however, were crushed by the empress dowager, Tz'u-hsi, in 1898 after the reform-minded Emperor Kuang-hsu worked to pass a series of dramatic changes. Following this defeat, the reformers did much of their work in exile. With the advent of the Open Door Doctrine in 1899 and 1900, inaugurated by Secretary of State John Hay, the Chinese viewed the United States as working against the excessive influence of other nations in China. The future of the reform movement in China seemed more promising after the Boxer rebellion in 1900 nearly destroyed the Manchu dynasty and the treaty system that European powers, the United States, and Japan had with the Manchu government while helping to strengthen resistance to the pro-Boxer empress (Chong 39). Leung Ki Chu (Liang Ch'i-ch'ao) was sent to the United States by K'ang to raise money and support for the reform movement. Leung Ki Chu's efforts were greeted favorably, and in 1903 as he headed to the West Coast, an American newspaper, the

San Francisco Examiner, for the first time publicly endorsed reform, fund-raising, and membership recruitment for the Emperor Protection Society (Chong 56). Sui Sin Far's glowing tribute to Leung Ki Chu in 1903, then, was in accord with popular sentiment.

She also cautions her American audience to consider Chinese reaction when crafting foreign policy and domestic law. Considering that the Chinese boycott of American products was still in effect following the renewal of the Chinese Exclusion Act in 1905 and that fears about Japanese dominance of China still prevailed, it is not surprising that she would appeal to American self-interest. With the death of the empress dowager and the emperor in 1908 and Sun Yat-sen's revolutionary efforts gathering momentum, the overthrow of the Manchu dynasty seemed imminent. Sui Sin Far responds to these political shifts by cautioning her western readers that their response to Chinese Americans will directly affect Sino-American relations: "Yet these Chinese, Chinese-Americans I call them, are not unworthy of a little notice, particularly as they sustain throughout the period of their residence here, a faithful and constant correspondence with relations and friends in the old country, and what they think and what they write about Americans, will surely influence, to a great extent, the conduct of their country-men towards the people of the United States" ("Chinese in America" 24).

In the short story "Scholar or Cook" (1909), Sui Sin Far stresses the sojourner status of her hero, Wang Lang, who though trained as a scholar is compelled to work as a cook in the United States in order to send money to his aging parents. While such a story develops a theme common throughout Sui Sin Far's fiction—that of the middle-class Chinese forced to accept working-class employment in America, a theme that creates intellectual agency for her characters—it also emphasizes the characters' unremitting connection to China.

Edith Eaton/Sui Seen Far/Sui Sin Far continually worked to validate the Chinese American presence in the United States through a complex series of rhetorical maneuvers that illustrate the contradictions inherent in the "immigrant acts" her work explores. Most broadly, within an American context, the new is a competitive work environment, modern technology, and individualism combined with the new ethic of gambling, promiscuity, drink, and indulgence unleashed in an increasingly secular American culture. Within this context, the new (white) woman is at once privileged but flawed—formally well educated but whose asserted independence often blinds her to the need for creating necessary coalitions across race and class. Yet at the same time, the positive aspects of the new ethic, which had been exclusively claimed as products of dominant American culture, either had their origins in China or will soon be claimed and refashioned by China, thereby promising increased power and influence on an international stage. The New Chinese Woman lays primary claim to divided skirts, vanity, and consumption. The New China, while increasingly open to western economic reform, offers spiritual groundedness to a crass age.

For Sui Sin Far, I argue, the rhetoric of the new becomes an important site of performative possibility with ultimately more options than pitfalls. While American-identified "new" Chinese men are defined principally by their willingness to adopt a Western work ethic, American-identified "new" Chinese women are defined by their roles as both cultural interpreters and signs of cultural assimilation. Sui Sin Far both claims and disavows the popularized and the traditional variants of the New Woman in a rhetorical strategy designed to evoke the fears her figure represents, which Chinese cultural values may assuage, and to claim the increasing validity of her assertiveness and intellectual independence. Like Pauline Hopkins, Sui Sin Far demonstrated the ability of her characters to adopt dominant bourgeois American ideals even when in refashioning them to include race and class consciousness, intersex solidarity, and spiritual strivings, the fault lines in those ideals are necessarily exposed. While like the New Negro Woman, the Chinese American New Woman's sexuality must be precluded, the New Negro Woman's relationship to commodity discernment and acquisition is always shadowed by the legacy of the commodification of black women during slavery. Sui Sin Far, by contrast, seems to invite her readers to consume China and Chinatown in much the same way readers of *The Westerner* were invited to consume the West, as an interest-bearing investment, a "'gold mine' . . . possessing not merely *inexhaustible* values, but *ever-increasing values*" (Trustee Company of Seattle). And yet that consumption, Sui Sin Far reminds her readers, is never of the "real thing," a kind of stable exotic "Other," but rather a dialectical process of, to use Lisa Lowe's term, always contradictory "immigrant acts."[16] Sui Sin Far, in other words, uses the rhetoric of the "new" generally and the New Woman specifically not to highlight perspectives the Chinese lack and must gain, or vice versa, but to demonstrate how central Chinese Americans are to the American progressive vision from which much of this "new" rhetoric emerges. Ultimately, the New Chinese Woman is Sui Sin Far/Edith Eaton herself, urging her white readers to acknowledge common ties and needs while highlighting the performative and therefore mutable nature of an American national identity the popular New Woman prefigures.

CHAPTER 5

Mary Johnston, Ellen Glasgow, and the Evolutionary Logic of Progressive Reform

> We are growing away from the four-footed—we are growing away
> from our sister the gibbon and our brother the chimpanzee—we
> are growing—we are changing—we feel the heavens over us and
> a strange new life within us—we are passing out, we are coming
> in—we need a new word.
> —Mary Johnston, *Hagar* (1913)

By 1913, the writing careers of Mary Johnston and Ellen Glasgow were firmly established. Johnston's historical romances *To Have and to Hold, Audrey, Sir Mortimer, Lewis Rand,* and *The Long Roll* had appeared on the best-sellers' lists in 1900, 1902, 1904, 1908, and 1911 respectively. Glasgow's realist work did not meet quite as much popular success—*Deliverance* made the best-sellers' list in 1904 and *The Wheel of Life* landed a spot in 1906—but her work was taken more seriously by literary critics who praised its realistic impressionism and "masculine virility."[1] As writers and close friends, Johnston and Glasgow took pride in their genteel Virginian heritage even as they espoused their commitment to socialism, women's suffrage, racial tolerance, and progressive reform.[2] Yet it was not until the publication of Johnston's *Hagar* (1913) and Glasgow's *Virginia* (1913) and *Life and Gabriella* (1916) that solving the woman question would be presented as the answer to the New South's economic and social turmoil.[3] Johnston's *Hagar,* with its contemporary setting, moments of documentary-realist style, and blatant advocacy of the New Woman cause, surprised readers and critics accustomed to her earlier, less polemical historical romances. While less overtly political in its project, Glasgow's *Virginia,* her first novel to focus on the development of a female protagonist, offered readers a naturalist narrative that exposed the futility of the southern lady's life based solely on romantic and maternal love. Three years later in *Life and Gabriella,* Glasgow crafted a southern heroine who is compelled to struggle alone to support herself and her two children after being deserted by her feckless, philandering husband.

As Johnston and Glasgow were writing their novels of the New South, they not only, like Wharton, relied on the philosophical, scientific, and social scientific literature of race, gender, and evolution but on a number of related discourses, all of which had as a foundation not just the changing socioeconomic order that Wharton addressed but the special place of the South in that order and in the national rhetorics of progress. They employed a series of extended conceits; Glasgow uses electricity (to signify modern, potentially disruptive energy) and Johnston uses the bridge (to signify both the new coalitions the new age demands as well as the industrial development the South seeks). Both use the more general trope of wave motion to suggest the power and potential chaos of that new energy; bridges traverse over it, electricity rides it. Their arguments about the "new" counteract some of the absences and errors of their northern counterparts.

Both Glasgow and Johnston cast a New Woman—a New Woman with varying degrees of commitment to feminism,[4] socialism, progressivism, and mysticism—as the figure best able to assuage the racial and economic anxieties of the developing New South. Defined principally by their genteel status and their desire for both economic independence and gradual social reform, these New Woman protagonists promise none of the social upheaval of an Undine Spragg. They are kin, in many respects, to what Julia Magruder describes as "The Typical Woman of the New South," who is not the typical new woman—in no section of the country had the "new-woman movement gained ground so slowly," but "an evolution of the past—an upward growth, a higher development" (Magruder 1687). Typified by the Christy Girl, she is proud but more "offhand in her manners with men" (1685). Similarly, Hagar's innate gentility tempers her advocacy of women's enfranchisement, progressive socialism, and transcendental mysticism such that it arouses only immediate family tension rather than the specter of widespread class conflict or marital strife. Indeed, Johnston and Glasgow express far less ambivalence toward the emergence of the New Woman than either Wharton, Hopkins, Cather, or Sui Sin Far because their new southern women retain a spiritual commitment to a southern agrarian past, which sustains vestiges of the old social order, even as they work to eliminate some of its worst abuses. Johnston and Glasgow offer their readers the promise that when visionary new (white) women make allegiances with like-minded new (white) men, the genteel white leadership, threatened during Reconstruction and more recent trends in immigration, would be strengthened.

Both Johnston and Glasgow ostensibly repudiate the Old South to embrace a vision of the New South not yet realized. Still clinging to the heroics of the Lost Cause, the Old South in their work becomes increasingly wasteful, inefficient, and isolated. Long-term southern residents have a regionally fixed worldview—charming but anachronistic—destined to wither in the fiercely competitive world of modern enterprise. And yet, as the Old South is critiqued, it is memorialized. Its patrician values are reconfigured as the New South develops, lest the crass

Howard Chandler Christy, "The Typical Woman of the New South."
Illustration in Julia Magruder, "The Typical Woman of the New
South." *Harper's Bazaar* (November 3, 1900): 1686. Courtesy of the
Newberry Library.

undercurrent of New South prosperity, commercialism, take over.[5] Like Johnston and Glasgow, who spent considerable time in New York but always considered Richmond their home, Hagar and Gabriella travel north to meet their personal and professional goals but return to the South for spiritual renewal in the lush, untutored environment of their family estates. Threatening dissolution to those who stay too long but offering a much-needed break from the trials of money getting, Hagar's and Gabriella's southern homes serve as bucolic sanitariums rejuvenating "higher" selves depleted in a northern marketplace. Johnston and Glasgow's vision of the New South represents struggle, opportunity, and connection, a place where the "fittest" women find professional fulfillment and political agency, where social Darwinist discourse validates upward mobility and inter-class relationships, and where the railroad connects all. Any lingering sectionalism is abolished in the New South through a tacit agreement of like-minded parties to "move forward." The evolutionary growth of the entire nation, these writers suggest, depends on the South's superior ability to select the best elements of old and new. Johnston and Glasgow offer, then, a new version of the romance of reunion. Rather than the northern gentleman wooing the southern lady toward the promise of regional reconciliation, the liberated new southern lady/state selects the best aspects of the northern element, thereby insuring the nation's race progress.

On May 24, 1910, Johnston wrote in her journal, "I have on hand a number of books on socialism. If I know anything about my own evolutionary process, I will sooner or later find myself identified with the movement."[6] Influenced by such gradualist socialist works as William Morris's *News from Nowhere* and Eduard Bernstein's *Evolutionary Socialism,* Johnston suggests in *Hagar* that economic crises under capitalism could and should be moderated by state action. Although Johnston was more heavily invested in socialist theory than was Glasgow (neither of whom, however, would become party members), both were familiar with socialist theory in the years prior to writing their New Woman fiction. In February 1911, Johnston was the guest of honor at a dinner for Max Eastman, socialist editor of *The Masses,* and in March of that year she attended her first socialist meeting in Richmond, a meeting where Eugene Debs spoke. When B. M. Dutton, leader of the Richmond Socialist Party, asked her to join the party, however, she refused:

> I with many others am profoundly dissatisfied with the structure of human society as it is today, and could wish very many fundamental changes. As a student of evolution, I think the three great world movements of today are 1st. The struggle of women against her age-long subjection to man. 2nd. The struggle of all western peoples toward a thorough-going democracy and collective ownership of all things necessary to subsistence. 3rd. The freeing of religion from dogmas. (quoted in Hanmer 26)

What is significant here is that Johnston implies that women's liberation was the necessary precedent to other movements. Women must become fully realized because the evolved woman or New Woman of the New South had cultivated those qualities—especially altruism—necessary for the advancement of the nation.

Glasgow was likewise committed to progressive economic reform and briefly called herself a Fabian socialist until it seemed to her the movement had become "flabby with compromise" (*Woman Within* 81). A good friend of George Walter McCormack (1868–1894), she read widely from his library, which included William Graham's *Socialism New and Old* and Francis A. Walker's *Political Economy* (Goodman 37). Her first novel, *The Descendent* (1897), featured a socialist and a New Woman as protagonists.[7] Yet by 1913, Glasgow's commitment to socialism had evolved into a desire for corporate-style reform. Like Wharton's *The Fruit of the Tree,* Glasgow's critically neglected *The Ancient Law* (1908) weaves a narrative of romance together with various progressive incorporation issues before her hero's vision of reform is realized.

In the spring of 1909, Johnston, Glasgow, and prominent social crusader Lila Meade Valentine helped to form the Equal Suffrage League of Virginia in Glasgow's Richmond home.[8] Although Glasgow had marched in one of the "great English Suffrage parades" with May Sinclair in 1909 and had published in 1912 a poetic call to action in *Collier's,* Johnston proved far more active in the suffrage struggle than her friend, who would resign from the league in 1911 after the death of her sister. In retrospect, Glasgow explained her waning interest in the cause as a fundamental belief in the ineffectiveness of the movement: "If women wanted a vote, I agreed they had a right to vote, for I regarded the franchise in our Republic more as a right than as a privilege; and I was willing to do anything, except burn with a heroic blaze, for the watchword of liberty. What I secretly felt, though I did not offer this as a reason for lukewarmness, was that, so long as the serpent continues to crawl on the ground, the primary influence of woman will remain indirect" (*Woman Within* 187). Yet for both writers, the political strategies that the league employed in its campaign to win voters would be clearly evident in their fictional works.

At the core of this strategy was an effort to redefine the role of the "southern lady" in the New South. Enshrined in the domestic sphere, the southern lady, according to the popular novelist Thomas Nelson Page, should lead a life of "one long act of devotion,—devotion to God, devotion to her husband, devotion to her children, devotion to her servants, to her friends, to the poor, to humanity" (Page, *Social Life* 38). As historians Anne Firor Scott and Marjorie Wheeler have pointed out, despite changing gender relations following the Civil War and Reconstruction, the ideal of the southern lady as "guardian and symbol of Southern virtue" still had tremendous appeal at the turn of the century (Scott 221; Wheeler, *New Women* 4). As Julia Magruder wrote in 1900 in *Harper's Bazaar,* "In no section, of course, has the new-woman movement gained ground so slowly as in the South" (1687). The New Woman of the New South, then, must draw on existing ideals of southern white womanhood even as she appeals to the latest theories of racial advancement: "The Southern woman of today is an evolution of the past—an up-

ward growth, a higher development; but as nothing is gained without some form
of loss, it may be conceded that she has lost, perhaps, some of the finer delicacy
that belonged to the lady, though she has acquired in its place the nobler, better,
and more serviceable qualities which make the ideal of womanhood" (Magruder
1687). For southern suffragists, allowing the beneficent southern woman to extend
her influence was necessary not only to their personal evolution but the region's
as well. Invoking the image of the southern lady, then, was both a reminder to
citizens of the Equal Suffrage League's own esteemed membership and an appeal
to cultural continuity in the face of tremendous change.

Johnston and Glasgow broadened the appeal of the southern lady image to
make her entrance into political and business life essential to the development
of the New South and ultimately to the nation. Even when they critiqued the
limitations of that role, they hoped to achieve legitimacy for women's suffrage
by invoking the legacy of the southern lady. In *Hagar,* the New Southern Woman
becomes the symbol of virtue and possibility for the entire nation. Like Glasgow's
Virginia, the eponymous protagonist Hagar is closer to the spiritual essence of
the nation's agrarian past, although Hagar is able to transfer that devotion to
settlement work or other progressive reform efforts. The money that Hagar earns
through writing, for example, supports the working-class Thomson, while Gabriella financially supports her family. Both acts reaffirm the popular image of
the southern lady's beneficence and sense of duty while justifying her immersion
in the marketplace.[9] The Gibson Girl, by contrast, had shed her veil of spiritual
beneficence—shopping in its own right was her duty. As Johnston and Glasgow
refigure the southern lady's legacy, they reformulate the tribal codes of exchange
upon which southern patriarchy rests. Instead of being an object of exchange
insuring patriarchal authority within the family system, both Hagar and Gabriella
choose to reify their own labor as white, female artists. And in marrying their
respective "new (white) men," they assure readers that even though class and
ethnic barriers may be more mutable in the new era, racial boundaries remain
comfortably fixed.

Both Glasgow and Johnston, like Charlotte Perkins Gilman, remind their readers that "newness" is an evolutionary process signaling the development not just
of southern women but of the entire nation. They both read Darwin's *Origin
of Species* and extended the logic of evolutionary development to the genesis of
the New Woman, the New South, and the new nation.[10] Given their dependence
upon changes in their environment for growth and advancement, their New
Woman protagonists are, in effect, new species who have developed favorable
lasting characteristics in the "struggle for existence."[11] As the ideal of the Old
South evolves into the New South in their fiction, it retains the moral advantage
of an exaggerated sense of community, "that disinterested love for all living crea-
tures [that is] the most noble attribute of man" (Darwin, *Descent* 1874). Yet J. R.
Raper's contention that Glasgow's commitment to Darwinism, with its "opposi-

tion to typological thinking," necessarily subverted racial and class divisions in Virginia society is premature. The discovery of new species meant an increasing need for distinctions according to type; a typological discourse pervades these novels, which to some extent retain racial and class hierarchies.

Like her friend Charlotte Perkins Gilman, Johnston used Frank Lester Ward's gynocentric theory, which he first presented in "Our Better Halves" (1888) and later developed in *Pure Sociology* (1903), as the basis for her trope of the New Woman.[12] For the reform-proponent Ward, the female was the "ancestral trunk" on the great genealogical tree upon which man is only grafted: "Woman *is* the race and the race can be raised up only as she is raised up . . . True science teaches that the elevation of woman is the only sure road to the evolution of man" ("Our Better Halves" 275). In *Pure Sociology,* which Johnston reported reading in 1911, Ward defines "gynocentric" theory as

> the view that the female sex is primary and the male secondary in the organic scheme, that originally and normally all things center, as it were, about the female, and that the male, though not necessary in carrying out the scheme, was developed under the operation of the principle of advantage to secure organic progress through the crossing of strains. The theory further claims that the apparent male superiority in the human race and in certain of the higher animals and the birds is the result of specialization in extra-normal directions due to adventitious causes which have nothing to do with the general scheme, but which can be explained on biological and psychological principles; that it only applies to certain characters, and to a relatively small number of genera and families. (296)

Ward, then, was also a committed Lamarckian; if women had had access to the same "adventitious causes," they too would have developed. Instead of greater gender distinctiveness being a sign of civilization as Darwin and Spencer had argued, Johnston used Ward to argue that progress lay in greater gender equity. The possibility for this gender equity would be found in the New South, not because women had a leg up there socially or politically, which they certainly did not, but because it was only in the South that woman was still primary. And as primary, the ancestral trunk of southern society, she could be trusted in sexual selection, in ways that the Gibson Girl, for example, certainly could not.

By, in effect, assuring readers that their New Woman protagonists would unite with new (white) men, both Johnston and Glasgow offered a vision of electoral political stability in conjunction with a moderate view on race matters. Both writers avoided the most blatant racist portraits in their fiction and occasionally made public statements that criticized the prevailing racist culture of the Jim Crow South. Johnston is perhaps best remembered for eschewing racist suffrage rhetoric when she resigned as honorary vice president of the Southern States Woman Suffrage Conference rather than be publicly associated with the racist

invective of its president, Kate Gordon. Glasgow once mentioned that she would
have been an abolitionist had she lived before the war (Godbold 244). In their
novels I examine here, neither Johnston nor Glasgow directly address the "Negro
problem" since it had been effectively "solved" in the preceding two decades by
a series of disenfranchisement measures. Positioning their black characters as
picturesque backdrop often associated with the rich soil or a lush tobacco crop
was a political strategy in and of itself. In the "second stage" of the women's suffrage movement in the South (roughly from 1909 to 1920), southern suffragists
rarely raised the race issue and were almost exclusively on the defensive against
those who argued that women's suffrage might jeopardize the newly reestab-
lished order of white supremacy (Wheeler, "Woman Suffrage Movement" 40).
As Charlotte Shelton observes, "As early as 1911, at the annual convention of the
United Daughters of the Confederacy, woman's suffrage was opposed on the
grounds that Negro women were allegedly more numerous than white women"
(20). The Equal Suffrage League countered such perceptions by publishing the
1910 U.S. Census figures for Virginia: the state's white women outnumbered the
Negro female population by 31,407 (Shelton 21). Furthermore, the league argued,
even in counties where there were black majorities, poll taxes, literacy tests, and
a yet-to-be invoked $250 property requirement would insure white dominance
(Lebsock 71). If women were enfranchised, Virginia suffragists argued, far from
being threatened by an influx of unruly black voters and the political corruption
that vying for new coalitions inevitably created—the "lesson" of Radical Reconstruction—the stability of the state would be enhanced. Indeed, as historian
Suzanne Lebsock notes, the southern suffragists' "central contention was that
white supremacy was not endangered and therefore not an issue" (71). Race and
sex were separable issues.

Covering the period from the 1880s to roughly 1913, *Hagar* begins with a bridge
metaphor that serves as a defining trope of the New Woman of the New South
and signifies both connective possibilities and necessary obfuscations. Even as
the bridge represents the New Woman's capacity for sectional reconciliation,
spiritual growth, and evolutionary advance, it also represents, to use Patricia
Yaeger's phrase, the "white South's economy of unknowing or racial blindness"
(108) to the violence of slavery and Jim Crow. The novel is framed by two bridge
scenes that reflect the change from an old to new southern order and suggest
Johnston's ambivalence about the growing industrialization of the South.[13] In
the first scene, the slow-moving packet boat glides down a Virginia river in the
long shadows of twilight. As "almost the last packet-boat in the state and upon
almost its last journey," the vessel with its "long, musical winding of the packet-
boat horn" promises to be replaced by the ubiquitous railroad: "the locomotive
would shriek here as it shrieked elsewhere" (3).[14] The gentlemen on deck tell war
stories wrapped in "[b]lue rings of tobacco-smoke" while the ladies placidly knit
(2). Along the banks a Negro and his mule "were now but a bit of dusk in motion,

and now were lit and, so to speak, powdered with gold-dust" (1). With its Confederate nostalgia, gendered locations, racial designations, and class privileges, this first image in the novel is a vision of the Old South that Johnston sees as both threatened with and destined for transformation. As symbols of industrial progress and human connection, the bridge and railroad promise to disrupt the isolated enclaves of genteel southern society. While Johnston sees this increasing connectedness as necessary for "growth," such change promises to disrupt long-established social hierarchies.

Hagar's willingness to forge alliances that bridge class and sex boundaries, but not racial boundaries, in order to further her intellectual and political ambitions demonstrates Johnston's selective repudiation of the old and commitment to the "new." If the North is a "pageant of impressions . . . hurrying crowds, the rush and roar, tramp and clangour, the color and bravura" (*Hagar* 188)—the energy and potential destructiveness of the male "katabolic" element—the South represents the more conservative "anabolic" energy.[15] Indeed, as Johnston writes in "The Woman's War," the male tends to be "more disruptive, destructive, energetic" while the female is "the more nutritive, the more constructive, the nearer to the womb of all things" (561). Together they are "[t]wo branches sprung from one root" (562). Johnston positions the South in *Hagar* as both a woman to be wooed and a natural resource to be developed. The urban masculine North represents the unbridled energy of that wave, while the agrarian feminine South provides the moral direction of the change that those waves will bring.

Johnston offers her readers a world in which gender and class designations are mutable but where racial designations are comfortingly fixed. Interracial antagonism promises not to be a barrier to white alliances because the progress of the nation depends upon a national unity of preestablished racial hierarchies even as it depends on the New Woman's advance. The bridge of change is anchored in a vision of perpetually agrarian Negroes. If desire represents social force, the African American characters are allowed no desire that would enable their own social development. None of the black characters in the novel are part of the larger "race struggle." At no time does Hagar attempt to form any political alliances with a black character, nor does Johnston include the history of Jim Crow violence in any of her documentary-style exposition of political turmoil. Only two black characters speak, and they appear briefly at the beginning and ending of the novel.

Indeed, while Hagar's two black playmates are associated with her creative development as an artist, they are depicted as caricatures of artists themselves. Hagar might be considered to have kinship with Mary Magazine—"named . . . for de lady what took her cologne bottle somebody give her Christmas, an' poured it on her han' an' rubbed Jesus' feet"—as another falsely maligned female biblical figure, but that kinship is necessarily limited by Mary's essential lack of literary sophistication (32). Too dependent on an oral tradition, she does not get the pun. While her surname may have inspired Hagar to publish her first story in the *Young People's Home Magazine,* Mary's association with such New Woman activity is merely figurative. At the end of the novel, she reappears as a "tidy co-loured maid" for the industrious and successful Hagar. Hagar does the "thinking, remembering, creating" while Thomson keeps the records and Mary serves tea.

Yet if the Negro characters in Johnston's work suffer an inability to create "Art," which positions them, as I will discuss in more detail later on, at the lowest point on the evolutionary scale, their nature as organic art, less spiritually edifying than physically restorative, equates them with an undeveloped nature that the Old South retains and the New Woman needs. Consider, for example, Johnston's description of her excursion with Ellen Glasgow, Carrie Coleman, and the Reverend Frank Paradise to a local tobacco factory in 1908:

> Worked until eleven to little effect. Then dressed and drove with Ellen Glasgow, Carrie Coleman, and Mr. Paradise to the tobacco factory—Ellen wishing him to see and hear the negroes. . . . Fourteen hundred negro men and women at work, all types and shades of colour and ages. Handkerchiefs twisted about their heads, or paper caps, standing at long tables stemming the tobacco, or bearing it in crates to a great trough or belt,—smiling, rolling their eyes, singing, now one or two male voices, now the whole long room,—the air warm and clogged with the tobacco-scent, all shades of brown, brown workers, brown leaf, brown walls and beams, now and then a note of red—it was Rembrandtesque. The voices very deep and rich; they sang *Roll, Jordan, Roll, Happy Land,* etc. etc. and they seemed to enjoy it as much as we did. A fine view of the river, and the hazy Indian summer shores. We were there two hours; it is a thing to see. ("Tea and Metaphysics" 3–4)

Johnston's "Rembrandtesque" vision of the tobacco factory—where the chiaroscuro effect of various shades of brown faces, tobacco leaves, walls, and beams mingle with the "rich" sounds of spirituals and the hazy warmth of Indian summer—supersedes any questions of race relations, working conditions, or even child-labor law, questions that we might expect considering Johnston's interests at the time. Seeming to have arisen organically from their rural environment, the tobacco workers are, quite literally, southern local color akin to *Hagar*'s "powdered with gold-dust" Negro seen from the bridge.

In Johnston's construction of Hagar's ancestral home, Gilead Balm, she reassociates the rhetoric of the "new" from a white urban consumer culture subject to decay to a southern agrarian refuge based on the tacit assumption of black nurturance. By naming Hagar's ancestral home after a well-known African American spiritual and giving her heroine the name of Hagar, the Egyptian maidservant whom Sarah gave to Abraham as his concubine and who is subsequently associated with the suffering of slave women, Johnston both affirms the history of slavery within the plantation household and divests it of its potency. Yaeger's reading of *Gone with the Wind* applies likewise to *Hagar* as a novel that "refuses to think what it knows about race—and therefore keeps reenacting the bizarre double structure of a character-driven plot that caricatures and dehumanizes blacks and an image-driven plot that makes black the color that one wants to become (in the service of recovering early object relations and desires) and makes white the most fractured, witless and monstrous of services" (108). In contrast to the moral and literal decay of the city, Gilead Balm enjoys an ever bountiful vegetative splendor: "the buds of the cucumber tree were swelling, the grass beneath was growing green, the ants were out in the sunshine" (104). Like the tobacco workers, the aptly named working-class Green family—Mrs. Green, Thomson, Maggie, and Corker—are depicted as "blatantly healthful" and relatively content rural guests (45). The old family dog "looked askance at a brand-new white butterfly on a brand-new dandelion" (104). Hagar returns three times to Gilead Balm, each time gathering nutritive energy by which she may continue her reform efforts. While the ideas of the local inhabitants may be ill-informed and misguided, the land provides an uncorrupted origin from which one may regenerate.

Indeed, the center of restoration in the novel is a southern resort known as "The New Springs," a place where "a lot of tired people come" (136).[16] An "all-day's climb from the nearest railway station," New Springs appears as a primordial landscape that welcomes northerners and southerners alike: "Up here you had wonderful views; you saw a sea of mountains, tremendous, motionless waves; the orb as it had wrinkled when man and beast and herb were not" (133). By addressing the reader in the second person, Johnston offers the uninitiated a travel guide to a virtually untapped southern resource. Johnston promises an end to sectionalism by offering the nation a New Springs that welcomes both the southern old—Colonel Ashendyne comes to meet his Civil War buddies—and the northern new—the settlement workers, Elizabeth Eden and Marie Caton, come to revive.

Hagar will rely on both the impressionism of "nature" and the keenness of Lost Cause "nobility" in her own development as artist reformer, but the latter provides her the necessary moral vision in her subsequent efforts toward social justice. While the novel contains many characteristics of what Nina Baym has identified as a typical sentimental overplot, its variation suggests Johnston's commitment to the legacy of the Old South. Like most sentimental women's fiction, Hagar is orphaned and neglected by her caretakers, must learn to survive on her own, and ultimately finds happiness in marriage and a spiritual faith "pried out of its patriarchal social setting" (Baym 42). Significantly, however, Hagar's tradition-bound guardians do not use deceit to hinder her progress. Their affection is guarded but genuine. While they try to persuade Hagar verbally to abandon her New Woman activities, they do not use more aggressive or dishonest methods to undermine her efforts toward self-determination. Her mail is always delivered and her money is her own. This modification of Baym's overplot suggests that Hagar's ties to the Old South will not be irrevocably severed. Her development as a protagonist depends on a southern code of honor.

Johnston charts Hagar's growth beyond that of sex parasitism through a teleological evolutionary logic—again revealing the influence of Gilman and Ward—which not only affirms her own evolved status but also her ability to read taxonomical distinctions "necessary" for society at large. Like Gilman, Johnston reminds readers that the nation's racial preservation must be balanced with the individual's self-preservation. In *Women and Economics*, Gilman writes,

> Love never yet went with self-interest. The deepest antagonism lies between them: they are diametrically opposed forces. In the beautiful progress of evolution we find constant opposition between the instincts and processes of self-preservation and the instinct and processes of race-preservation.... these two forces work in opposition. We have tied them together. We have made the woman, the mother,—the very source of sacrifice through love,—get gain through love,—a hideous paradox. (97–98)

Given the genetic possibility of indifference as the daughter of the frustrated neurasthenic New Woman Maria, the precocious twelve-year-old Hagar makes her appearance in the novel with a question to her fashionable yet tradition-bound aunt, "[W]hat is evolution?" (2). The question casts the frame on the preceding image of the packet boat: What must evolve? Evolve to what? While Miss Serena keeps up with the fashions—"She sat very elegantly on the camp-stool, a graceful, long-lined, drooping form in a greenish-grey delaine"—she is grossly behind in the new thought and is appalled by Hagar's question (2). Like the gentlemen's tobacco-hazed vision, Miss Serena's vision is limited by the haze of costly garments and sentimental novels. Only Hagar sees the convicts working on the railroad under guard, an empathetic perspective indicative of her racial inheritance. The product of her father's worldliness and her mother's guarded frustration, Hagar must look beyond her family to answer her own question. Hagar's reading of Darwin's *Descent of Man* is, in fact, the first turning point in the text, the first moment when she knowingly dissents from parental authority in favor of rational scientific discourse. Her developing precociousness is defined by her ability to distinguish between seemingly similar experiences, to employ a taxonomical ordering system in her observations of the world around her:

> She was not aware that she observed that which we call Nature with a deep passion and curiosity, that beauty was the breath of her nostrils, and that she hungered and thirsted after the righteousness of knowledge. . . . In conversation she would have applied the word "pretty" indiscriminately to the flushed sky, the star, the wheeling swallows, the yellow primroses. But within, already, the primroses struck one note, and the wheeling swallows another, and the sky another, and the star another, and, combined, they made a chord that was like no other chord. Already her moments were distinguished. (11–12)

Her growth throughout the course of the novel would follow a similar progression from false generalizing to true specification. When the female English novelist Roger Michael visits Hagar's boarding school, she places similar weight on making typological distinctions. When Michael compares southern girls to New England and English girls, "She noted exceptions to type." Just as readers of *Life* would be encouraged to identify various Gibson Girls like so many products, readers here are encouraged to act both as social ethnographers and savvy consumers; the activity is portrayed as a decidedly "modern" and "northern" activity.

Within this evolutionary logic, the "negro on the towpath," by his position in the novel, suggests the influence of a neo-Darwinian, eugenics-based "descent of man" ideology when it comes to race, where heredity takes precedence over environment in the production of variation and where natural selection becomes the primary mechanism of evolution.[17] Singing "For everywhere I went ter pray, / I met all hell right on my way," the Negro would seem to be a subversive presence (4). But framed within the text—Johnston's depictions of black characters almost always appear as the last human figures in general descriptive paragraphs—he becomes part of a nostalgic vision safely gesturing to the margins of genteel white culture, defining gentility by his lack of it. Moving from images of country gentlemen to ladies, Negro, mule, serpent, gnats, and finally flies, the first scene of the novel establishes a hierarchy that reinforces the racist biological-inferiority arguments used to justify the New Paternalism. As historians such as Don Doyle have demonstrated, while such a devotion to evolutionary social change ameliorated some of the harshest effects of urban life—child labor, illiteracy, poor working conditions, and the convict lease system—it left intact the ideology of the unfit unable to evolve. Indeed, the very absence from the novel of major black characters suggests their inability to compete in the rigors of natural selection. "Outcasts from evolution," to use John S. Haller Jr.'s phrase, they are languishing in the wake of civilization's advance.

The metaphysical or New Thought discourse in the novel corroborates this worldview, opening the paths of spiritual evolution to a select few, namely the New Woman, who can access enlightenment in a way that signals her racial advance. Johnston reportedly had her first "psychic" experience in 1906 and devoted much of her subsequent life to the exploration of mystical experience. While her religious education was based on Christianity—she grew up a Baptist—it became increasingly eclectic after she withdrew her membership from the Baptist church in 1895 (Cella 28). She read books on magic, fetishism, ancient and modern religions as well as numerous books by William James, whose *Varieties of Religious Experience* sanctioned the exploration of mysticism. In a journal entry for April 1908, she recalled, "Ellen Glasgow here this morning. We talked the Upanishads, Spinoza, Kant. To merge the self into the Larger Self and All—we both want that"

("Tea and Metaphysics" 6). In 1910, Johnston recalled discussing reincarnation and metaphysics with Glasgow, and in July 1912, Johnston noted in her journal, "New conception of space and time. Cosmic consciousness. This century to be a great spiritual one, etc." Five months later, she began writing *Hagar* and felt her voracious reading had greatly contributed to her "considerable inner growth."

Johnston's exploration of mysticism and her reliance on the reform Darwinist perspective of Lester Ward allowed her to refigure notions of desire and selfhood, goals central to the New Thought movement, the turn-of-the-century woman's movement, and proponents of progressive social reforms in general (Satter 11, 10). Indeed, as Beryl Satter has argued, the New Thought movement became an important tool for those who wanted to prove that the "New Woman could help redeem a race and a nation now threatened with moral dissolution" (12). Even as Johnston's transcendentalist discourse in *Hagar* enables her to reiterate the importance to the nation of an underindustrialized but spiritually ennobling South, it also allows her to develop a measuring device by which to distinguish between desirable and undesirable New Women. This strategy of discernment was key to a South committed to disenfranchising "unfit" citizens and to members of the Equal Suffrage League pressured to exploit the "Negro problem" in order to win the vote.

Hagar's capacity for a kind of transcendental belief system is her racial inheritance. While her mother is dying—unable to be both southern lady and New Woman—the young Hagar is sent to play and sees a divine presence in the world around her: "God in the sand, God in me, God here and now . . . Then God also is trying to grow more God" (53). Yet her religious vision, the pinnacle of which is apprehension of the fourth dimension,[18] accepts the ascendancy of only those imbued with a sense of God's immanence, a group that must then "name" what it has discovered in a great teleological mission. That the climactic turning point of the novel confirms Hagar's role as both physical and cultural anthropologist, albeit a spiritual rather than a professional accreditation, foreshadows and legitimates her role as race leader. At a meeting with other free thinkers, she defends women's development: "We shan't . . . get into the Fourth Dimension while we have a shrivelled side" (255). The "shriveled side" of humanity is also the "shriveled side" of the nation. Starkly confronted with her family's deep resentment of her activities in the suffrage movement, Hagar realizes that her education—both at home and abroad—has enabled her access into the liberating world of the fourth dimension: "Inner freedom, ability to work, personal independence, courage and sense of humour and a sanguine mind, breadth and height of vision, tenderness and hope" (318).

Even as Hagar's ability to realize a fourth dimension signifies the extent of her evolution, the black characters in *Hagar* have no access to the fourth dimension and therefore no possibility of realizing the vision of the New Woman, New Man, or New South. Hagar's edifying and progressive religious belief system is contrasted with black playmate Jinnie's allegiance to "old," provincial African superstitions: "You jes' hab to believe dem. Dey're true! My lan'! Goin' ter church an' readin' de Bible an' den doubtin' erbout ghosts!" (55). The narrative voice frames Jinnie's exposition derisively, "The piece of ancient African imagination, traveller of ten thousand years through heated forests, was fearsome enough. 'Ugh!' said the children and shivered and stared.—It took the sun, indeed, to drive the creeping, mistlike thoughts away" (55). Monstrous and uncanny, regression is to be feared even as, in some sense, it is desired.

Hagar's romantic relationships similarly suggest the perils of regression and the imperative of enlightenment. Her first suitor, Mr. Laydon, is a traditional yet romantic instructor at Eglantine, Hagar's finishing school. Hagar's response to him reflects not only her growing awareness of her sexuality but also, paradoxically it seems, her growing sensitivity to suffering: "something that clung to soul and body, something strange, sweet and painful, something that, spreading and deepening with great swiftness, suffused her being and made her heart at once ecstatic and sorrowful" (79). On their journey to see a production of *Romeo and Juliet* in a neighboring town, Johnston offers her first interjection of documentary-style realism, which reflects this newfound sensitivity (94–95). While Laydon is apparently oblivious to the life struggles around him, Hagar notes, "A drug store—a wine and liquor store . . . ; amber and crimson, green and blue, broken and restless arrived the lights through the filmy glass . . . headlines 'Homestead'; and underneath, 'Strong Hands of the Law'" (95). The pastiche of images connoting urban squalor and turmoil reflect a similar kind of social unrest endangering the South that Glasgow presents in *The Ancient Law*. While Johnston does not use electricity, as Glasgow did in her novel to describe this potentially destructive energy, she presents these images in a fragmented form to suggest their power to overwhelm the coherence of the linear narrative.

Her next suitor, Ralph Coltsworth, has a southern genteel heritage and family connection as Hagar's cousin, but he represents a primitive desire and paternalism she must resist. Committed only to a principle of economic growth, he is "tied by greed to a million whirring wheels; bound by a vitiated inheritance to that utter gargoyle, that nightmare monster, *decadence*" (Johnston, "Woman's War" 566). At New Springs, the place of spiritual rejuvenation, he declares that he wants "first to make fifty millions, and then . . . spend fifty millions" (151). As he continues his suit, Ralph increasingly comes to represent an ancestral throwback, a "featherless biped" intent on dominating the "minds and fortunes of men" and assuming his rightful dominion over women (307, 368).

Hagar's successful suitor, John Fay, as his name suggests, is much less traditionally masculine. A bridge builder who has learned to "manage men" rather than conquer them, John Fay is the long-awaited "new man" (352). His economic and romantic success is a testament that the new economy does not demand men like Ralph, that women and men are becoming increasingly recognizable as part of the same "root." His proposal of marriage and commitment to having children assures readers that this "fit" woman will continue her evolutionary legacy.

The final scene of the novel is the obverse of the placid river and packet boat that opened the novel. Hagar and Fay take a boat excursion and get caught in a tremendous storm: "Now it laboured in the black trough of the waves, now it staggered upon the summits" (386). Significantly, however, neither of them captain the boat nor does the novel end with the storm. The novel ends, in fact, with their avowals of love for one another and Fay's commitment to take up the Woman Movement in the United States rather than his work in South America: "There are a plenty of bridges to be built in the United States" (390). For Johnston, the flux that the storm generates represents a chaos to be ridden through rather than an energy to be harnessed, so it is not surprising that the bridge, which depends on the stability of landed support, serves as a central metaphor for the text, framing the opening and closing scene.

Fay is a man from neither North nor South nor East nor West and his ascendance suggests a fundamentally different literary vision of sectional reconciliation than that offered in earlier decades. Fay becomes like the fairy of Hagar's first story, bringing Hagar to a new world beyond the bitter divide of sectional and gender conflict. Indeed, her first published story is "[a]bout fairies and a boy and a girl, and a lovely land they found by going neither north nor south nor east nor west" (113). If regional differences construct gender differences, then obscuring regional boundaries necessarily obscures gender boundaries. Any social disequilibrium such a move might suggest, however, is stabilized by a spiritually and scientifically ordained racial hierarchy. With Mary Magazine as her servant, Hagar remains a lady; with picturesque Negroes in the background, she remains an artist.

As they chart the concomitant evolution of the New Southern Woman and the New South, Ellen Glasgow's *Virginia* and *Life and Gabriella* likewise demonstrate an ambivalence toward the Old South and selective embrace of the new. The Old South in *Virginia* is everything stationary: nostalgia for the Lost Cause, the southern lady, an agrarian economy, and docile Negroes. The new in these novels is, in the broadest sense, change: changing gender roles, increasing racial strife, developing industrial economies, emerging technologies. The new is electricity, speed, efficiency, force, Wall Street, the railroad, divorce, suffrage, interracial violence, and settlement work. In *Virginia,* especially, Glasgow creates a South where the legacies of slavery erupt into the violence of Jim Crow, and while the New Southern woman is linked to this struggle metaphorically, she distances herself actually. Her triumph is, for the most part, conceived of as a personal domestic or professional success.

Much of the debate about this novel has focused on the extent to which Glasgow presents a feminist vision in her depiction of the character Virginia's rise and fall. Elizabeth Ammons and Anne Goodwyn Jones fault the novel for what they see as

Glasgow's capitulation to the romantic idealism of the southern lady (Ammons, *Conflicting Stories* 171; Jones, *Tomorrow* 248–49). Pamela Matthews sees Glasgow in *Virginia* coming to a "full realization" that "[s]exual oppression equals race oppression" (82). In Susan Goodman's recent biography of Glasgow, Goodman notes how Glasgow links both race and gender oppression in the novel to offer a larger indictment of regional idealism: Virginia, the state, practices a kind of "evasive idealism" that "has negatively determined the status of women, the plights of black Southerners, and the state (or state of mind) of Virginia" (127). Glasgow, Goodman argues, suggests that "the problem of the South—and of Virginia—will only be corrected when the spirit of 'patriarchal tyranny' passes" (127). I argue, however, that Glasgow's commitment to an evolutionary logic in which white women struggle to evolve and blacks permanently lag precludes any consistency in her presentation of racial protest even as it forecasts white woman's advancement. While Glasgow attacks the sexual exploitation of the slave household and criticizes her heroine for her blindness to the legacy of the plantation system, she creates her black characters as picturesque local color and perpetuates the myth of old retainer loyalty. Indeed, Glasgow ultimately undercuts the significance of her racial protest, in much the same way that Johnston did, by redeploying the rhetoric of slavery to define the plight of southern white bourgeois women rather than African Americans under Jim Crow.

Glasgow intended *Virginia* "to be the candid portrait of a lady; and nowadays, as I am made increasingly aware, the lady has become almost as extinct as the dodo" (preface ix). While Virginia is a victim of her selfless devotion to her husband and her children, her martyr status is decreasingly satirized as the novel progresses: "Although, in the beginning, I had intended to deal ironically with both the Southern lady and Victorian tradition, I discovered, as I went on, that my irony grew fainter while it yielded at last to sympathetic compassion. By the time I approached the end, the simple goodness of Virginia's nature had turned a comedy of manners into a tragedy of human fate" (Glasgow, preface x). Yet Glasgow's sympathetic rendition of Virginia's decline does not mean an indictment of her New Woman characters as conquerors. Rather it suggests that Glasgow, like Johnston, longs to retain some vestiges of the southern lady in the New Woman, especially in the personal ethics that Virginia sustains despite adversity.

The tensions in Glasgow's narrative—which moves, to some degree, from ironic detachment to romantic sentimentalism—are most evident in Glasgow's use of flower imagery to define Virginia's character. The frontispiece to the 1913 edition depicts Virginia carrying and framed by flowers, nearly overwhelmed by the bouquet she carries. When we are first introduced to her character, she and her friend, Susan Treadwell, "floated, like wind-blown flowers" (4). Virginia wears a Jacqueminot rose in her hair and physically exudes flowerlike characteristics to become "the feminine ideal of the ages" (5). Framed and defined by flowers, she becomes a veritable garden. As J. R. Raper has observed, the garden represented for Glasgow the sheltered life, the life apart from the rigors of natural selection but a space that nurtured ethical development. As Pamela R. Matthews notes, Glasgow often portrayed the beauty of nature as a means of spiritual healing (49). It was a contradiction embraced by evolutionary theorists such as Thomas Huxley—Huxley's work was a part of Glasgow's library (Tutwiler 4)—where the "garden" would become the only guarantee to righteousness in modern society. In "Evolution and Ethics" (1902), Huxley maintained, like John Stuart Mill in "Nature" (Mill was also well represented in Glasgow's library)—that the ways of nature, reflected in the evolutionary process of the animal world, were to be conquered, not obeyed. It was only in the artificial environment of the "garden" that "justice" could thrive (Raper 55). Yet Glasgow also cautions her readers that if as "wife and mother, she [Virginia] approaches perfection . . . it is a law of our nature, as of all nature, that change only endures, and the perfect mould must be broken" (preface xvii). All the elements of the new, which seem to have the rigors of natural selection as their foundation, promise to disrupt the garden sanctuary. As in *Hagar*, the rhetoric of Darwinism legitimates the New Woman's ascent even as the garden imagery reminds us of the ethical foundation of Virginia's character.

Indeed, as an emblem of the rural splendor of the state and "the feminine ideal of the ages," Virginia represents the devotion to an ultimately paradoxical idea, vegetative stasis. She is static in mind even as her beauty flourishes: "The chief object of her upbringing, which differed in no essential particular from that of every other well-born and well-bred Southern woman of her day, was to paralyze her reasoning faculties so completely that all danger of mental 'unsettling' or even movement was eliminated from her future" (22). As in *The Ancient Law*, characters more attuned to the Old South are associated with the lamplighter and the gaslight. Virginia's beauty can withstand neither the glare of the electric light nor the reflection in the shop window. Her being is completely opposed to the modern ideal of speed, movement, and artifice.

Virginia's New Woman companion, Susan Treadwell, by contrast, is associated with the dynamism of the industrial age: "The stronger of the two, she dominated the other, as she dominated every person or situation in life, not by charm, but by the force of an energetic and capable mind" (6). But contrary to Undine, she retains an allegiance to family and friendship ethics when she foregoes going to college to care for her ailing mother and sustains her friendship with the increasingly isolated Virginia. Susan has the same "power to command events" that her father does, and as Anne Goodwyn Jones notes, "the verb *want* is consistently applied to Susan and rarely to the other women" (Glasgow, *Virginia* 363; Jones 244). Yet because Susan's ambitions are tempered by sympathetic attachments or vice versa, she seems immune to the assault of time, which Virginia can only endure. While Virginia becomes haggard with age, Susan, like Gabriella and Hagar, becomes better looking.

The novel is divided into three sections: "The Dream," "The Reality," and "The Adjustment," which reflect most broadly Glasgow's vision of Virginia's necessary transition from the Old South to the New, and, more specifically, her conviction that women's advancement was integral to that progress. "The Dream" is the falseness of the Virginian ideal for which Virginia and her romantic interest, Oliver, fall. Yet, in many respects, Oliver Treadwell appears to be of the new order—his two ruling texts are *The Origin of Species* and *The Critique of Pure Reason*. When he stakes out his own literary independence, facing the wrath of his Uncle Cyrus, he is writing a play about a "new woman" with a past (128). Yet Oliver has little insight into how the legacies of the old affect him: his "distinctly formulated philosophy" is to apply general principles loosely (128). So the "classic phrases, 'women are like that,' and 'women think so queerly about things,' were on his lips as constantly as if he were an average male and not an earnest-minded student of human nature" (128). He too, like Virginia, upholds the ideology of the southern lady: "He understood now the primal necessity of woman, not as an individual, but as an incentive and an appendage to the dominant personality of man" (115). While clever and bold in some respects, ultimately "he stood merely for one of the spasmodic reactions against the dominant spirit," making him, like Virginia, a human being "born to be wasted" (129):

> he was pathetically ignorant of his own place in the extravagance of Nature. With the rest of us, he would have been astounded at the suggestion that he might have been born to be wasted. Other things were wasted, he knew, since those who called Nature an economist had grossly flattered her. Types and races and revolutions were squandered with royal prodigality—but that he himself should be so was clearly unthinkable. Deep down in him there was the obstinate belief that his existence was a vital matter to the awful Power that ruled the universe. (129)

As Cecelia Tichi points out in *Shifting Gears*, in an era that increasingly lauded the efficiency ethic, waste was a source of anxiety, connoting dysfunction and danger (63). The implied author's comments here foreshadow Oliver's squandering of both his talent and his marriage.

The second and third sections of the novel chart Oliver's failure to succeed as a serious playwright, his growing success in the commercial theater market, his consequent realization of Virginia's "intellectual limitations" (307), and his dalliances with other more modern women, dalliances rationalized as evolutionary by-products of the new age. As Oliver accuses Virginia of essentially wasting too much time on the children—an expenditure of energy that is subsequently validated by her son's serious illness—he "wastes" his sexual energy first with Abby Goode and then with Margaret Oldcastle. Ironically, the women whom he courts, who are also strongly associated with instinctual behavior, seem more intrinsic to race advancement. "[B]ouncing, boisterous" Abby Goode relishes the fox hunt and Atlantic City but is rewarded with marriage at the end of the novel (304). Margaret Oldcastle, the popular actress in Oliver's plays, has a "flame-like personality" reminiscent of Priscilla Batte's vision of the "spirit of commercial materialism" rising from the "ashes of a vanquished idealism" (486, 13). Her flame burns both the remnants of Oliver's idealistic devotion to his wife and then Virginia herself. Neither a "pretty doll" nor a "voluptuous enchantress," Margaret Oldcastle had worked her way up in the theater business through "hard work, self-denial, and discipline" (442), the "Oldcastle" virtues that suggest her relative permanence in an age of flux. When Virginia goes to confront her rival, she falters, and the implied author reminds readers of the epic, evolutionary meaning of Virginia's failure and Margaret's success:

> She stood not only for the elemental forces, but for the free woman; and her freedom, like that of man, had been built upon the strewn bodies of the weaker. The law of sacrifice, which is the basic law of life, ruled here as it ruled in mother-love and in the industrial warfare of men. Her triumph was less the triumph of the individual than of the type. The justice not of society, but of nature, was on her side, for she was one with evolution and with the resistless principle of change. (486)

The rhetoric of natural and sexual selection combine here to suggest the necessary destructive force of the New Woman's triumph over the old. Margaret Oldcastle is both the chaos of wave motion, the "resistless principle of change," and, as her name suggests, the foundational ethic at the root of evolutionary progress.

As Oliver's characterization suggests, the "new man" is portrayed far less sympathetically in *Virginia*. On the one hand, Cyrus Treadwell, the wealthiest citizen of Dinwiddie as the founder of a profitable cigarette manufacturing company, has a commitment to industrial innovation in his tobacco works, which suggests the drive and entrepreneurial spirit necessary for the new southern economy. He is also continually associated with the dynamism of railroads, the foremost image of the New South. According to Goodman, Glasgow patterned Cyrus after her uncle Joseph Reid Anderson and her father, Francis Glasgow, who were instrumental in the development of the Tredegar Iron Works, a major supplier of iron for both the Confederacy and the developing New South.[19] Yet the fact that the iron works relied heavily on slave labor and then on prison labor was a source of anxiety and social debt for Glasgow. Indeed, as Goodman notes, "In various manifestations, economic and sexual, the thing not named but imagined—the 'real' relationship between her family and their black employees—would become for Glasgow a moral debt and the subject of fiction" (Goodman 12). In the three chapters of the novel that focus on Cyrus as contradiction, "he stood equally for industrial advancement and domestic immobility" (362).

All of the Cyrus chapters include his rejection of either his wife or his daughter's needs, a reminder of his nostalgic connection to his old Confederate war buddy

Gabriel, and a rejection of his former mistress, the black domestic Mandy, and their illegitimate child, Jubal. The chapter in which the Treadwells are first introduced focuses on Cyrus's neglect of and tyranny over his wife but also includes Gabriel making an appeal to Cyrus to employ their son and Cyrus barely acknowledging Mandy when he passes her in the house. In the next Treadwell chapter, Cyrus is introduced sitting alone and spitting on the sunflowers bordering his house, metaphorically seeking to destroy the feminine garden of ethics (163). He then refuses to allow Susan to go to college, appearing to her in his moment of summary dismissal "as soulless as a steam engine" (164–65). The local boarding-house proprietor Mrs. Peachey then arrives to notify him that Oliver has fallen in love with Gabriel's daughter, Virginia. And finally, Mandy approaches Cyrus complaining of a stitch in her side. When he does not reply, her expression turns "half scornful, half inviting, yet so little personal that it might have been worn by one of her treetop ancestors while he looked down from his sheltering boughs on a superior species of the jungle. The chance effect of light and shadow on a grey rock was hardly less human or more primitive" (173). It is significant that this passage can not be clearly attributed to Cyrus; rather it is more likely that of the implied author, especially in the last sentence, which suggests an aesthetic sense that Cyrus would not have. While Glasgow subsequently critiques Cyrus's sexual predation as having created the fallen Mandy, she suggests here that Cyrus's fall was a merging with the "primitive" element, making the real threat of Cyrus's "domestic immobility" racial reversion. While, as Goodman notes, Jubal's later murder of a white policeman "functions as a warning" to southerners refusing to recognize the consequences of white men's sexual exploitation of black women (Goodman 128), the social critique, I would argue, is directed against the primary sin, miscegenation.

The sequence of events in these chapters reflects the extent to which Glasgow refigures the black struggle against Jim Crow abuse and terror into the New Woman's struggle against the legacy of the southern lady. The third Treadwell chapter occurs at the end of "The Reality" and before "The Adjustment" section. The chapter begins with Susan asking her father if she may marry with his consent. While he at first puts up obstacles, he eventually relents and Susan triumphs. Susan then tells her father that Mandy has been looking for him because her son will be lynched for shooting a policeman. Cyrus's "help" is in the form of a $50 bill. Gabriel then appears, and in a conversation with Cyrus about the murder, they discuss what kind of action should be taken. While Cyrus espouses the "eye for an eye" ethic, Gabriel argues that whites have the responsibility to set a moral example: "We stand for civilization to them; we stand even—or at least we used to stand—for Christianity. They haven't learned yet to look above or beyond us, and the example we set them is one that they are condemned, for sheer lack of any finer vision, to follow" (370). If Cyrus represents the disastrous consequences of the sexual exploitation of black women by white men and the hypocritical denials that follow, then Virginia's father, Gabriel, represents the equally disastrous consequences of paternalism. When Gabriel leaves Cyrus and continues his journey to visit a former slave, Aunt Mehitable, he seems, however, to have been rewarded for the ethic he espouses. The "essence of the spring . . . awakened and gave him back his youth" (372). Arriving at his former slave's log cabin, he muses on the "picturesque" sight before him: "People may say what they please, but there never were happier or more contented creatures than the darkeys" (374). He reflects on the innate difference between him and his former mammy: "He could make laws for her, but no child of a white mother could tell whether those laws ever penetrated that surface imitation of the superior race and reached the innate differences of thought, feeling, and memory which constituted her being" (375). Mehitable warns him there is going to be trouble following the white man's murder, and Gabriel begins his journey home. On his way, he happens upon two white men harassing Mehitable's grandson, and Gabriel, "the ordinary man" turns "hero." Feeling the old fury of Civil War battle, Gabriel strikes one of the attacking men and is killed; like his biblical namesake, Gabriel becomes the avenging angel who destroys the wicked.

Glasgow makes Cyrus pivotal to each of the Treadwell chapters to suggest the legacy of the Old South in the new. These are, indeed, well-trod events, dominant southern paradigms, often repeated. Cyrus's nostalgia for Gabriel and the Lost Cause, combined with his hard-hearted New South ambition, are the roots of his domestic, economic, racial, and sexual oppression. And meanwhile, "The Problem of the South," remains unsolved; neither the hardheaded Cyrus nor the romantic Gabriel offer an answer. Gabriel's more beneficent paternalism is Cyrus's tyranny in a different guise. At the same time, Cyrus's racism mirrors his sexism; his disavowal of Mandy's claim is akin to his disavowal of his daughter's ambition. Although Susan gains her agency by claiming her right to marry her love interest, Mandy loses her agency over her son. Likewise, Gabriel's paternalism denies Mehitable's agency, just as Virginia has lost hers. Yet Jim Crow violence spurs no resolution at the end of this second section of the novel even as the ascendancy of the New Woman is made inevitable.

Strikingly, Glasgow uses similar language to describe the enslavement of blacks and the oppression of the southern lady, the struggle against Jim Crow racism and the triumph of the New Woman. Early in the novel, Virginia reflects, "She let her mother slave over her because she had been born into a world where the slaving of mothers was a part of the natural order, and she had not as yet become independent enough to question the morality of the commonplace" (54). Later in the novel, Glasgow describes Jubal's murder of the white policeman as "The old blood crimes that never ceased where the white and the black races came together! The old savage folly and the new freedom! The old ignorance, the old lack of understanding, and the new restlessness, the new enmity!" (376). The phrase "new freedom" would be used to describe Margaret Oldcastle's triumph over Virginia in the subsequent chapter. While this appropriation and refiguring of racialized rhetoric suggests Glasgow's efforts to link the struggles of African Americans and white women, the fact that Jubal's "new freedom" results in violence and his fate is left unknown suggests the extent of Glasgow's significant unease with a black "restlessness" turned "enmity." While Susan announces Mandy's presence, she never directly involves herself with Mandy's plight.

And so, by the end of the novel, the New Woman apparently triumphs while the New Negro disappears. Virginia's story takes center stage. Completely alienated from her two "very modern" daughters (464)—Lucy a "pre-flapper" and Jenny a social reformer (454)—Virginia returns to Dinwiddie, then goes back to New York to make one last attempt to save her marriage but fails. The "freewoman" self-made, Margaret Oldcastle, who is "one with evolution" faces no narrative reprisals for her role as mistress. At the very end of the novel, in complete despair, Virginia returns again to Dinwiddie where, at long last, she receives a telegram from her beloved son Harry saying he will return. Harry's return, his assertion of filial loyalty above workaday profits, again indicates the extent to which Glasgow seeks to retain vestiges of the southern lady in the developing New South. The New Women in this novel may have prevailed but none have sons who return.

Glasgow originally conceived of *Life and Gabriella*, subtitled *The Story of a Woman of Courage*, as the second book in an uncompleted trilogy of "American womanhood" (Goodman 136). Written as a companion novel to *Virginia* and covering a later period, from 1894 to 1912, *Life and Gabriella* describes the eponymous heroine's failure in marriage to the drunken and philandering George Fowler and subsequent success both in business, as proprietor of a dress shop, and in love, with the self-made man Ben O'Hara. The frontispiece by C. Allan Gilbert features a short-haired, serene-faced premodern girl doing a traditionally feminine activity, sewing, but the caption startles in its assertiveness, "I want to be happy, but it depends on myself." Unlike *Virginia*, most of the novel takes place in a northern urban setting, and it deals more frankly with sexual issues, which may reflect the fact that Glasgow wrote it in the relative freedom of New York rather than more socially conservative Richmond (Goodman 137) as well as the changing social mores of the later period. Indeed, in *A Certain Measure*, Glasgow describes Gabriella as a product of a new age: "Although Gabriella lived only a decade later than Virginia, a whole era of change and action, one of the memorable epochs in history, separated the two women. The younger woman, a character of native energy and independence, blessed with a dynamic philosophy and a quick relish for the immediate, was, in a measure at least, the symbol of an advancing economic order" (97).

The novel is divided into two major sections: "The Age of Faith" and "The Age of Knowledge," which reflect the primary literary genre and social characteristic associated with the old and new order. For the former, sentimentalism and Christian faith define the age, while the New South is characterized by realism,

C. Allan Gilbert, Frontispiece from Ellen Glasgow, *Life and Gabriella: The Story of a Woman's Courage* (New York: Doubleday, 1916). Author's collection.

invention, and professionalism. The central conceit of the sentimental ethic is the blooming flower, and in the first half of the novel Gabriella evinces the flower ethic of romantic womanhood. In the "Mirage" chapter, she continually blooms in George's presence (93, 106). George, however, crushes her geraniums, which are symbols of the garden ethic, and foreshadows his actions to come (107).

Realism is brought with the electric light and the keener knowledge it enables.[20] It is under the power of the electric light that George's face appears "as if it were held under a microscope," and Gabriella notices for the first time the essential dullness of George's character (150). Once clouded by the haze of romantic longing, her vision is now cleared: "For a flashing instant of illumination she saw him with a vision that was not her own, but a stranger's, with a pitiless clearness unsoftened by any passion" (150). And when the strung out and nearly dead George stares blankly at the electric light in the mirror at the end of the novel, we are reminded of *Sister Carrie*'s Hurstwood, another character who suffers greatly for being out of step with the new electric age (441).[21]

While George is fundamentally unable to make the transition from faith to knowledge, Gabriella has all of the qualities that make her successful in the new economy. Foremost among these is the will to struggle and survive, which she apparently inherits from her father and namesake, Gabriel.[22] As in *Virginia,* where Cyrus was "force degraded" and Susan was "force refined," force or energy is a central trope used to define the nature of Gabriella and the qualitative nature of the new. Like Emily Brooke in *The Ancient Law,* Gabriella has a "radiant energy" (302), while her "new man" O'Hara is "irrepressibly energetic" (407). Together they create a veritable electric circuit: "And through her magnetic sense of his nearness there flowed to her presently a deeper and clearer perception of the multitudinous movements . . . For the first time, flowing like a current from the mind of the man beside her, there came to her an understanding of her own share in the common progress of life" (470). Because of this energy, Gabriella continually revitalizes herself as she ages.

Gabriella then capitalizes on this energy by developing a carefully cultivated work ethic. As she works to establish an increasing foothold in Madame Dinard's dress shop, she notes Madame's frequent failures in economy, industry, and efficiency, the central tenets of the Taylorist ideal, qualities essential to profitable expansion. At one point Gabriella exclaims, "The waste of time and misdirected energy are appalling. The business would be worth three times as much to anybody who could give her whole attention to it" (351). At the same time, Gabriella embraces the new psychology of successful marketing. Newness is good value— practical American design rather than overpriced Parisian fashions (275)—as well as the psychology of salesmanship, taking an interest in people (63). Gabriella brings the "finer gift of personality to the selling of hats" (71).

Yet newness is also the new ethic of quick marriages and easy divorces. Gabriella's stoicism when relating George's infidelity suggests a disturbing lack of embarrassment, a frankness characteristic of a new era: "And though she was unaware of its significance, her action was deeply symbolical of the failure of the old order to withstand the devastating advance of the new spirit" (238–39). Florrie, who seduces Gabriella's husband and then leaves him for a more advantageous match, is a woman who "ought to have been a failure. But she was not a failure" (225). Seemingly amoral but "surprisingly successful" (402), Florrie is the ethically dubious new type that Wharton represents in Undine. And like Undine, Florrie is often associated with a potentially destructive wave motion. She "seemed to float with all the elusive, magic loveliness of a sunbeam" (63). Her figure is "long, slender, sinuous," and her hair was like "melted gold in . . . [its] large loose waves" (491). If the new ethics are not morally dubious, they may reflect a dizzying lack of direction. Gabriella's daughter Fanny "dabbled in kindergarten, wood engraving, the tango, and settlement work, she was studying for the stage, and had fallen in love with a matinée idol" (370–71). Fanny also dabbles in the suffrage movement but never shows any lasting conviction for a particular cause (377–78).

As in *The Ancient Law,* the direction that new energy is to take is the central issue debated within the novel. Funneling it through speculating is portrayed as inherently nebulous and potentially dangerous. The Fowler men gain and lose their money from speculating although we never learn exactly what stocks they trade. Gabriella realizes her status is determined by the fluctuating demands of the marketplace: "This inadequate sum, she concluded with a touch of ironic humour, represented the exact value in open market of her marriage to George" (261).

In many respects, Glasgow seems to endorse a much more proprietary capitalist model of development in this novel, where the individual's ability to manufacture goods at a price the market will support is upheld rather than a more bureaucratic cooperative organization backed by the sale of securities. The pervasive Darwinist rhetoric in this novel, which legitimates both Gabriella's and O'Hara's assent, seems to impede the coalitions Gabriella may have made with her fellow workers. Coming home from work one evening, she feels that, "A subtle distinction divided her from the over-dressed shopgirls around her as completely as her sex separated her from the portly masculine breadwinner in the opposite seat" (349). Gabriella has "the aristocratic racial outline of the Carrs" (349), which allows her to retain "[i]n the whirlpool of modern business . . . the finer attributes which Nature had bred in her race" (349). And the fact that the black presence in the novel is almost nonexistent, appearing almost exclusively as picturesque backdrop (116, 123, 141, 156) and only in "The Age of Faith" section, suggests the extent to which African Americans are left behind as the (white) New Woman claims her rightful racial inheritance.

And yet what we are left with in *Life and Gabriella* is, in many respects, an extension of the New Woman's role in *Virginia* with ultimately an economic vision more corporate than socialist. Gabriella's "vein of iron" evokes Francis Glasgow's role in the Tredegar Iron Works, which went public in 1866. With her ideals of efficiency and hard work, she seems to be establishing a meritocracy essential to corporate growth, and her circuit-like connection with the working-class, slangy, Irish American O'Hara suggests that class differences must be bridged in the new era to ensure success. O'Hara too has aspects of the corporate personality. Although a self-made man, he seems to have a corporate ethos in his development of Bonanza City. His gift of a church, theater, and library signify his commitment to creating stable communities crucial to forming a reliable work force upon which a corporate culture would depend (416). Gabriella's "racial" and personal characteristics have paved the way for her economic ascent as well as for her limited coalition-building across class boundaries. But that same "subtle distinction" of her character fundamentally precludes her acknowledgment of the legacy of Jim Crow. Even as they signify restorative health to an overcivilized nation and white guilt for the sins of slavery, the Negro characters in Johnston's and Glasgow's fiction are destined to lag behind, bereft of the "ennobling" qualities that define southern gentility and ineluctably marginalized from the evolutionary narrative in which the (white) New Woman eventually succeeds.

CHAPTER 6

Willa Cather and the Fluid Mechanics of the New Woman

On November 16, 1895, in a column on the current literary scene for the *Lincoln Courier,* Willa Cather praises Henry James as "that mighty master of language and keen student of human actions" but wishes he would write "about modern society, about 'degeneracy' and the new woman and all the rest of it" (*World* 275).

Nearly a year later in a biographical sketch on the wives of presidential candidates William McKinley and William Jennings Bryan for the socially conservative *Home Monthly,* Cather lauds both women as New Women. She begins her sketch of Ida McKinley by praising her graciousness and charm but then focuses on her skills as a businesswoman. Having worked in her father's bank "before the advent of the business woman, and certainly before the 'New Woman' was dreamed of," she could do her work "better and more thoroughly than any man" (*World* 309). Cather then assures her readers that after Ida Saxton's courtship and marriage to Major William McKinley, her "life and interests have been those of her husband, as, in one way or another, actively or passively, every woman's must be" (310). She concludes her sketch by noting Mrs. McKinley's devotion to children, elegant social affairs, and music.

Mrs. William Bryan, by contrast, would offer the nation a quite different New Woman type. Socially awkward and unfashionable, Mary Bryan was instead "a student and a thinker, a woman burning with enthusiasm, the votaress, perhaps the victim, of great ideals which she believes practicable" (*World* 311). As valedictorian of her college class, an avid reader, an attorney admitted to the bar in Nebraska, clubwoman, wheelwoman, and expert swimmer—while still devoted to her husband's political career and her children—Bryan is "the 'New Woman' type at its best" (311–12).

Finally, on February 4, 1899, Cather wrote in a review for the *Lincoln Courier* that the "jovial, natty" comedienne and male impersonator Johnstone Bennett was "a hail-fellow-well-met, and the trimmest tailor-made New Woman of them all" (*World* 543). Cather praises Bennett's "frank," "frolicsome," and "boyish" demeanor combined with her "downright grit" as a professional woman. Bennett

Johnstone Bennett, n.d. Merriman Scrapbooks. Curtis Theatre Collection. Courtesy of the University of Pittsburgh Library System.

had refused to cut short her performance despite a painful abscess on her toe (Bennett).

Cather's deployments of the New Woman trope in her journalism—a trope at once associated with modernity, "degeneracy," professionalism, education, "downright grit," and gender transgression—reflect her fascination with the power and danger of a figure that must be contained. Indeed, for Cather, the New Woman figure had a certain cachet even as her transgressiveness necessitated boundaries. Successful in business or in law, the New Woman's first allegiance was to her family. However "frank" and "frolicsome" she may be as a male impersonator, her professionalism was beyond reproach.

Yet Cather's literary reviews during the same period display far less fascination with and far more hostility toward both the sociopolitical implications of New Woman activities and the creation of coalitions with other New Woman writers. Even as Cather praised Du Maurier's *Trilby,* she lambasted Sarah Grand's widely popular feminist novel exposing the sexual double standard, *The Heavenly Twins,* as "atrocious" and decried its "cheap, vulgar, ignorant discussions of questions that should not be touched outside of a medical clinic" (*World* 132). Emma Frances Brooke's *The Superfluous Woman,* a feminist novel describing the political and sexual awakening of a young woman, was similarly a "dreary waste of paper" with "no one flash of truth that gives the book a right to be" (*Kingdom* 406). While praising George Sand and George Eliot as the only "two real creators among women authors," Cather lamented the feminine mind's "hankering for hobbies and missions" (*Kingdom* 406). In a review of Christina Rossetti's work occasioned by her death in December 1894, Cather noted that Rossetti's poetic limitations hamper most erudite women: "[l]earning and a wide knowledge of things does not seem to help women poets much. It seems rather to cripple their naturalness, burden their fancy and cloud their imagination with pedantic metaphors and vague illusions" (*World* 146). Ouida had talent but spoiled it with her poor craftsmanship and humorlessness, prompting Cather to wonder "why God ever trusts talent in the hands of women, they usually make such an infernal mess of it" (*World* 275). Similarly, the authors of the *Woman's Bible,* edited under the direction of Elizabeth Cady Stanton, were hopelessly unqualified to undertake their task because they were "without scholarship, without linguistic attainments, without theological training, not even able to read the Bible in the original tongues" (*World* 539). In *The Awakening,* Miss Chopin created an inferior Creole version of *Madame Bovary.* Given Chopin's "exquisite and sensitive, well-governed . . . style," why, Cather asks, did she devote her narrative to "so trite and sordid a theme" (*World* 697). By contrast, Cather celebrated male writers such as Homer, Emerson, Whitman, Stevenson, Kipling, and Carlyle for their virile aesthetic sensibility, prompting Cather biographer Sharon O'Brien to assert that Cather equates "creativity both with paternity and with an aggressive, phallic masculinity" (148).

For Cather, it appears, women had only one gift, and that was the power of feeling: "The women of the stage know that to feel greatly is genius and to make others feel is art" (*World* 146). As Elsa Nettels notes, even if Cather gave many female performers acerbic reviews, she saw the potential for women to exhibit real creative power on the stage (124). The eccentric and popular actress Sarah Bernhardt, known for her exercise routines and commitment to dress reform, had "one of the greatest artistic careers of the last fifty years, one of the most strenuous and ambitious and most rich in achievement" (*World* 813). The actress Minnie Maddern Fiske had a "penetrating intellect . . . like a searchlight, she has only to turn it upon a character to master it. . . . [H]er modernness is the compelling power in her acting. . . . She has that ardent sympathy which is the very root of all realistic art" (*World* 659). The great American soprano Lillian Nordica was abundantly endowed with that "practical and aggressive form of courage in America termed 'grit'" (643). She was a "splendid Amazon warrior" (644) even as she embodied the "best in American womanhood" (646). Such a disparity in Cather's estimation of women's aesthetic potential between the two disciplines suggests her conviction of male intellectual superiority in writing and women's emotional superiority on stage, what Nettels describes as an essential "gender divide" in her fiction.

Given that anxieties about the feminization of American culture were often directed against women writers, it is not surprising that Cather would privilege female performers whose artistry was more embodied and arguably less threatening to established gender stereotypes. And yet, as Judith Butler has argued, Cather's privileging of male authorship may only be an apparent privileging, an attempt to dissimulate lesbian desire pathologized in turn-of-the-century medical discourse. As a lesbian, Cather identifies with the male protagonist in her fiction in order to express what would be a taboo desire for her female protagonist (*Bodies* 148–49).

No matter how this apparent "gender divide" is read, it is symptomatic of a host of contradictions in Cather's work that have fueled much of the recent critical debate. How, critics have asked, can one reconcile Cather's antifeminist statements, seemingly privileged male narrative voices, endorsement of white privilege, and use of ethnic stereotypes with her lesbianism, portrayal of strong, often transgendered female protagonists, critiques of patriarchal privilege, and positive portrayals of ethnic communities? The New Woman—a figure continually criticized for blurring conventional gender roles, forming dangerous attachments to other women, and assuming the vices associated with ethnic Others—lies at the intersection of all of these critical debates and offers Cather a performative model for intervening in the sociopolitical concerns of her era.

Invariably a source of anxiety because of her association with women's personal freedom, the New Woman was also an overdetermined figure that embodied other anxieties of Cather's age: dehumanizing technological advances, a burgeoning immigrant population, bitter class conflicts, the closing of the frontier, and the medicalizing of homosexuality. While Wharton constructs a New Woman that was hard to define but functioned as a modern force potentially destructive to venerable old New York values, Cather carefully defines her New Woman and cautiously celebrates her by showing her to be a necessary, if potentially threatening, element of the newly emerging social order. As performers who, to use Judith Butler's terminology, "subversively repeat" some received gender and sexual roles, ethnic stereotypes, and class designations, Cather's New Woman characters pose only a necessary, albeit limited, threat to compulsory heterosexuality, ethnically and religiously motivated nativist sentiment, professional hierarchies, and the masculinized solid mechanics of the machine age. Yet because these characters are remarkable exceptions who pay a varying price for their extraordinariness and are uninterested in recruiting others, their threat is contained. In Cather's fictional world, if the New Woman is ethnically marked as nonwhite, her transgressions are generally sexual in nature in keeping with the prevailing ethnic stereotypes. In contrast to her white counterparts, she is most often punished for her transgressions. If she is white and male-identified, she must demonstrate sexual restraint or renunciation—especially if her desire is coded lesbian—intellectual acumen, and a savvy embrace of modern innovation before she is deemed a modern phenomenon to be celebrated. If she is white and female-identified, she is allowed more sexual expressiveness but a range of exceptionalness that does not extend beyond the feminized power of feeling.

As I will demonstrate, Cather uses the overdetermined wave motif to define her New Woman protagonists as essential figures of the modern age even as she first displaces the anxiety these characters create onto safer targets—a western landscape already marked as the site of social-political transgression and a group-identified ethnic other—and then refigures that anxiety as an inevitable but naive response to a new but necessary modern social force.[1] Epitomized ultimately by Thea Kronborg in *The Song of the Lark,* the triumph of this new force, racialized as white and gendered as female, is proof of the legitimacy of the New Woman's evolutionary success and Others' evolutionary failure. Indeed, while most critics see Cather as creating ever more emancipated female protagonists culminating in Thea Kronborg, they fail to acknowledge that that emancipation is increasingly predicated on validating both the social Darwinist triumph of an essentially white Thea and a complex appropriation and refiguration of a dark Other. For even as the currents of the Other prove dangerous, the taut performance of whiteness, bourgeois class identity, conventional gender roles, and compulsory heterosexuality falters as it appears to triumph: feeling stifled by codes of professionalism, Protestant prohibitions, and individual isolation, white characters continually seek out the company of ethnic Others; eastern effete culture is exposed for its shallowness; savvy female characters succeed professionally while their male counterparts stumble; seemingly happy marriages conceal destructive turbulence.[2] The modern bourgeois ethic of progress crushes even as it produces prosperity.

Set in a western ranch town, "Tommy the Unsentimental" was published in the *Home Monthly* a month before the Bryan and McKinley sketch in the same magazine. The story reveals a similar strategy of containing the New Woman's transgressions and thereby remains in accord with the socially conservative editorial goals of the magazine. In the inaugural July 1896 issue, the magazine assured readers it would present wholesome, elevating fiction: "*The Home Monthly* is not ambitious of becoming a dignified review, nor is it to be used only as a vehicle for the dissemination of fashion gossip and culinary recipes. It is equally certain that it should not be made a mere purveyor of sensational and unwholesome fiction. . . . Nothing need be said further than that these pages will be kept clean and pure in tone, and that all plans for *The Home Monthly* center in the aim to entertain, to educate, to elevate" (quoted in Byrne and Snyder 4). Given such a policy, it seems surprising that Cather would present a female protagonist who would flout conventional gender roles and sexual designations in nearly every aspect of her life. Her appearance is decidedly unfeminine: "Tommy was not a boy, although her keen gray eyes and wide forehead were scarcely girlish and she had the lank figure of an active half grown lad" ("Tommy" 63). She plays whist and billiards, drinks cocktails, earns the respect of her father's business friends, and demonstrates her father's savvy business sense when she saves the bank of the inept but likeable Jay Ellington Harper. She shows an unseemly interest in another woman, Miss Jessica, her school friend from the East—"a dainty, white, languid bit of a thing, who used violet perfumes and carried a sunshade" (66). With its homoerotic overtones—"The Old Boys said it was a bad sign when a rebellious girl like Tommy took to being sweet and gentle to one of her own sex" (66)[3]—their relationship would be considered dangerous within the sexology discourse of the period. And, most strikingly within the context of the story, she rides a bicycle, which, Patricia Marks has observed, is one of the signature New Woman activities.[4] When there is a run on his bank and Harper panics, Tommy rides her bicycle the twenty-five miles to save it.

Sharon O'Brien views "Tommy" as an iconoclastic story that "mocks the Victorian ideal of womanhood" while demonstrating "the professional woman's ability to outdistance less competent men" (229–30). In this respect, she sees "Tommy" as Cather's "alter ego" and the story as a "veiled but rebellious self-disclosure" (230). Judith Butler notes, however, that Tommy pays for her transgressions. At the end of the story, Tommy both takes the place of her father and renounces her own lesbian desires, in effect demonstrating the costs of a woman identifying with patriarchal power and privilege (*Bodies* 161). Indeed, Tommy's business ethic, her "particularly unfeminine mind that could not escape meeting and acknowledging a logical conclusion" ("Tommy" 63), does not jeopardize the ultimate romantic relationship between her conventionally feminine friend,

Miss Jessica, and Jay Harper. Although Tommy herself was "immensely fond" of Harper, she essentially gives Miss Jessica to him when she declares, "as soon as it is convenient, Jay, I wish you'd marry her and be done with it" (70). Significantly, Miss Jessica's feelings in the matter are unrevealed; she becomes a mere object of exchange. By validating Tommy's final act of renunciation in which she instigates the exchange of women that insures patriarchal dominance, Cather ultimately contains the transgressive potential of Tommy's behavior and remains in accord with the socially conservative editorial goals of the *Home Monthly.*

And yet, Cather also effects containment by displacing the danger of Tommy's transgressions onto a western setting. Here Tommy's New Woman accomplishments are respected: "People rather expect some business ability in a girl there, and they respect it immensely" (*Twenty-four Stories* 63). By contrast, the East offers either moral dissipation or physical lassitude. Jay Harper was sent West by his father when "he had made a sad mess of his college career, and had spent too much money and gone at too giddy a pace down East" (63). The languid Miss Jessica, a thorough product of eastern feminine culture, is reduced to tears after physical exertion.

But it is the bicycle ride through the rugged, unforgiving western terrain that represents the climax of the story, the height of Tommy's transgression as a New Woman figure, and Cather's mapping of a "safe" place. On the one hand, Tommy's activity is sanctioned as part of a larger cultural shift celebrating women's greater athletic activity. Writing for *Good Housekeeping* in 1912, Anna de Koven declares "The hoydenish tomboy, who was the despair of the mother of the past generation, is to-day just the normal girl whose keen love for outdoor sports is the pride of the family" (150). Yet the landscape Tommy and Miss Jessica ride over evokes a more dangerous representation of New Woman sexuality in its wavelike imagery: The road "is rough, hilly and climbs from the river bottoms up to the big Divide . . . running white and hot through the scorched corn fields and grazing lands" ("Tommy" 67). While Tommy is riding, she feels only the "throbbing, dazzling heat that had to be endured. Down there in the valley the distant bluffs were vibrating and dancing with the heat" (68). Miss Jessica would likewise see wavelike motion in the stifling hot landscape: "[she] found it harder than ever to breathe, and the bluffs across the river began doing serpentines and skirt dances" (68). Tommy's posture on her bicycle would also have been read as sexually charged. Feeling overwhelmed with exhaustion, Miss Jessica cattily observes, Tommy "sat very badly on her wheel and looked aggressively masculine and professional when she bent her shoulders and pumped like that" (68). As Ellen Gruber Garvey notes, Tommy's riding style—the bent-over posture favored by speeders rather than the decorous upright posture that women were supposed to follow—would have been considered dangerous by some turn-of-the-century physicians. Writing for the *American Journal of Obstetrics and Gynecology* in 1895, Dr. Robert L. Dickinson cautions that the friction on the clitoris and labia due to an ill-adjusted seat would only be exacerbated by the posture of "stooping forward" and the "warmth generated from vigorous exercise" (33–34).

Butler argues that Miss Jessica's distasteful response to Tommy's riding style suggests her rejection of Tommy's desire even as her vision of "serpentines and skirt dances" reflects the extent to which she is caught up in it. Yet Butler does not consider the dynamics by which Cather both represents Tommy's sexuality and displaces the anxiety it causes Miss Jessica through the landscape. The "throbbing," "dazzling," "vibrating" and "dancing," "serpentine" heat—which in its "hotter still" wind emanation fuels Tommy's journey ("Tommy knew that the wind was their only chance")—is also "sickening" and "destroying" ("Tommy" 68).[5] By acknowledging the heat's destructiveness while ultimately affirming its power—embracing that heat allows Tommy to save the bank—Cather, I argue, endorses the potential if not the actuality of Tommy's sexuality.

Any residual danger caused by Tommy's transgressive desire is finally displaced onto an ethnic Other. When Tommy arrives at the bank, she is met by a flustered Jay trying to stave off a score of angry Bohemians—"They just came down like the wolf on the fold. It sounded like the approach of a ghost dance"—declaring "We want 'a money, want'a our money" ("Tommy" 69). Conjuring images of ravenous ferocity and primitive tribalism, the Bohemians' demands pose a more tangible threat to the established order, both romantic (Jay would lose his viability as a suitor if the bank defaults) and social (Tommy's father would lose a valuable asset; the community a valuable service provider). Cather implies that Miss Jessica would also be victimized if the Bohemians held sway. Left "all bunched up by the road like a little white rabbit" (70), she is, metaphorically at least, a potential victim of the "wolf on the fold." What I am suggesting here is that Cather displaces Tommy's dangerous sexual desire not only by cross-gender identification, as Butler argues, but also through a series of regional and ethnic codes, which help to write New Woman desire as both a necessary performance in a western landscape and a safer idiosyncratic alternative than angry Bohemians with a dangerous group consciousness.

Published in *Cosmopolitan* in April 1900, "Eric Hermannson's Soul" (1900) presents a decidedly different New Woman, one who defies fewer gender conventions but who is allowed, provisionally, a direct sexual expression that Tommy is not. A cosmopolitan actress from the East, Margaret Elliot is "one of those women of whom there are so many in this day, when old order, passing, giveth place to new; beautiful, talented, critical, unsatisfied, tired of the world at twenty-four" ("Eric" 98). The story creates a series of contrasts: the hard landscape of the Nebraska Divide versus the cosmopolitan but effete East; the asceticism of the Free Gospellers, intent on "saving" the wayward on the Divide, versus the pagan appreciation of nature that demands physical expression; the boldly courageous, ethnically marked Eric Hermannson versus Margaret's overcivilized, cynical fiancé. The story traces two liberations, that of Eric Hermannson, the "saved" but miserable Norwegian, and that of Margaret, the privileged but aimless traveler to the West. For Eric, Margaret represents "an entirely new species of humanity," who awakens his long-repressed desires. He falls in love with her, and, renouncing the proscription against dancing and music that the Free Gospellers have imposed, he offers her an evening of revelry and sexual awakening at a farewell town dance. For Margaret, Eric offers a life force not crushed by the passionless rounds of her Brahmin life.

Indeed, in the letter Margaret receives from her fiancé, he describes both a theatrical performance and a painting with the critical distance of someone intellectually engaged but physically and emotionally removed. Within these works of art, he suggests, women should please a male viewer by conforming to the setting of which they are a part. Speaking of the lead female role in *As You Like It,* he writes, "Miss Harrison reads her lines well, but she is either a maiden-all-forlorn or a tomboy; insists on reading into the part all sorts of deeper meanings and highly colored suggestions wholly out of harmony with the pastoral setting" ("Eric" 110). When he describes his recent purchase of a painting that features a woman in an exotic African setting, he again describes how his pleasure is determined by the degree to which the female figure and then Margaret conform to the pictorial fantasy: "The drapery of the female figure is as wonderful as you said; the fabric all barbaric pearl and gold, painted with an easy, effortless voluptuousness, and that white, gleaming line of African coast in the background recalls memories of you very precious to me" (110). What is interesting here is that Cather contrasts these images of women in nature—a carefully crafted nature in which women should seamlessly blend for the pleasure of the male gaze—with the untamed element of the West, where the expanse of the horizon and the "burning stars" reflect Margaret and Eric's mutual passion but especially the female protagonist's sexual awakening (114). When they share a kiss at the top of a windmill tower, "the riotous force under her heart became an engulfing weakness" (116). As she climbs down from the tower, the stars again respond, this time to her erotic state of confusion: "the drunken stars up yonder seemed reeling to some appointed doom" (116). Cather's use of pathetic fallacy here—with "burning" and "drunken stars"—emphasizes the force of the feminized New Woman's desire—no longer is she simply in harmony with nature, but, instead, she is dramatically redirecting it. Even, however, as "Eric Hermannson's Soul" presents the West as a transgressive space for women, it, like "Tommy the Unsentimental," predicates the New Woman's freedom on an ultimate renunciation. The ethnic and class transgressions of a long-lasting relationship with Eric are not realized. Margaret returns to the East, giving up Eric and returning, one may surmise, to her fiancé.

Published as the first story in *The Troll Garden* (1905), "Flavia and Her Artists" has been considered Cather's most negative portrait of the New Woman in the guise of the story's title character Flavia.[6] Devoid of any aesthetic sensibility herself, Flavia's ambition is to collect artists whose currency she determines has sufficient value. All of the artists are to some degree satirized: the erudite but ponderous third-person narrator, Imogen, the specialist in a "well-sounding branch of philology" (7); the "militant iconoclast" Frau Lichtenfeld (8), a woman of "immense stature" who strides down a hillside "in a very short skirt and a broad, flapping sun hat" (9); the actress "Jimmy" Broadwood, reminiscent of "a nice, clean, pink-and-white boy who has just had his cold bath, and come down all aglow for a run before breakfast" (8); Will Maidenwood, the editor of *Woman,* who becomes "faint after hurting his finger in an obdurate window" (14); and the supercilious "fat and bald" Monsieur Roux, who reportedly declared that he "had never met a really intellectual woman" (17).

Yet, in the end, it is Flavia who is most cruelly satirized when Monsieur Roux publishes an article exposing her to the derision of all and prompting the departure of most of her artist guests. Entitled "Roux on Tuft Hunters; The Advanced American Woman As He Sees Her; Aggressive, Superficial and Insincere," the article offers a "satiric characterization of Flavia, a-quiver with irritation and vitriolic malice" (25). Flavia, however, does not see the article and blames her well-meaning husband for the sudden departure of her artists. Imogen finally declares Flavia's husband, the supposed philistine, to be "a pillar of sanity and law" in a "house of shams and swollen vanities" (30). On the one hand, the story satirizes the woman who claims to be "advanced" but is so insecure in her ideas that she parrots those of others and builds a salon based on popular opinion rather than on her own informed aesthetic sense. On the other hand, the story satirizes the dilettante artists, the poseurs, who are willing to participate in Flavia's gatherings for reasons of economic convenience, curiosity, or flattery. Yet of all the artists, "Jimmy" Broadwood escapes most of the censure. As her name suggests, "Jimmy" has the broader vision to see the folly of both her "artist" compatriots and her hosts. And of all three characters who explicitly transgress conventional gender appearance and behavior—Frau Lichtenfeld and Will Maidenwood being the other two—only Jimmy's is validated.

At the same time, the story distinguishes between the poseurs and the real artists through ethnic markers. When Jimmy denounces the other artists, she uses an ethnic slur, calling them humorless "gypsy-dago" people (13). For the dinner that turns out to be a showcase of pretense, Flavia has chosen an Orientalist décor, characterized by darkness and exoticism: "There was about the darkened room some suggestion of certain chambers in the Arabian Nights, opening on a court of palms" (13). By contrast, in the morning after the dinner, Jimmy looks "fresh and encouraging" in her "stiff, white, shirt bosom," "dark blue-and-white necktie," "wide rolling collar," and "white rosebud in the lapel of her coat" (20–21). What I argue is that by associating the dark "gypsy-dago" people with a languid exoticism and a stale affectedness and the white Jimmy with freshness, crispness, and insight, Cather affirms both Jimmy's usurpation of the narrator's power to read the preceding events and the legitimacy of what now appears a worldly-wise gender transgression.

It is not until *Alexander's Bridge* (1912), however, that Cather associates the

New Woman with all the anxieties of the modern. Based on an actual engineering disaster, the collapse of the Quebec Bridge in August 1907, the novel was serialized in the muckraking magazine *McClure's* as "Alexander's Masquerade." The novel offers an extended parallel between the bridge builder Bartley Alexander's romantic and professional life. While torn between whether he should pursue an affair with the New Womanish Hilda Burgoyne, an old flame who brings back all the excitement of his youth, or remain faithful to Winifred, his beautiful but "very proud, and just a little hard" wife from the East (47), Alexander must decide how, given cost and labor tensions, to complete successfully the "longest cantilever in existence," the great Canadian Moorlock Bridge. Cather uses this conceit to suggest the tensions between two modern ethics: the newfound, "fluid," sexual expressiveness of the New Woman versus the relentless and dehumanizing machine-age ethic, which Cecelia Tichi describes as "gear-and-girder technology" (*Shifting Gears* 16). Even as Cather evokes, contains, and displaces the threat of this female-identified New Woman's sexuality, she also makes it an intrinsic element in the new mechanical age.

The novel begins with a contrast between the solidity of Boston's gravely colored houses—Alexander would later be compared with the cracked façade of a building—and moves to the "moist spring earth and the saltiness that came up the river with the tide" (3). Presented as the "tamer of rivers" (8), Bartley is himself an embodiment of "gear-and-girder" technology. He is described as a machine—"his head seemed as hard and powerful as a catapult, and his shoulders . . . strong enough . . . to support a span of any one of his ten great bridges" (8)—and a tireless machine at that: "[t]he machinery was always pounding away in this man" (11). The female characters, by contrast, represent the wavelike, chaotic element inextricably linked but at odds with this "gear-and-girder" force. His wife, whom he met during work on his first bridge, suggests both the wave energy of water and the dynamo. She contains "stormy" possibilities, and "for all her composure and self-sufficiency, she seemed to [Wilson] strangely alert and vibrating, as if in her, too, there were something never altogether at rest" (12). The Bloomsbury-raised, Irish actress Hilda, who is single and supports herself, offers a greater degree of turbulence as an ethnically marked New Woman.[7] Unlike Winifred, she has more than the suggestion of a "vibrating element"; she has something "utterly wild and daft" (22). As Bartley is increasingly drawn to Winifred, he gazes out onto the water (28, 48) until his once solid resolution is overcome by the motion of the sea: "Deep down in him somewhere his resolution was weakening and strengthening, ebbing and flowing. . . . He was submerged in the vast impersonal grayness about him, and at intervals the sidelong roll of the boat measured off time like the ticking of a clock. He felt released from everything that troubled and perplexed him" (50–51). The once regular but relentless, pumping machinery now takes on the properties of fluids even as fluids take on the properties of machinery. Hilda's London is "red and roaring and murky" where the "undulating tramp, tramp of the crowd . . . was like the deep vibration of some vast underground machinery" (63). In her last meeting with Alexander, Hilda arrives at his New York rooms soaked by rain (71). When Alexander is called to return to his current troubled bridge project, he travels over his first bridge and feels the increasing power of water to destroy: "the sound of the rushing water underneath, the sound which, more than anything else, meant death; the wearing away of things under the impact of physical forces which men could direct but never circumvent or diminish" (78). Ultimately, when his latest bridge collapses because of insufficient structural support, the terrified French Canadian bridge builders pull him under and he drowns.[8]

With this conclusion, Cather does not, as most have argued, simply indict Bartley's gear-and-girder technology and its associations with a rugged masculinity; neither does she simply indict the destructive wave force that kills him. Rather Cather charts a shift in the energy dynamic of the new age. It is on his journey across the Atlantic to see Hilda that Bartley grows passive, where he feels his resolution "ebbing and flowing" like the tide, his whole being immersed in the "vast impersonal grayness about him." And because of his relationship with Hilda, Alexander fails to receive the crucial telegram in time to prevent the fatal bridge collapse. These events suggest what Luce Irigaray has described as the failure of a masculinized solid mechanics to deal with a feminized fluid mechanics.[9] If men as subjects are associated with rigidity and logic, women as objects are the effusive turbulent Other that must be contained. This gendered water dynamic, with its wavelike sexual overtones, becomes more pervasive and more threatening, gradually overtaking the gear-and-girder force of the engineer.[10] Hilda represents, then, in some respects, what Bram Dijkstra describes in *Idols of Perversity: Fears of Feminine Evil in Fin-De-Siècle Culture* as the predatory siren figure, which arose as a defense against the threat to male patriarchal power that the New Woman generated:

> In the popular lore of the years around 1900, the sea was ultimately passive, and woman was the creature of the sea, water being her symbol: totally yielding, totally flexible, yet ultimately all-encompassing and deadly in its very permeability. Her predatory sexuality was the tool with which nature tried to "draw back by cohesion and [refund] into the general watery surface" of the ocean of undifferentiated instinctual life the individualized "drop" representing the male intellect in Joseph Le Conte's scheme for evolutionary development. (265)

And yet, crucially, Cather does not simply create a polarity between a rational masculine solid mechanics and an irrational feminine fluid mechanics. Instead she charts the emergence of a new wave energy that drives the new age: "the deep vibration of some vast underground machinery" (63).

In my view, then, Cather's novel does not, as Marilee Lindemann maintains, ultimately reject "one of the major tropes organizing the story of desire in Western culture, the figure of the woman who falls and brings a man down with her" (introduction to *Alexander's Bridge* xxix). Rather than "bystanders only, symbols in and spectators of the drama of his self-destruction" (xxx), Winifred and Hilda, especially, play an active part in Alexander's destruction. "[T]otally yielding" and "totally flexible" to Bartley's wishes while being increasingly associated with dangerous fluidity, Hilda's allure becomes all-encompassing and deadly. By equating "death and love," "the rushing river and his burning heart" (78), Cather ultimately relegates Hilda to the "undifferentiated instinctual life" of the rushing river. The illustrations by F. Graham Cootes in the original serialized version confirm this. In the third illustration, captioned "Are You Going to Let Me Love You a Little Bit Bartley," Cootes emphasizes Hilda's role as seductress, yielding but manipulative in Bartley's embrace.

And yet if the New Woman's sexual transgression is threatening, it is also a natural force to be reckoned with rather than quelled by an eastern culture of refinement. As Janis Stout suggests, Alexander's failure is also coded as a critique of eastern culture. Educated in the West, Alexander leaves to come East where he cracks; Winifred is beautiful but "very proud, and just a little hard." Alexander's engineer's ethic, born in the West but stultified in the East, makes him unable to compensate for the wavelike force embodied by the new cultural developments that Hilda, most prominently, represents. Significantly, the novel ends with Hilda and Alexander's old friend Wilson gazing into the fire, an image that evokes Alexander's fantasy of returning to his boyhood West, camping and gazing into a fire on his journey to his failing bridge (77). The ending of the story not only indicates Cather's tacit endorsement of a West that would represent the New Woman's sexual freedom—Hilda evokes all of the excitement of his youth, the "rough days of the old West" (28–29)—but also a critique of an eastern gear-and-girder ethic unable to compensate for the impact of fluid forces.

As in "Tommy," the threat of the chaotic fluid element is displaced onto an ethnic Other associated with a dangerous group consciousness. Alexander twice reflects on the pressures not only of cost-cutting measures but of steel strikes and general industrial unrest on his U.S. bridge projects. When Bartley first plunges into the water after the bridge collapse, he rises to the surface and feels sure that he will survive. It is only when another part of the bridge collapses and the French Canadians fall on top of him that he is pushed under and drowns. As Lindemann notes in her introduction, this final scene reveals Cather's anxieties about the "power and the size of the labouring class," an anxiety highlighted in an article on the repercussions of union violence that ran concurrently with "Alexander's Masquerade" (xviii).[11] It also serves, in effect, to take Hilda, and by extension the New Woman, off the hook. She may have driven him into the water but the French Canadians drowned him.

Some years later Cather repudiated *Alexander's Bridge* as "unnecessary and superficial" and generally inferior in quality,[12] while she praised her subsequent novel, *O Pioneers!* (1913), as "spontaneous" and original, drawing on material she knew well (97, 98). Noting the considerable change in style, setting, and theme between the two novels—from pseudo-Jamesian to an expansive Jewett, from relatively unfamiliar Boston and London to home-town Nebraska, from failed male protagonist to successful female protagonist—most critics have, in effect, agreed with Cather's own estimation. Yet the parallel elements are crucial in understanding the points of divergence. Both novels explore the consequences of sexual transgression, the threat and promise of the ethnic Other, mechanical forces versus dangerous fluidity, and the pleasure and danger of the New Woman's emergence. And I am certainly not the first to suggest that Alexandra Bergson is in some ways akin to Bartley Alexander: from the word play (Alexander to Alexandra and the reversal of initials—B.A. to A.B.) to the unflagging drive that propels them to acts of creation that change the landscape.[13] In both novels, Cather presents an overdetermined New Woman who embodies the cultural flux of the period even as in *O Pioneers!* she offers the New Woman as remedy to the fear that change produces. By exploring the ways Cather exploits anxieties about ethnic difference and industrialization as she makes her case for the New Woman in *O Pioneers!,* I would like to complicate rather than reject the feminist content of this novel.[14]

In *Willa Cather: Queering America,* Marilee Lindemann argues that Alexandra's triumph at the end of *O Pioneers!,* a triumph celebrated by most feminist critics, should be viewed with regard to its costs: "Alexandra's triumphant personhood is considerably more vexing ... when viewed along the axes of ethnicity and sexuality as an allegory of nation-building predicated on the repudiation or containment of the 'queer' and emblematized in skin so smooth and white it is said to possess 'the freshness of the snow itself'" (46). Lindemann defines the "queer" as "bodily difference that is perceived as socially unassimilable, whether that difference is a matter of sex or gender 'troubles,' racial or ethnic otherness, or nonnormate physical appearance or ability—or, as is frequently the case, some combination of these factors" (47). While I agree with Lindemann that Cather constructs Alexandra to appease early-twentieth-century fears of race suicide, I do not believe Alexandra represents a complete disavowal of the "queer." Most notably, through the trope of the New Woman, Cather demonstrates both the power and failure of whiteness—as it represents sexual repression and a Taylorist efficiency ethic—to offer women who transgress gender codes, and arguably compulsory heterosexuality, a coherent or stable identity. The allure of the ethnic Other remains, even when seemingly banished from the text.

Early on Alexandra manifests all the "downright grit" of the professional New Woman, subverting the expectations of her gendered identity as she demonstrates the "force" and dynamism of the modern engineer. She is a "tall, strong girl, and she walked rapidly and resolutely, as if she knew exactly where she was going and what she was going to do next" (14). She wore a "man's long ulster" and "carried it like a young soldier" and directed her gaze toward the horizon (14). Rejecting the "flirtatious instincts of a clothing drummer," she responds with a glance of "Amazonian fierceness" (15). Because she has inherited her grandfather's "force" and intelligence (28–29), she is given the leadership responsibility for the family farm, and with "the strength of will, and the simple direct way of thinking about things out" along with her commitment to farming as a professional enterprise, she conquers the land: "It was Alexandra who read the papers and followed the markets, and who learned by the mistakes of their neighbors. It was Alexandra who could always tell about what it had cost to fatten each steer, and who could guess the weight of a hog before it went on the scales closer than John Bergson himself" (28). And when she refuses to disavow her relationship with Carl, she refutes her brothers' assertion that "The property of a family belongs to the men of the family" (153).

Despite a feminine physical appearance—most notably her "shining mass of hair" (15)—both her rejection of conventional gender roles and her cross-dressing would have evoked all the fears of what the leading European sexologist of the time Richard von Krafft-Ebing had described as the "Mannish Lesbian": "The masculine soul, heaving in the female bosom, finds pleasure in the pursuit of manly sports, and in manifestations of courage and bravado. There is a strong desire to imitate the male fashion in dressing the hair and in general attire, under favorable circumstances even to don male attire and impose in it" (418–19).[15] By creating the new term "Mannish Lesbian," Krafft-Ebing, as Carroll Smith-Rosenberg notes, "linked women's rejection of traditional gender roles and their demands for social and economic equality to cross-dressing, sexual perversion, and borderline hermaphroditism. . . . physical disease again bespoke social disorder" (*Disorderly* 272). Though more ambivalent in his conclusions, English sexologist Havelock Ellis likewise maintained that female gender crossing was an indication of lesbianism. For Ellis, a wide range of "masculine habits," all of which could be applied to Alexandra, signaled the "psychic abnormality" of inversion, or a biologically determined attraction toward the same sex: "the brusque energetic movements, the attitude of the arms, the direct speech . . . the masculine straightforwardness and sense of honor, and especially the attitude towards men, free from any suggestion either of shyness or audacity" (153). Such fears would only have been exacerbated by Alexandra's long delay in marrying, a decision that likely precludes the possibility of children while prompting charges of race suicide.

Yet Cather defines Alexandra's sexuality, I would argue, as neither lesbian nor heterosexual but rather as having elements of both—fluid—what Irigaray describes as "unending, potent and impotent owing to its resistance to the countable" (111). Unlike Bartley, Alexandra comes to accept this fluid element both in herself and in her relationship to her environment.[16] After returning from a scouting mission in the river country, Alexandra has a new found sense of the potential of the high land: "For the first time, perhaps, since that land emerged from the waters of geologic ages, a human face was set toward it with love and yearning. It seemed beautiful to her, rich and strong and glorious. Her eyes drank in the breadth of it, until her tears blinded her. Then the Genius of the Divide, the great, free spirit which breathes across it, must have bent lower than it ever bent to a human will before" (64).

While some critics have viewed this passage as a sign of masculine possession, where Cather offers Alexandra's justification for developing the land, others view this passage as a kind of feminine dispossession, where Alexandra gives herself over to the land. What I would suggest here is that we have both. The land emerges from the water; Alexandra drinks in the land; the water emerges again from her in the form of tears. And later in the novel, the water is even more clearly marked as a sexual element found in the land but often not obviously evident: "Her personal life, her own realization of herself, was almost a subconscious existence; like an underground river that came to the surface only here and there, at intervals months apart, and then sank again to flow on under her own fields. Nevertheless, the underground stream was there, and it was because she had so much personality to put into her enterprises and succeeded in putting it into them so completely, that her affairs prospered better than those of her neighbors" (183). Even as it is repressed, the water element continually reemerges to enhance Alexandra's relationship with the land and understanding of herself.[17] Often coded in both feminine and masculine terms—the "swell of the prairie" receives travelers "into its bosom" even as its "vast hardness" suggests a "land [that] wanted to be let alone, to preserve its own fierce strength" (21)—the land as an object of desire cannot be read as indicating either Alexandra's heterosexual or lesbian erotic life. As Susan Wiesenthal notes, the hermaphroditic Alexandra's unabashed love and yearning for this hermaphroditic land suggests a "subtle celebration of the hermaphroditic and perhaps even bisexual sensibility" of Alexandra's erotic life (53).

And yet, I would not go so far as O'Brien to suggest that through this water imagery Cather implicitly endorses Alexandra's more organic creative process over Alexander's gear-and-girder ethic (391). Even as the Taylorist ethic is critiqued, aspects of it are valorized, while unchecked fluidity brings disaster. Indeed, for Alexandra's Bohemian friend Marie, the water imagery represents a sexual pining for Alexandra's brother Emil that will end in ruin. When Carl sees them walking through the pasture on the way to the pond, he notes that "the golden light seemed to be rippling through the curly grass like the tide racing in" (117). Emil and Marie then walk to the pond where Emil kills the wild ducks, foreshadowing their own murder by Frank, Marie's husband. When Frank later intrudes on Emil and Marie, who have just made love, he hears a "murmuring sound, perfectly inarticulate, as low as the sound of water coming from a spring, where there is no fall" (235). As he recognizes the lovers through the leaves of the mulberry tree, he hears "Again the murmur, like water welling out of the ground" (235). The water element, dangerous both in its conductivity and its aversion to boundaries, the water that Alexandra had almost succeeded in keeping underground, has welled up out of the earth and laid waste.

At the same time, the unchecked energy of solid mechanics also proves deadly. Even as the land increasingly seems to welcome technological intervention, the fate of Amédée suggests the human costs of embracing a solid-mechanical efficiency ethic. Amédée is killed both by the ceaseless energy of the thresher "driven by a stationary engine [that] fed from the header boxes" (217) and by his reckless refusal to turn the machine off. Even when in intense pain, he does not stop the machine: "How can I? I got no time to be sick. Three thousand dollars' worth of new machinery to manage, and the wheat so ripe it will begin to shatter next week" (218). Alexandra, by contrast, cautiously embraces scientific and technological change. Apart from crop rotation, the only technological improvement to the land that Alexandra is directly responsible for is the building of a new silo, the first on the Divide.

Alexandra's land management success lies both in her caution, her ability to see order within the natural environment, and her erotic identification with the land. She looks at the stars and thinks of "vastness and distance, and of their ordered march." She seems to understand "the great operations of nature, and . . . the law that lay behind them" and consequently develops "a new consciousness of the country" (68). Marie, on the other hand, lifts her face to the "remote, inaccessible evening star" (222). With Alexandra's "new relation" to the land coupled with a profound identification—"She had felt as if her heart were hiding down there, somewhere, with the quail and the plover and all the little wild things that crooned or buzzed in the sun"—the land welcomes human management: "the brown earth . . . yields itself eagerly to the plow; rolls away from the shear, not even dimming the brightness of the metal, with a soft deep sigh of happiness" (74). With requited love, the land offers itself to Alexandra for her arrangement. Known for its "most unusual trimness and care for detail," for its "order and fine arrangement," Alexandra develops one of the richest farms on the Divide (80–81).

Yet this order also extends to a racial and ethnic taxonomy that, in effect, acts as a governing principle for people on the Divide. As Marilee Lindemann has demonstrated, in accordance with the rise in nativist discourse at the turn of the century, the narrator continually relies "quietly but systematically on physical appearance as a means of judging and classifying individuals" (40). So Alexandra's brothers grow "more and more like themselves" (55). Lou is "apt to go off at half-cock" while Oscar is "as indolent of mind as he was unsparing of his body" (55, 56). At the church bazaar, we are given a catalogue of different ethnic types. The "French and Bohemian boys were spirited and jolly, liked variety, and were as much predisposed to favor anything new as the Scandinavian boys were to reject it. The Norwegian and Swedish lads were much more self-centred, apt to be egotistical and jealous" (192).

Marie's type, however, is most significant for my purposes, because it is in accord with prevailing stereotypes of Bohemians and the iconoclastic New Woman
at the turn of the century. In a review for the *Nebraska State Journal* in 1896,
Cather described Bohemianism as "a rebellion against all organized powers and
that in itself is defeat, for victory is with the organized powers of the universe"
(*World* 295). That same year, while hard at work as editor for *Home Monthly,* she
reprimanded her friend Mariel Gere for accusing her of acting Bohemian, noting
that lately her only wildness was in racing streetcars on her bicycle (*Calendar* 6).
By some measures, Emil performs Bohemianism more than Marie—he delays
pursuing a profession to travel in Mexico, returns to his community in Mexican
costume, smokes "terrible-smelling Mexican cigarettes and talks Spanish" (193),
gets along better with the French than the Swedes or Norwegians (192), and pursues
the married Marie. Yet his experience with the Other is marked by what bell hooks
describes as the process within commodity culture whereby "ethnicity becomes a
spice" (21). He quite literally shops for and then sells the coveted accoutrements of
the ethnic Other he appropriates (that is, via the turquoise shirt studs). By contrast,
just as Clara Vavrika's "wildness" is intrinsic to her identity as "The Bohemian
Girl" (1912), Marie's ethnic identity determines her performance. Indeed, with her
dark skin, ethnic heritage, convent escape, free-spiritedness, and sexual transgression, Marie both performs and is ethnically marked as Bohemian. Even though
she struggles to end the relationship with Emil based on the moral strictures of
her Catholic upbringing, she is positioned by Alexandra as a temptress.

Marie's association with the orchard reinforces her marginal but powerfully
evocative presence. Unlike Alexandra who feels a spiritual affinity for the vast
expanse of the Divide, a Divide that promises the creation of wealth, Marie declares a pantheistic love for trees, which suggests her ties to the past: "The Bohemians, you know, were tree worshipers before the missionaries came. Father
says the people in the mountains still do queer things, sometimes,—they believe
that trees bring good or bad luck" (138). Before she is murdered in Emil's arms,
she walks down to the orchard, an orchard drenched with the scent of waiting
flowers suggesting sexual temptation: "the evening air was heavy with the smell
of wild cotton. The fresh, salty scent of wild roses had given way before this more
powerful perfume of midsummer. Wherever those ashes-of-rose balls hung on
their milky stalks, the air about them was saturated with their breath" (221).

And, finally, Marie is associated with urban forms of dissipation. As a child, her
uncle brought her a mechanical toy, a "Turkish lady sitting on an ottoman and
smoking a hookah" (127). The Eastern European woman smoking was a classic
image of the debased New Woman, a figure portrayed in advertising as more
sexually available than the most popular variant of the New Woman, the statuesque and inviolable Gibson Girl. Carl notes that Marie's eyes, while "the color of
sunflower honey, or of old amber," have a sparkle that suggests the bubbles that
"rise in a glass of champagne" or "sparks from a forge" (125). Similarly, in "The

Bohemian Girl," Clara Vavrika is illustrated tying a "wine-colored ribbon about her throat" (307) while in her eyes there "shone something fiery, like the yellow drops of Tokai in the brown glass bottle" (322–23).[18] Marie's father, in fact, runs a successful saloon, while her husband dissipates his energies at local barrooms or in ill fits of temper. The fact that the first kiss between Marie and Emil at the French Church Bazaar occurs when Marie is wearing a traditional Bohemian costume and Emil a Mexican costume further demonstrates the ethnic typing of their sexual transgression.

Alexandra, by contrast, seems to transcend her ethnic type to become a racial type best suited to developing the land. While her mind was replete with "force" and intelligence, it was also "slow, truthful, steadfast. She had not the least spark of cleverness" (61). Her Swedishness is almost always associated with her whiteness. Though tan in the summer, "where her collar falls away from her neck, or where her sleeves are pushed back from her wrist, the skin is of such smoothness and whiteness as none but Swedish women ever possess; skin with the freshness of the snow itself" (84–85). She is surrounded in "milky light" when Carl sees her at dawn. And when Carl sees her with Marie, he describes her as "the Swedish woman so white and gold, kindly and amused, but armored in calm" (124). Her mind is described as "a white book, with clear writing about weather and beasts and growing things" (185), a description that serves to link whiteness with the professionalization of agriculture. Rather than relying exclusively on Old World oral tradition in her farming practice, Alexandra consults a university-educated farmer for advice. She anticipates the "vast checker-board" of wheat and corn fields, the white roads and right angles (73). Her farm is noted for its "symmetrical pasture ponds . . . [and] a white row of beehives in the orchard" (81). If Amédée fails because he is more French than he is white, then Alexandra succeeds because she is more white than she is Swedish. Whiteness becomes order becomes wealth.

Yet at the same time, Alexandra dreams of escape from the weight of whiteness, which is coded as efficiency, professional expertise, and wealth accumulation. In an image reminiscent of Bartley's fantasy on the ship—"submerged in the vast impersonal grayness about him"—Alexandra fantasizes she is weightless (50–51). She feels herself transported by "one very strong man," who carries her as "easily as if she were a sheaf of wheat" and appears "yellow like the sunlight" with the "smell of ripe cornfields about him" (185–86). Both of these fantasies emerge at moments of sexual repression. For Bartley, it is his struggle to repress his desires for Hilda; for Alexandra, to repress her carnal knowledge of Emil and Marie. Rather than succumbing to the erotic potential of her vision, Alexandra "would stand in a tin tub and prosecute her bath with vigor, finishing it by pouring buckets of cold well-water over her gleaming white body which no man on the Divide could have carried very far" (186). As social anthropologist Mary Douglas notes, cleansing rituals signify an attempt "to create and maintain a particular culture, a particular set of assumptions by which experience is controlled" (128). Alexandra takes little pleasure in consumer culture per se, decorating her house because it's expected rather than as a means of self-definition. And yet as a sort of rebellion, she embraces the unassimilated Old Mrs. Lee, the Bohemian and free-spirited Marie, and Ivar, the "queer" Norwegian, who is associated with wild sod, wild ducks, and Old World traditions (38–41).

Alexandra's dreams of escape reach a critical point after the murder of Emil and Marie. Grief-stricken, she wanders through a rain storm and finally accepts the dark Other, the subconscious water/sexuality element: "Ever since Emil died, I've suffered so when it rained. Now that I've been out in it with him, I shan't dread it. After you once get cold clear through, the feeling of the rain on you is sweet. It seems to bring back feelings you had when you were a baby. It carries you back into the dark, before you were born; you can't see things, but they come to you, somehow, and you know them and aren't afraid of them" (250). Alexandra's full immersion in the water brings her to a moment of fetal completeness, before social strictures necessitate that the sexual desires of the body be suppressed and the divided self emerges. To use Marianna Torgovnick's words in a different context, the passage represents the desire for the "utopian primitive" where "the wish for 'being physical' . . . [is] coextensive with 'being spiritual'; the wish for physical, psychological, and social integrity . . . [is] a birthright, within familial and cultural traditions that both connect to the past and allow for a changing future" (245). We do not have, then, a final repudiation of the "queer," as Lindemann argues, but an ambivalent, vexed longing for it. The same "manly" traits that define Alexandra's success as a farmer and icon of whiteness create her profound sense of alienation that, in turn, necessitates a return to the Other, which can then be funneled into the self.

After her immersion in the rain, Alexandra again has the fantasy of weightless transport but with a significant difference. She knows who the man is, and she does not wash herself afterwards: "His white cloak was thrown over his face, and his head was bent a little forward. His shoulders seemed as strong as the foundations of the world. His right arm, bared from the elbow, was dark and gleaming, like bronze, and she knew at once that it was the arm of the mightiest of all lovers; She knew at last for whom it was she had waited, and where he would carry her" (251). I agree with those critics who see this cloaked "mightiest of lovers" as death,[19] which, as in *Alexander's Bridge*, suggests the pleasure and danger of immersing oneself in the fluid element. Through this dream image, Alexandra conquers her fear of death as fluid—a fluid element that is both a "dark and gleaming" ethnic Other and an unbound sexual expression—while asserting her power over it.[20] In a gesture that both absolves her conscience and serves as proof of that power, she subsequently works to free the imprisoned Frank Shabata. Having lost, during his incarceration, his English, his dandy accoutrements, his farm, and all the veneer of his assimilated identity, Frank, like Ivar, is a most vulnerable recipient of Alexandra's beneficence, and by some measures, the darkest Other. Visiting Frank in prison, Alexandra notices that with his shaved head, "the conformation of his skull, gave him a criminal look" (260), and he looks "not altogether human" (261). In 1910, *McClure's* devoted an essay to the results of Franz Boas's seminal ethnographic study based on the head measurements of 30,000 New York immigrants. Even though Boas's work undermined the logic of biological racial typing—skulls did appear to change through time—his work, and the coverage it received, reflected common apprehension about the "swarthy" and "recalcitrant" immigrant Other, especially the Bohemian whose head combined the "largest measurements of both Sicilian and Jew" (Hendrick 46). Having visibly degenerated, then, Frank's only hope is to be on "his good behavior" (259).

Coding the fluid through ethnic signifiers diverts attention away from the transgressiveness of her final romantic choice, Carl, the effeminate steel-engraver turned prospector to whom Alexandra expresses a deep friendship and finally a romantic longing. When Carl finally returns, they walk together to the pond where Emil and Marie often met, revisiting the danger of their secret love and reminding readers of the duck shooting that foreshadowed the murders. But then the water takes on more positive associations. Alexandra longs to take an ocean voyage to Alaska: "I haven n't [*sic*] been on the water since we crossed the ocean, when I was a little girl" (271). Her family homestead appears as water: "On every side the brown waves of the earth rolled away to meet the sky" (272). The final paean to the land, reminiscent of Alexandra's embrace of the high land early in the novel, again suggests a fluid relationship to the earth: "Fortunate country, that is one day to receive hearts like Alexandra's into its bosom, to give them out again in the yellow wheat, in the rustling corn, in the shining eyes of youth!" (274). Receiving and giving, sensitive to pressures, "easily traversed by flow," "mix[ing] with bodies of a like state," "already diffuse 'in itself,' which disconcerts any attempt at static identification," the land contains many of what Irigaray defines as fluid properties (111).

By beginning the conclusion with the danger of the fluid and ending with the power of the fluid to mark the profound significance of Alexandra's journey, Cather makes her case for the New Woman. Unlike the gear-and-girder ethic that necessitates firm resolution, sharp distinctions, and clear-cut measures, the fluid element of permeability, diffuseness, and perpetual motion allows the contradiction of simultaneous possession and dispossession; Alexandra can own and develop the land, transgress gender and sexual boundaries, embrace and manage the ethnic Other, can be a New Woman, all without really seeming to.

On the one hand, then, Alexandra's whiteness, as represented by her farm, her modern vision, and her personal self-control, is presented as a more important legacy than any children would be. The New Woman of the midwestern frontier, as an ad for the *Country Gentleman* demonstrates, may have "farmed a thousand acres, and invented the corn harvester and baler," but she also "raised nine children." Like Bohemianism, whiteness in this text is as much a performance as a denotation of ethnic origin or skin color, and it is the performance of whiteness that Cather offers as a salve to anxieties over new waves of immigrants and technological change. And yet the longing for the repressed element remains in this novel, a longing that suggests a marked instability in the sociocultural dichotomies—between white and ethnic Other, fluid and solid mechanics, West and East, New Woman and Old—that increasingly defined America's hegemonic voice at home and abroad at the turn of the century. In a seemingly paradoxical conclusion, maintaining Alexandra's successful "white" farm means recognizing and harnessing that dark, fluid element—be it her Irish foreman, Ivar, Frank, the land, or her own sexuality—a job for which Cather's white New Woman is aptly designed.

In *The Song of the Lark* (1915), Cather creates arguably her most fully realized New Woman protagonist. Cather, in fact, urged her editor at Houghton Mifflin to market the novel to women's colleges since such an audience might well appreciate the novel's "aggressive careerism" (*Calendar* 53). Thea Kronborg, the protagonist of the novel, refuses both to be stymied by the parochial values of her

Six million American women are working for wages!

Teachers, stenographers, shop girls, factory hands—they are shut up in the cities, tired, unhappy, poor in health and wealth.

To these the great out-of-doors is calling, and

The COUNTRY GENTLEMAN

is pointing the way to opportunity. Already a million women have heard the call, and from their farms they are beckoning to their sisters of the cities:

"Come and be farmers!"

THE NEW WOMAN

This woman farmer raised nine children, farmed a thousand acres, and invented the corn harvester and baler shown below.

Other woman farmers are tilling the soil, raising poultry, developing orchards, breeding livestock, making homes in the great out-of-doors.

The new woman of the future is the woman farmer!

Courageous, independent, but still womanly, she is leading the men on Uncle Sam's homesteads. Plucky, energetic, willing to work, she is finding her place in the fields, the meadows, the feed lots, the orchards, the poultry yards—and she is earning health and wealth and happiness.

Are you one of the Six Millions?

The Country Gentleman will help you!
If you want to raise chickens the ways of success are told
In The Country Gentleman
If you want to grow vegetables and fruits the last word is
In The Country Gentleman
If you are planning your flowers for next spring the best methods are
In The Country Gentleman

Come back to the land and be happy!

THE COUNTRY GENTLEMAN
Five cents the copy at all newsdealers $1.50 a Year
The Curtis Publishing Company, Independence Square, Philadelphia, Pa.

"The New Woman" advertised by the *Country Gentleman* in the *Ladies' Home Journal* (October 1913). Courtesy of the University of Iowa.

small-town upbringing or the Victorian ideals of decorous womanhood, and in so doing she crosses class and ethnic boundaries, affirms her sexuality, and finds her voice to become a world-renowned diva. It is a voice closely linked with a water and wave force, and, in fact, water-wave imagery characterizes Thea more than any of Cather's previous female protagonists. To channel successfully such water-wave motion, Thea Kronborg works relentlessly, forsakes familial bonds (she does not visit her dying mother and becomes estranged from most of her siblings), and rejects traditional feminine romantic fulfillment (her final marriage is barely mentioned, while children are out of the question). Her racial inheritance and her unique status as "artist" enable her to direct her force, while those with weaker constitutions dissipate theirs. Whereas in *Alexander's Bridge* and *O Pioneers!* the gear-and-girder ethic is still constructed as a powerful ideal posing a viable threat to the fluid, in *The Song of the Lark,* the gear-and-girder ethic is at once repudiated—Ray Kennedy is killed by the railroad he loves, and Thea rejects those "who made her spine like a steel rail" (269) and harnessed. Indeed, while the fluid wave force becomes central, signifying at once sexual liberation, artistic inspiration, and the new technologies of the modern era, the railroad represents the social Darwinist force directing that energy. What sets this novel apart in its feminist content is not simply that Thea has gained artistic success and a measure of sexual freedom, but that Thea acts as her own engineer, so to speak—unlike Sister Carrie and Undine—ultimately managing and directing her own wave force. And yet while most critics celebrate this novel for its seemingly uncompromising feminist vision, they neglect to consider the nature of Thea's triumph that necessitates both a troubling reconciliation with the human costs of her ascent and a complex reappraisal of an alternately energizing and dehumanizing modernity.

Like Alexandra, Thea's whiteness becomes a defining aspect of her character—from Dr. Archie who marvels at her little-girl body, "so neatly and delicately fashioned, so soft, and so milky white" (10) to the Mexicans who marvel at her hair and fair skin: "'Blanco y oro, semejante la Pascua!' (White and gold, like Easter!)" (230). But fundamentally that whiteness is linked to a purity, invulnerable to taint, which the novel's most startling incident reveals.

Toward the end of the first section of the novel, a tramp, filthy and feverish, enters Moonstone and tries to run a sideshow outside the local saloon. With his "bony body grotesquely attired in the clown's suit," the tramp exhibits a "box of snakes," passes the hat, and promises that when a dollar is collected, he will "eat 'one of these living reptiles'" (135–36). The tramp's display of snakes in front of the saloon symbolizes the evils of drink—(in an earlier scene Mrs. Kronborg encountered two hoboes with a drinking "affliction")—and of sexual licentiousness, dirt, and disease—all of the urban social problems that *McClure's* had exposed and railed against. The town responds by banishing the hobo: the marshal arrests him; the saloon keeper kills his snakes; the constable releases him and tells him to "get out of town, and get quick"; and when the tramp later hides in a freight car, he is put out yet again. But he does leave a message for the town, an "ugly, stupid word, chalked on the black paint of the seventy-five-foot standpipe which was the reservoir for the Moonstone water-supply; the same word, in another tongue, that the French soldier shouted at Waterloo to the English officer who bade the Old Guard surrender; a comment on life which the defeated, along the hard roads of the world, sometimes bawl at the victorious" (136). When a week later, the town water starts to "smell and taste," the townspeople then learn the truth. The tramp had drowned himself in the town well, poisoning the water supply. Several adults and half a dozen children die, although the Kronborgs, who have their own well, are not affected.

I pause here on this incident because it encapsulates Cather's fascination with and anxiety about marginalization, purity, and waste, preoccupations central to her conception of the New Woman. The word the tramp leaves, we imagine, was "shit," and the tramp, treated like abject refuse, quite literally becomes abject refuse, which the town cannot discard, hard as it may try. A distinct marker of modern progress, water purity was essential for urban growth and was of especial interest to muckrakers of the period. The town's inability to eject the tramp despite their bureaucratic handling of him—from the saloon keeper's first alarm, to the marshal's arrest, and finally to the constable's incarceration—suggests both the failures of an apparently efficient bureaucracy and the potentially dire social consequences when human capital becomes waste.

Deeply disturbed both by the townspeople's hypocrisy and her own—all implicitly claiming a Christian worldview while shunning someone most in need—Thea goes to see Dr. Archie. Dr. Archie's response to the tramp episode offers an apology for the social Darwinist ethic that would validate Thea's rise to operatic diva: "Ugly accidents happen, Thea; always have and always will. But the failures are swept back into the pile and forgotten. They don't leave any lasting scar in the world, and they don't affect the future. The things that last are the good things. The people who forge ahead and do something, they really count" (139). Even as Dr. Archie makes legitimate Thea's rise to stardom—she will "forge ahead," "she counts"—so too does he validate the tramp's demise in obscurity: now he is an "accident," a "failure . . . swept back into the pile and forgotten." Dr. Archie's reading of the tramp episode and Thea's acceptance of that reading suggest the extent to which Cather was departing from the muckraker's "social Christianity" in *McClure's* in favor of a social Darwinist worldview that privileges Thea's essential isolation from others, predicated in part by her purity.[21]

An admirer of Emile Zola, Rudyard Kipling, Stephen Crane, and Frank Norris, in particular—Norris "is big and warm and sometimes brutal, and the strength of the soil comes up to him with very little loss in the transmission" (*World* 747)—Cather would use the logic of naturalism and empire to legitimate Thea's success.[22] The language of force, desire, and conquest, arguably three defining ethics of naturalism, is used throughout *The Song of the Lark*. Thea yearns to tap into the "fragments of the [Cliff Dweller's] desire" (321), and Fred longs to have Thea touch her "real force" (333) even as he notes the "force of her determination" (344). Thea's whiteness is defined not only by her essential purity, desire, force, and determination but also by an ambition characterized as imperialistic conquest at different key moments in the text. When she recalls a trip with her father to a reunion of old frontiersmen in Laramie, Wyoming, she is most impressed by one old frontiersman's story of having heard the first telegraph message to cross the Missouri River: "Westward the course of Empire takes its way" (54). For Thea, this message was one she would never forget, one that reminds her that the "spirit of human courage" lived "up there with the eagles" (55). A short time later in the novel, that message is reinforced when during a music lesson, Wunsch advises Thea that "The world is little, people are little, human life is little. There is only one big thing—desire. And before it, when it is big, all is little. It brought Columbus across the sea in a little boat, *und so weiter*" (75–76).

But, more significantly, the social ills the muckrakers so railed against become a backdrop against which Thea's success becomes that much more striking. We learn that Thea's music teacher, Harsanyi, lost his eye in a mining accident: "He held no grudge against the coal company; he understood that the accident was merely one of the things that are bound to happen in the general scramble of American life, where every one comes to grab and takes his chance" (183). And, seeing a consumptive girl on the train to Moonstone, Thea feels not sympathy but contempt: "She smiled—though she was ashamed of it—with the natural contempt of strength for weakness, with the sense of physical security which makes the savage merciless" (217–18).

Thea's social Darwinist struggle for artistic success is defined by water and wave motion characterized in part by the urban chaos of which she must both become a part and insulate herself against if she is to succeed. Her voice is like "the murmur of water" (77), "a goldfish darting among creek minnows" (235), "a river of silver sound" (412). For Thea's voice instructor, Bowers, when Thea sings, "Her whole back seemed plastic, seemed to be moulding itself to the galloping rhythm of the song" (270), reflecting the "river of sound" she produces. But it is only when this "river of sound" becomes part of the larger urban current that a true operatic star emerges. After attending her first concert in Chicago, Thea leaves the concert hall to enter a "furious gale"; the "streets . . . full of cold, hurrying, angry people," "cars . . . screaming," "street lights . . . gleam[ing]" (200). Taking the wrong streetcar, she is ejected in front of a saloon where two men proposition her. For the first time, Thea becomes "conscious of the city itself, of the congestion of life all about her, of the brutality and power of those streams that flowed in the streets, threatening to drive one under" (200). Cather makes this scene the defining moment of Thea's transition to womanhood. Rather than fleeing this scene of immigrant influx, sexual vice, economic struggle, dirt, noise, and confusion, Thea embraces the struggle to become part of the urban current: "All these things and people were no longer remote and negligible; . . . they were there to take something from her. Very well; they should never have it. . . . She would live for it, work for it, die for it; but she was going to have it, time after time, height after height. She could hear the crash of the orchestra again, and she rose on the brasses. She would have it, what the trumpets were singing! She would have it, have it,—it!" (201). That "it"—which is both Thea's artistic gift and her desire for artistic acclaim—sets her apart and signifies both her biological superiority—she already has "it"—and social Darwinist advantage—she has the right to have "it."

At the same time, Thea represents both the power of the modern machine— speeding, forceful, and dynamic—and a rejection of it. As a child, "She used to drag her mattress beside her low window and lie awake for a long while, vibrating with excitement, as a machine vibrates from speed" (140). Harsanyi sees the source of Thea's voice in machine terms: "Everything about her indicated it,—the big mouth, the wide jaw and chin, the strong white teeth, the deep laugh. The machine was so simple and strong, seemed to be so easily operated" (188). Fred notes that "even a stupid woman could get effects with such machinery" (449). And yet it is a machinery neither definitively electric nor gear and girder. Even though Thea is associated with railroad-driven manifest destiny and effulgent light (191), she guards herself against a "steel rail" sensibility and longs to flee the glare of electric lights. To describe Thea's climatic final performance of the novel, Cather uses inorganic and organic metaphors to define Thea's voice, a move that reflects a profound ambivalence about the meaning of Thea's triumph and by extension about the shifting technologies of the new era: "While she was on the stage she was conscious . . . that her body was absolutely the instrument of her idea. Not for nothing had she kept it so severely, kept it filled with such energy and fire. All that deep-rooted vitality flowered in her voice, her face, in her very finger-tips. She felt like a tree bursting into bloom. And her voice was as flexible as her body" (478). Given the sheer force of the modern antagonistic currents, how long would that bloom be able to survive?

Indeed, it is the modern current from which Thea must both engage and disengage. While at first Thea's well is private—the private Kronborg well allowed the family to escape the tramp's disease—and thereby free of the taint of social ills that affect the larger streams of life, later, once she has suffered the stress of fighting those modern currents, her well must be renewed by a new "pure" source. Like Alexandra, Thea learns to channel the energy of an ethnic Other—an Other extinct and therefore pure, or alive and potentially dangerous—apart from the urban aggression of which she is now a part. It is with the remains of the Cliff Dwellers, a people long gone and therefore free of the sexual taint of Bohemianism, that she discovers how to access this pure energy source:

One morning, as she was standing upright in the pool, splashing water between her shoulder-blades with a big sponge, something flashed through her mind that made her draw herself up and stand still until the water had quite dried upon her flushed skin. The stream and the broken pottery: what was any art but an effort to make a sheath, a mould in which to imprison for a moment the shining, elusive element which is life itself,—life hurrying past us and running away, too strong to stop, too sweet to lose? The Indian women had held it in their jars. In the sculpture she had seen in the Art Institute, it had been caught in a flash of arrested motion. In singing, one made a vessel of one's throat and nostrils and held it on one's breath, caught the stream in a scale of natural intervals. (304)

By creating this "sheath" or sacred vessel, Thea can be both in the stream of life and separate from it. The scene evokes Henri Bergson's élan vital where "life appears in its entirety as an immense wave which, starting from a center, spreads outwards, and which on almost the whole of its circumference is stopped and converted into oscillation" (290). At the turning point of the novel, Thea can indulge in a romantic tryst with Fred Ottenburg without having to face social censure. By contrast, both Wunsch and Spanish Johnny, diminished by distance and time, pay for their transgressions and end up impoverished itinerant workers, outside the élan vital of American life. At the end of the novel, the "gray-haired little Mexican" Spanish Johnny comes alone to see Thea perform: "Then he walked down Broadway with his hands in his overcoat pockets, wearing a smile which embraced all the stream of life that passed him and the lighted towers that rose into the limpid blue of the evening sky" (479). Unable to direct life's currents, he becomes part of the popular commercial entertainment that Thea explicitly rejects—a "feature of Barnum and Bailey's" Mexican band—a less pernicious evil than the contaminating tramp but part of low-brow culture, which within Thea's world is mere social detritus (478). Even the people of Moonstone who are also cut off from urban life's currents—"a stagnant" pool only refreshed by outside waterways (490)—have their children to bring refreshment.

Thea, then, not unlike Undine, is both part of the evolutionary current and a force that drives it. She is distinctly modern, not as electricity per se or commercial indulgence but as a representative of both feminine sexual desire and masculine naturalistic energy, combined in a new era driven by wave force. Free from the fallen-woman stigma that would characterize other female stage performers, Thea represents a newly spiritualized, newly masculinized, vital force, which both reflects the rise of nativist sentiment during the period and, in some sense, is a rebellion against it. The tramp, Wunsch, and Spanish Johnny all become, to use Dr. Archie's phrase, "failure[s] . . . swept back into the pile and forgotten," but they are failures made now nostalgic, part of the currents we cannot stop and few of us can master.

CONCLUSION

The trouble is that just as the introduction of the elevator has been
so rapid that many people's stomachs are not yet adjusted to the motion, so the changes in the social condition of women have been so
sudden that many men's prejudices have not yet their "sea legs."
—Louise Connoly, "The New Woman," *Harper's Weekly,* June 7, 1913

In 1905, Charles Dana Gibson made a dramatic life change. Fearing that his staple
pen-and-ink drawings would give way to the more exciting world of color—Rem-
ington, Parrish, and Frost had already made the transition—Gibson relinquished
both his lucrative contracts with *Collier's* and *Life* and his future book illustrating opportunities to embark on a European tour to study oil painting. The stock
market crash of 1907, however, brought him back home. Having lost both his
life savings and any pretensions of moving beyond the light social satire of the
Gibson Girl image, he now had to return home to churn out what had become a
ubiquitous if somewhat tired cultural icon. While publishers still sought him out,
Gibson surely realized that his vision of American womanhood was increasingly
at odds with the direction American women seemed to be heading. When in its
January 1913 thirtieth birthday issue *Life* offered a retrospective of its career amidst
an exciting array of social, political, and technological developments, the magazine placed a Gibson Girl on its cover; she was the one great, glorious constant
among all of that change. Gibson himself could keep up with the fashions—the
new shorter terraced skirts, the coronets of braided hair and the Merry Widow
hats—and keep up with the changing social conventions—automobile driving,
dashing to parties, dancing, and having fun—but he was uncomfortable with
American women's seemingly increasing free-floating morality. And so it must
have been with some relief, when at the advent of World War I, he could return to
the public a Gibson Girl whose stature and inviolability represented the power of
a liberty-loving nation. With Uncle Sam at her side, the mighty Columbia would
face down the tyrannous Kaiser.

While the rise of the flapper in the late teens and twenties brought the final
death knell to the Gibson Girl, *Life*'s homage in 1913 signified both her fading
cultural authority and the end of an era. Indeed, the *New York World* noted in
the same year the demise of the Gibson Girl and the coming of the flapper. The
Gibson Girl marked a capitalist culture in transition. While she would collect

men—more men than she ever needed in this age of capital accumulation—she took time to manage herself and others. Her large bust suggested bounty, if not nurturance; her corseted small waist suggested control. While competing with members of her own sex for attention, she would encourage men to compete for her. In a period devoted to developing a large, stable, and skilled workforce, she offered the carrot of personal incentive more often than the stick of ill consequence. The fact that Gibson drew her in the working as well as in the middle and upper classes suggested his commitment to the social mobility necessary for a merit-based workforce. Here was an American nation with the resources and commitment to become a world leader, a nation eager for growth and bound for imperial expansion.

At the same time that the Gibson Girl suggested a confidence in prosperity and growth, she also worked to relieve crises in American identity by healing old conflicts and creating new possibilities for national unity. When Boston Brahmin Gibson married the widely touted Southern belle Irene Langhorne in 1895, their union signified a symbolic end to tensions between the North and South (Fox 22). In an era of rising anxieties about the divisive effects of labor agitation, urbanization, new immigrants, and imperialist ventures at home and abroad, the Gibson Girl's whiteness and capacity for discernment promised racial progress and national unity. The Chicago Columbian Centennial of 1893 featured thirty-nine Gibson drawings as emblems of national prestige while Daniel Chester French's Columbia appeared like a "monumental" Gibson Girl. As the "veritable queen of the kingliest of races," she would "carry forward into the wilds the standard of civilization" (Christy 12–15). Frederick Jackson Turner may have pronounced the frontier closed in 1893, and Roosevelt's National Park system may have signaled the end of a vast unbounded wilderness, but the Gibson Girl offered new frontiers to conquer, new large-game trophies to be won. Unlike the Steel-Engraving Lady of an earlier generation, who offered her family a safe domestic haven, men had to work for the Gibson Girl in order to fulfill her insatiable desire for material goods. Because she both represented and assured the progress of the race, men could indulge her juggling of suitors, her entomologist-like probing. In the face of modern upheaval, the Gibson Girl offered the heft of inviolability and the promise of maternity. On the cover of *Life* in 1905, James Montgomery Flagg offers a circular world map, where a Gibson Girl-style head sports hair in the shape of Africa and Asia; Madagascar is her earring. "A Map of the World: As Seen by Him" the caption reads; the Gibson Girl is the center of the world and developing nations her accessories. By at once taming the dark continent and Asian menace, urging her male suitor to foreign conquest all while creating boundaries against the very foreign element she appropriates as part of her sexual iconography, this "Map of the World: As Seen by Him" is more imperative than we might imagine.

The writers I examine also offered anodynes to what they saw as destructive,

James Montgomery Flagg, "A Map of the World (as Seen by Him)." Illustration. Cover of *Life* (March 23, 1905). Courtesy of the Newberry Library.

atomizing modern trends, namely fears that the material age had brought with it a spiritual void, a fervor for conquest, and the persistent threat of economic irrelevance. Johnston's and Glasgow's New Woman protagonists, for example, rejected consumerism—it signified a northern, potentially corrupt materialism—while they affirmed a ruggedly pastoral, mystical South as a vacation refuge. Similarly, Sui Sin Far offered male and female characters whose filial duty and honor code reveal a spiritual centeredness increasingly lost in a hedonist American culture. She more often granted her Chinese American female protagonists, however, the privileged role of cultural interpreters who demystified the contradictions of race, class, and sex prejudice in a supposedly democratic American nation. Cather similarly celebrated a New Woman protagonist who flouts traditional gender roles while repudiating both an unchecked, dehumanizing, "gear-and-girder" efficiency ethic and the chaos of unchecked fluidity—defined, most notably, as ethnically marked sexual dissipation. Hopkins grew increasingly disillusioned with the ideological possibilities of the popular New Woman and the Washingtons' New Negro. By investing her "talented tenth" female protagonist with renewed spiritual authority, Hopkins gave her the agency to sanction a return and recolonization of Africa. By contrast, Wharton's New Woman protagonist represents a social Darwinist marketplace ethic that weeds out those relatively noble but hopelessly anachronistic men who struggle to act as her provider. Incorporation offers the only hope that her force—modern in expression but age old in form—may be harnessed.

As the second decade of the twentieth century wore on, the new was increasingly associated with all of the signature elements of American high modernism. Freud's work became readily available to intellectual and scientific communities. Undine's savage energy anticipated the frenetic motion and "primitive" desire that characterized Stravinsky's phenomenal ballet, *Le Sacre du printemps.* Debuting in May 1913, the performance created a sensation both in Paris and the United States with its Dionysian celebration of a young woman's dance to the death as the price of spring renewal. The ballet seemed to reject the ethics of rationality, balance, and self-discipline, all that Gibson's archetype of American womanhood had stood for. The explosive Armory Show of 1913 introduced Americans to modern European aesthetic movements and suggested a Western tradition in revolt. In February 1915, despite the resistance of the NAACP and others, D. W. Griffith's film *The Birth of a Nation,* which heralded the end of Reconstruction and the birth of the Ku Klux Klan, became a smash hit and presaged an increasing eugenic anxiety later critics would see as a defining element of modern literary culture. With the introduction of long-range artillery, the machine gun, and mustard gas, World War I proved to be the most mechanized, deadly, and disillusioning conflict the West had ever experienced. By the early 1920s, women's suffrage was won, Prohibition was in effect, waves of racist mob violence were sweeping the South, the Harlem Renaissance had begun, John Held's flapper was all the vogue, and T. S. Eliot's "The Wasteland" defined an era.

While the Gibson Girl represented a quest for economic growth and race progress, the flapper represented a leisure culture working ever harder to spend money but not necessarily to attract the best mate. When she was not dancing the Charleston, her languid posture suggested a Euro-American disillusionment with all that the Gibson Girl stood for. As Gibson drew the flapper, she was sketchy, impressionistic, harder to pin down. Held's flapper images for *Life* suggested a woman whose very plasticity was humorous but disconcerting. Too busy or too listless to represent the nation, flappers abandoned their corsets (although they bound their breasts), bobbed their hair, wore long-waisted, loose-fitting dresses, and played. Even as they physically appeared more akin to a Taylored ideal, they signaled a new generation of women devoted to greater mobility and greater fun.

The writers I have examined shared an ambivalence, at best, toward many of the cultural and literary trends associated with the flapper and emerging high modernism. The "new erotic"—leisure—and consumption ethics, eugenics, and increasing professionalization, as well as the commitment to modernist fragmentation appear at odds with the predominant reform idealism in the work of most of these writers. With the exception of Cather, whose works arguably become more modernist in style after 1913, the writers who continued to enjoy popularity well into the twentieth century—that is, Glasgow and Wharton—continued in a more or less realist style. While publishers were apparently at last soliciting Sui Sin Far's work at the time of her death in 1914, her previous work reflected an ambivalence toward a "new" consumption ethic so often deployed as part of a larger Orientalist logic. Pauline Hopkins's divinely inspired true New Woman couched in the sentimental overplots of popular fiction, did not find support in an increasingly patriarchal and professionalized black literary culture. After she began the short-lived *New Era* journal in 1916, her literary career ended. Under the wing of the Washington machine, Margaret Murray Washington continued unabated her work at Tuskegee and in the black women's club movement—she was president of the National Association of Colored Women (NACW) from 1912 to 1918—but turned her attention to women's role in international affairs after World War I. In 1922, she would be the leading force behind the creation of the International Council of Women of the Darker Races (ICWDR), which was devoted to "education, political affairs and social uplift" (Rief 13–15). After the financially unsuccessful *Hagar,* Mary Johnston abandoned contemporary political fiction and returned to writing historical romances with an increasingly metaphysical bent. Her developing commitment to the theosophical movement, a movement that offered the promise of evolutionary progress toward a period of blissful stasis, suggested her increasing disillusionment with a material, profane age. Her books never again became best sellers. With *The Age of Innocence* (1920), Edith Wharton did, however, achieve both popular and critical acclaim. Yet much of Wharton's work was commercially successful after World War I, it received mixed reviews, and not long after her death, her literary reputation was in decline (Benstock 460). Only recently has this later work been critically recuperated in a sustained way as a conscious attempt on Wharton's part to engage more directly in the contemporary political and social debates of her time.[1] By contrast, Glasgow and Cather wrote what has generally been recognized as some of their best work in the late teens and twenties. In *Barren Ground* (1925), Glasgow presents arguably the apotheosis of her New Woman figure in Dorinda Oakley, and for some critics Cather would do the same in *My Antonia* (1917).

Yet by 1914, all that had made the New Woman of 1895 "new" was not so new anymore, and the rhetoric of the "new" had become associated with different but related social trends. In 1913, the *New Freewoman* appeared, a short-lived magazine whose title suggested that personal liberation was to be the dominant theme in the decade to come. The "new ethic" of quick marriages and easy divorces had become the "new erotic ethic" of sex in the age of increasingly available contraception. Eugenics, the "term that had hardly as yet come into general use," was increasingly deployed to bolster nativist arguments (Johnston, *Hagar* 251). With Woodrow Wilson's presidential victory in 1912, his "New Freedom," which sought to regulate trusts to ensure free competition, appeared to win out, albeit temporarily, over Roosevelt's "New Nationalism," which accepted large corporate combinations as progress but sought tougher regulations on corporate wrongdoers. Washington's "New Negroes" would become Alain Locke's "New Negroes"—spiritually emancipated, self-determined but with an international race consciousness and centered in a "prophetic" Harlem (Locke 3–16). The corresponding renaissance of black woman's writing that emerged in the 1890s would not reappear until the late teens and twenties. The New Woman as Gibson Girl or suffragette became the socially transgressive flapper or the politically minded feminist. Feminists, as Nancy Cott has observed, no longer felt they needed the mantle of true womanhood to have their say. Refusing the Christian moral authority of the old bourgeois matron, feminists could abandon the New Woman and the behavioral boundaries she represented. Such a shift suggests an even greater emphasis on individualism, which Cott sees as having increasingly undermined a broad-based feminist movement, especially after the passage of the Nineteenth Amendment.

As I have reimagined turn-of-the-century American New Woman literary history, I have attempted to create "cultural dialogics" of literary discourse that too often has been simplified. The New Woman as potentially erratic force, high-minded spiritual leader, or tough self-made professional reflects more than debates about women's changing roles in American culture. An overdetermined trope linked to Progressive-era issues that still resonate in our time, the New Woman embodies the fears and desires of a modern nation working ever harder to create new false needs for newly individuated consumer citizens, even as it represents the call of many women for collective action to ensure equal rights. It is that tension—between the New Woman singular shopping in the marketplace and the new women plural marching in the streets—that frames much of the imagined future in these texts.

At the same time, the emergence of the New Woman is also the story of individual female writers striving for success in their respective but connected literary communities. Marked by region, race, class status, and political and social affiliations, these writers create New Woman characters who often reflect and interrogate the social positioning of their creators. While attempting to forge some coalitions, these writers disavow others; while acknowledging the sociopolitical limitations within which their New Woman protagonists live and work, they affirm some of those limitations, while rejecting others. In our arguably postfeminist period, their narratives remind us of how difficult it is to forge crosscultural coalitions, let alone those protean enough to evolve and strong enough to endure.

NOTES

Introduction

1. Fleissner draws here from Sheila Jeffreys, *The Spinster and Her Enemies.*

2. Consider the following recent studies of the New Woman: Amy Kaplan's "Romancing the Empire" (2002) explores how the New Woman in popular historical romances of the period becomes a model for imperial subjects in the New Empire (*Anarchy,* 92–120). Margaret Finnegan's *Selling Suffrage: Consumer Culture and Votes for Women* (1999) explores the ways in which suffragists employed the logic and the rhetoric of consumer culture. Beryl Satter's *Each Mind a Kingdom: American Women, Sexual Purity, and the New Thought Movement, 1875–1920* (1999) looks at the ways in which the New Thought movement negotiated changing conceptions of gendered "mind, matter, spirit, selfhood, and desire" even as it depended on a racialized evolutionary discourse for its logic (10–12). And Laura Behling's *The Masculine Woman in America, 1890–1935* (2001) explores the literary, artistic, and rhetorical strategies used to contain the "sexually inverted" woman.

3. Whether or not the term "New Woman" was capitalized varies considerably. Unless context dictates otherwise, I will generally capitalize the term to emphasize its constructed nature.

4. Catherine Gilbert Murdock's *Domesticating Drink: Women, Men, and Alcohol in America, 1870–1940,* 9. Frances Willard, president of the Women's Christian Temperance Union (WCTU) was a vocal proponent of the New Woman. In an 1896 interview with the British feminist newspaper the *Woman's Signal,* Willard claims, "The demand for new women is a demand by men who want women with sunny spirits, a friendly outlook in life, with scientific knowledge of how health should be preserved . . . women who are an active, industrial, and educational factor in the world's work ("Miss Willard").

5. "Fire Fly" attributes this quote to a "Mr. R." I am indebted to Dominika Ferens for sending me copies of Eaton's work in the *Gall's Daily News Letter.*

6. See Alison Berg's "Reconstructing Motherhood: Pauline Hopkins's *Contending Forces* and the Rhetoric of Racial Uplift" in *Mothering the Race: Women's Narratives of Reproduction, 1890–1930.* Pauline Hopkins's first novel, in particular, "insists that as long as black women did not hold title to their own bodies and those of their children, they could not be emancipated—and emancipating—mothers" (51).

7. See Michael Tavel Clarke's "The Growing Woman and the Growing Jew: Mary Antin, the New Woman, and the Immigration Debate" ("These Days" 241–81).

8. See Dorothy Berkson, "'A Goddess behind a Sordid Veil': The Domestic Heroine Meets the Labor Novel in Mary E. Wilkins Freeman's *The Portion of Labor*" in *Redefining the Political Novel: American Women Writers, 1797–1901.*

9. See "The Girl of the Period," in the *Gall's Daily News Letter,* Feb. 8, 1897.

10. See William Leach, *Land of Desire: Merchants, Power, and the Rise of a New American Culture,* especially 50, 73, and 104–6.

11. See chapter 8 of Luce Irigaray, *This Sex Which Is Not One.*

12. Consider, for example, the debates about Jane Addams's role at Hull House, which Rivka Shpak Lissak summarizes in her book *Pluralism and Progressives: Hull House and the New Immigrants, 1890–1919* (1989). Was Addams ultimately committed to "Anglo-American conformity, cosmopolitanism (or the melting pot), [or] cultural pluralism"? (7).

13. According to Peter J. Bowler in *The Eclipse of Darwinism,* the term "neo-Lamarckism" was coined in 1885 by the American scientist Alpehus Packard to describe those who wished "to establish the inheritance of acquired characteristics as an alternative to Darwinism" (59). As Cynthia Eagle Russett notes in *Darwin in America: The Intellectual Response, 1865–1912,* even though by 1900 American natural scientists strongly supported Darwinism, many also embraced Lamarck's theory in large part because Lamarckianism offered scientific support for the efficacy of education in improving humanity (10). Yet as Russett points out in *Sexual Science,* a Lamarckian worldview was not necessarily an optimistic one. It could emphasize the ways in which the negative traits of ancestors appeared in subsequent generations. Degeneration occurred when these negative traits, traits such as alcoholism or criminality, occurred in subsequent generations (200).

14. In the 1880s, August Weismann developed his theory of germ plasm, where a separate substance in the cell nucleus was responsible for transmitting hereditary information. Unable to affect the genetic information passed to the next generation, the body was in a sense only a "host" for its own germ plasm. Weismann "purged Darwinism of all its original Lamarckian connections and proclaimed natural selection as the only mechanism of evolution." Weismann's "hard" heredity became known as "neo-Darwinism" (Bowler 41).

15. See Elyse Blankley, "Beyond the 'Talent of Knowing': Gertrude Stein and the New Woman," 196–209.

16. Phyllis Eileen Steele provides a helpful overview of much-neglected New Woman literature in her dissertation, "Hungry Hearts, Idle Wives, and New Women: The American Novel Re-examines Nineteenth-Century Domestic Ideology, 1890–1917" (1993).

17. See, for example, Barbara Bardes and Suzanne Gossett's *Declarations of Independence: Women and Political Power in Nineteenth-Century American Fiction* (1990) for a discussion of how (white) women's desires for autonomy were debated in popular fiction of the nineteenth century. Their study recovers neglected precursors to New Woman texts such as Mary H. Ford, *Which Wins? A Story of Social Conditions* (1891); Annie Nathan Meyer, *Helen Brent, M.D.* (1892); and Lillian E. Sommers, *For Her Daily Bread* (1887).

18. Here Felski draws on the work of Teresa de Lauretis, who, in turn, draws upon Foucault to define the "technology of gender" as "not a property of bodies or something originally existent in human beings, but 'the set of effects produced in bodies, behaviors, and social relations,' in Foucault's words by the deployment of 'a complex political technology'" (3).

19. Shirley Marchalonis's *College Girls: A Century in Fiction* (1995) is an exception to this trend. She notes that those women who chose to attend college "carefully and consistently avoid[ed] using the term" (35).

20. See Lois Banner, *American Beauty* (1983); Martha Banta, *Imaging American Women: Idea and Ideals in Cultural History* (1987); Patricia Marks, *Bicycles, Bangs, and Bloomers* (1990); and Rosemary Hennessy, *Materialist Feminism and the Politics of Discourse* (1993).

21. See June Sochen, *The New Woman in Greenwich Village, 1910–1920* (1972); Mary Jo Buhle, *Women and American Socialism, 1870–1920* (1981); and Rosalind Rosenberg, *Beyond Separate Spheres: Intellectual Roots of Modern Feminism* (1982).

22. See Sandra Gilbert and Susan Gubar, *No Man's Land: The Place of the Woman Writer in the Twentieth Century,* vol. 2 (1989); Laura Doan, *Old Maids to Radical Spinsters: Unmarried Women in the Twentieth-Century Novel* (1991); Marianne DeKoven, *Rich and Strange: Gender, History, Modernism* (1991); Ellen Kay Trimberger, "The New Woman and the New Sexuality: Conflict and Contradiction in the Writings and Lives of Mabel Dodge and Neith Boyce" (1991); and Esther Newton, "The Mythic Mannish Lesbian: Radclyffe Hall and the New Woman" (1991).

23. See Kathy Peiss, *Cheap Amusements: Working Women and Leisure in Turn-of-the-Century New York* (1986); Susan Glenn, *Daughters of the Shtetl: Life and Labor in the Immigrant Generation* (1990); and Marjorie Wheeler, *The New Woman of the New South* (1993).

24. In "The New Woman as Cultural Symbol and Social Reality," Ammons discusses Cather's *The Song of the Lark,* Mary Austin's *A Woman of Genius,* Jessie Fauset's *The Sleeper,* Angelina Weld Grimké's *Rachel,* Edith Wharton's *The House of Mirth* and *Summer,* in addition to Sui Sin Far's *Mrs. Spring Fragrance.* In *Conflicting Stories,* Ammons includes works by Frances Ellen Harper, Charlotte Perkins Gilman, Sarah Orne Jewett, Alice Dunbar-Nelson, Kate Chopin, Pauline Hopkins, Gertrude Stein, Mary Austin, Sui Sin Far, Willa Cather, Humishuma, Jessie Fauset, Edith Wharton, Ellen Glasgow, Anzia Yezierska, Edith Summers Kelley, and Nella Larsen.

25. Felski is drawing here on the work of Nancy Fraser in *Unruly Practices: Power, Discourse, and Gender in Contemporary Social Theory* (1989).

26. See also Carla Willard, "Timing Impossible Subjects: The Marketing Style of Booker T. Washington," 651–56.

27. Lois Banner documents this shift in ideals of American beauty by citing an editorial in the *New York World,* Jan. 5, 1913 (*American Beauty* 166).

Chapter 1: Selling the American New Woman as Gibson Girl

1. According to Ellis, "The actively inverted woman . . . may not be . . . what would be called a 'mannish' woman . . . [I]n the inverted woman the masculine traits are part of an organic instinct which she by no means always wishes to accentuate. The inverted woman's masculine element may in the least degree consist only in the fact that she makes advances to the women to whom she is attracted" ("Sexual Inversion in Women" 148).

2. By contrast, I found comparatively little evidence of temperance workers being satirized within the pages of *Life,* probably because their cause was in keeping with the generally conservative stance *Life* took on social issues.

3. Gibson illustrated Abbe Carter Goodloe's *College Girls* (1896) and the College Girl issue of *Life,* May 20, 1909.

4. See Banner, *American Beauty,* 154. I do not mean to conflate these images, however. As Carolyn Kitch notes in her recent book, *The Girl on the Magazine Cover,* Fisher's "girl" was more demure and conventionally pretty than Gibson's. The Christy Girl, likewise, was less haughty and more pretty than the Gibson Girl, while Flagg's "vamps" tended to be saucier and more provocative (57). All, however, are easily recognized as variations on a type popularized first by Gibson.

5. See *Stories of New York* (New York: Scribner's, 1893), 187–214. In addition, the novel

in which Undine appears, *The Custom of the Country,* was prominently advertised in the pages of *Life* (see, for example, May 29, 1913, 1096).

6. As Martha Banta points out, however, in *Imaging American Women,* Gibson was more ambivalent about U.S. imperialist missions abroad than Christy. Consider, for example, Gibson's two political cartoons in the aftermath of the Spanish-American War: "On August 11, 1898, Charles Dana Gibson pictures Columbia as a gracious, albeit towering, figure who suggests to Spain, the sullen runt, 'come, let us forgive and forget' . . . But two weeks later, Columbia in a bathing dress—as aloof as a society belle disdainful of associating with her inferiors—asks herself, 'Do I want to go in with that crowd?'" (555).

7. See Martha Banta, *Imaging American Women* (211–12) and Richard Marschall's contribution to *American Humor Magazines and Comic Periodicals* (147).

8. Thirty-nine of Gibson's drawings were exhibited alongside Will Bradley's book designs in the Liberal Arts Building at the Fair (Koch 71).

9. Military imagery had long been used by the more radical branches of the suffrage movement, especially in England. In *The Gender of Modernity,* Rita Felski suggests the significance of this revolutionary rhetoric: "The pervasive use of militaristic metaphors in feminist discourse sought to countermand such images of disorderly feminine bodies by creating a counter-image of a well-disciplined army marching inexorably toward success" (169).

Chapter 2: Margaret Murray Washington, Pauline Hopkins, and the New Negro Woman

1. Frances Willard was president of the Women's Christian Temperance Union from 1897 until her death in 1898 and cofounder of the General Federation of Women's Clubs in 1889. Ellen Henrotin was a labor organizer, social reform advocate, and prominent Chicago clubwoman. She was president of the General Federation of Women's Clubs from 1894 to 1898. Mary Dickinson was a poet and novelist and president of the National Council of Women from 1895 to 1897 (*Booker T. Washington Papers* 4:239).

2. See "Women's Department" 118, and "Famous Men of the Negro Race. Booker T. Washington" 441.

3. In the capital-intensive world of magazine and newspaper publishing, Washington offered a wellspring of financial support. By 1900, he supported and controlled the Chicago *Conservator,* the *Colored Citizen* of Boston, the *New York Age,* and the *Colored American* of Washington (Abby Arthur Johnson and Ronald M. Johnson, "Away from Accommodation"). When the *Colored American Magazine* of Boston suffered financial difficulties a year after its inception due to Elliott's suggestion that the Co-Operative also publish books (among them Pauline Hopkins's novel *Contending Forces*), Walter Wallace wrote confidentially to Booker T. Washington requesting funds (*Booker T. Washington Papers* 6:184–85).

4. My analysis is in part indebted to Walter Benn Michaels's "The Souls of White Folk." Michaels argues, "For Dixon, the reincarnated souls of the clansmen were a way out of acknowledging the inevitable impurity of one's own racial identity and a way into imagining a racial identity that could serve as the defining characteristic of one's national identity" (199). Michaels does not, however, consider the role of gender in constructing these "souls of white folk."

5. See Abby Johnson and Ronald Johnson, "Away from Accommodation," 329–30.

6. See *Life,* Apr. 21, 1904, 387.

7. In 1895 Margaret Murray Washington organized the Tuskegee Woman's Club, composed of faculty and spouses of faculty members, to provide educational lectures. The club also started a school for children of poor workers on a nearby plantation settlement. Active in the growing black women's club movement at the turn of the century, she became president in 1896 of the National Federation of Afro-American Women, which later merged with the National League of Colored Women and became the National Association of Colored Women (NACW). Washington served as president of the NACW from 1912 to 1918 (Hine 1234).

8. Even though Washington puts the onus on black Americans to prove their civilized state rather than on whites to end racist affronts and vigilantism, her final "Of One Blood" assertion seems surprising given Booker T. Washington's public accession to segregation policy in his Atlanta Compromise speech the same year. The key, it seems, is audience. Margaret Washington's "New Negro Woman" was published in *Lend a Hand,* a journal begun by the Boston Unitarian minister and writer Edward Everett Hale and devoted to philanthropy and reform (see Mott 4:742). See also Carla Willard's fascinating "Timing Impossible Subjects: The Marketing Style of Booker T. Washington" for her analysis of how Washington fashioned his message for the white, professional-managerial class audience in late-nineteenth- and early-twentieth-century mass periodicals.

9. Booker T. Washington also stressed the Christian aspects of hygiene in his writing about Tuskegee in *Up from Slavery:* "'The gospel of the tooth-brush,' as General Armstrong used to call it, is a part of our creed at Tuskegee. No student is permitted to remain who does not keep and use a tooth-brush . . . It has been interesting to note the effect that the use of the tooth-brush has had in bringing about a higher degree of civilization among the students" (102–3).

10. See Martha Banta's *Taylored Lives: Narrative Productions in the Age of Taylor, Veblen, and Ford* for a brief analysis of the significance of Booker T. Washington's management ideals as a precursor to Frederick Winslow Taylor's published work (330 n. 13).

11. See also Hallie Brown, *Homespun Heroines and Other Women of Distinction* (1926), 228, from the Digital Schomburg, http://digilib.nypl.org/dynaweb/digs/wwm97253/@Generic__BookView.

12. Carla Willard notes this disjunction between industrial education and a model of education more closely aligned with Du Bois's "Talented Tenth" ("Timing Impossible").

13. The letter to Bruce is in the John E. Bruce Papers in the New York Public Library.

14. Founded by Josephine St. Pierre Ruffin in 1893, the Woman's Era Club was composed of approximately one hundred and fifty women who worked on committees devoted to literature, civics, philanthropy, domestic science, and race work (Cash 79).

15. See Siobhan Somerville's "Passing through the Closet in Pauline Hopkin's *Contending Forces*" (1997). According to the *Oxford English Dictionary,* the first English reference to "sapphism" to mean "homosexual relations between women" appeared in print in 1890, though it may well have been circulated in nonprint form earlier.

16. I am indebted to Teresa Faden Alto for pointing out the origins of Dianthe Lusk's name.

17. See my "'kin' o' rough jestice fer a parson': Pauline Hopkins's *Winona* and the Politics of Reconstructing History." Hopkins's source for much of her work on John Brown was Franklin B. Sanborn's biography, *The Life and Letters of John Brown: Liberator of Kansas and Martyr of Virginia* (1885). Sanborn quotes a letter from Dianthe Lusk's

brother, Milton Lusk: "She was my guiding-star, my guardian angel; she sung beautifully, most always sacred hymns and tunes; and she had a place in the woods, not far from the house, where she used to go alone to pray. . . . After my sister's death he [John Brown] said to John, his son, 'I feel sure that your mother is now with me and influencing me'" (33–34).

18. See Theophus H. Smith, *Conjuring Culture: Biblical Formations of Black America*, 126. In broad terms, Smith defines conjuring as a "magical means of transforming reality" as well as "cultural performances that involve curative transformations of reality by means of mimetic operations and processes" (4–5). In "Pauline Hopkins and the Hidden Self of Race," Thomas Otten notes that "Moses's use of omens and plagues was . . . seen as a sort of conjuring" (250).

19. Otten notes that the Reuel/Moses connection would have suggested Moses', and hence Reuel's, Ethiopian roots in part because Hopkins, like other black intellectuals of the period, believed that Egypt owed much of its cultural legacy to Ethiopia. In addition, "by marrying Zipporah, [Moses] introduces Ethiopian blood into the Old Testament lineage; though Moses's father-in-law is usually said to be a priest of Midian, the book of Numbers implies that he is Ethiopian. And though his name is usually given as Jethro, the first time the Old Testament mentions him, he is called Reuel" (250).

20. Her words are reminiscent of John Brown's final prophetic words, "I, John Brown, am now quite *certain* that the crimes of this *guilty land* will never be purged *away* but with blood" (Sanborn 620).

21. Jim Titus may be a reference to "a notorious proslavery scoundrel named [Colonel] Titus, one of the Buford party from Alabama" (Sanborn 311).

Chapter 3: Incorporating the New Woman in Edith Wharton's The Custom of the Country

1. Wharton began writing *The Custom of the Country* in late 1907 or spring 1908 and worked on it intermittently even after its serial publication in *Scribner's Magazine* began in January 1913. In the intervening years, she published *Ethan Frome* (1911), *The Reef* (1912), and a series of stories. Wharton partially blamed the relatively weak sales of *Ethan Frome* on Scribner's poor printing and advance advertising. When Scribner's did not agree to her price for the serial rights of *The Reef,* she chose to publish the novel with D. Appleton and Company, a contract that Fullerton helped to negotiate. She returned to Scribner's to publisher *The Custom of the Country* the following year.

Due to his mental illness, infidelities, and financial blunders, Teddy was increasingly difficult to live with, and Edith filed for divorce in 1913. Edith began her yearlong affair with Morton Fullerton in 1908. Teddy sold The Mount rather abruptly in June 1912 while Edith was on her way to Paris. See R. W. B. Lewis, *Edith Wharton: A Biography*; Cynthia Griffen Wolff, *A Feast of Words: The Triumph of Edith Wharton*; and, most recently, Shari Benstock, *No Gifts from Chance: A Biography of Edith Wharton*.

2. I am indebted here to Dale Bauer, who, in *Edith Wharton's Brave New Politics*, defines "cultural dialogics" as "the varying intensity of a writer's engagement with material history as revealed through the layers of cultural references with which a writer deepens her work; moreover, cultural dialogics reveals how internalized the cultural voices are even as the writer interprets and evaluates their directives in orchestrating among cultures a 'dialogic encounter'" (4).

3. In *The Corporate Reconstruction of American Capitalism, 1890–1916*, Martin Sklar defines the proprietary competitive ethic as "capitalist property and market relations in which the dominant type of enterprise was headed by an owner-manager . . . in which such enterprise was a price-taker, rather than a price-maker, price being determined by conditions of supply and demand beyond the control of the enterprise" (4).

4. Sklar defines the "corporate reorganization of industry" or "corporate reconstruction" as "not simply the *de jure* incorporation of a property otherwise managed *de facto* along proprietary lines, but the capitalization of the property in the form of negotiable securities relatively widely dispersed in ownership, a corresponding separation of ownership title and management function, and management of the enterprise by bureaucratic administrative methods involving a division, or a specialization, of managerial function, and an integration, or at least a centralization, of financial control" (*Corporate Reconstruction* 4).

5. See Martin J. Sklar, *The United States as a Developing Country: Studies in U.S. History in the Progressive Era and the 1920s.*

6. Undine was likely modeled after Selma White, the heroine of Robert Grant's best-selling *Unleavened Bread* (1900). Socially ambitious yet ever provincial, Selma rationalizes her own morally dubious ascent to social prominence. In a letter to the novelist, Wharton praised his "objective" portrayal of certain American types: "Selma, I think her as good in her way as Gwendolen Grandcourt. Every stroke tells, & you never forget the inconscient quality of her selfishness; you never fall into the error of making her deliberately false or cruel . . . 'Unleavened Bread' in fact seems to me one of the best American novels I have read in years" (*Letters* 41).

7. See Jennie Kassanoff, "Corporate Thinking: Edith Wharton's *Fruit of the Tree*": "1907 saw Wharton's literary earnings drop to half of what they had been in 1906. Although Charles Scribner explained that 'the book had been well received everywhere,' he attributed its limited sales to the 'great and sudden change in business conditions' caused by the financial panic of 1907." Wharton herself could only wistfully agree: "It is too bad that I coincided with the Knickerbocker trust!" (29).

8. See also Claire Preston's description of Moffatt's activities as a corrupt financier: "The kinds of productive activity in which we see him more typically engaged seem to involve strategic 'booming' of new towns and companies, and other mostly abstract schemes which seem to rely on numerical legerdemain, hype, and low cunning, more than on any solid investment or production" (109). Preston compares Moffatt to Jay Gould, the so-called "Mephistopheles of Wall Street" (110).

9. In this respect, you could see him as what Christophe Den Tandt calls the corporate androgyne—"male protagonists whose willingness to develop a supreme form of masculinity paradoxically involves the appropriation of feminine features . . . [They] derive their heightened power from an ability to bracket off their sense of individuation and to merge with entities modeled as feminine bodies—the urban market, the corporation" (640).

10. See letter to Sara Norton, May 29, [1908]: "On board ship I've been deep in Kellogg's Darwinism Today, which is admirably done (do you know it?) & am following it with Lock's Heredity & Variation" (*Letters* 146).

11. Wharton was also influenced by Joseph-Arthur de Gobineau (1816–1882) and Georges Vacher Laponge (1854–1936), pan-Germanic apologists for racial hierarchy. In a letter to Morton Fullerton on Sept. 22, 1911, Wharton describes reading "a rather good book of E.

Seillière's, 'Les Mystiques du Néo-romantisme,' . . . In this, the chapter on the Pan-German idea, built up on Gobineau & Vacher de Laponge (whom I used to talk to you about) would interest you, I know" (*Letters* 257). Diplomat, novelist, and historian, Gobineau advocated the need for a chiefly Teutonic "racial aristocracy." French anthropologist Laponge was likewise a "student of the Aryan race" (*Letters* 258 n. 8).

12. See Sklar's *The United States as a Developing Country* for a useful overview of the changing social relations during the incorporation period.

13. In "Corporate Thinking: Edith Wharton's *The Fruit of the Tree*," Jennie A. Kassanoff argues that Wharton's novel endorses firm regulation of the markets by an "elite group of corporate financiers": "*The Fruit of the Tree* marshals a complex set of images to articulate Wharton's deeply rooted political fear of a country adrift in the twentieth century, divorced from genealogical, class-based sources of stability" (31). While I certainly agree that Wharton endorses some forms of market regulation, she also offers, as I have sought to demonstrate, significant critiques of those corporate financiers in charge of regulating production.

14. I disagree then with Ellen Dupree, who argues that Wharton refuses "to permit Justine's perspective to be absorbed in that of Amherst and the male text. Instead, she provides an ending in which the feminine is disturbingly present" ("New Woman" 60).

15. Undine's susceptibility to reversion may also be due to the "crossing" of her parents. In his chapter "Mendelism," Lock writes, "The phenomenon of so-called *reversion on crossing* has long been familiar to biologists. . . . The phenomenon consists in the appearance, in the offspring of a cross, of a character which was not visibly present in either parent, and in many cases this character can properly be regarded as ancestral—it is a character which has been lost by both parents in the course of their divergent evolution from a common primitive form" (188).

16. Edith Wharton to Mary Cadwalader Jones, February 1912, Edith Wharton Papers, Beinecke Library, New Haven.

17. Edith Wharton to Edward Wharton, July 6–8, 1910, Edith Wharton Papers, Beinecke Library, New Haven. Wharton's literary earnings were considerable. According to Shari Benstock, Wharton earned $42,790.06 in 1906 although she earned only a third of that in 1907. She earned $14,000 in 1908. In October 1913, Scribner's paid $6,000 for serial rights and a royalty advance of $7,500 for *The Custom of the Country* (284).

18. See Grant McCracken's analysis of possession and divestment rituals in *Culture and Consumption* 85, 87.

19. See Celia Lury, who cites McCracken's use of term "possession rituals" to refer "to rituals involving the collecting, cleaning, comparing, showing off and even photographing of possessions . . . it is in rituals such as these that the performative capacity of goods is made visible; through performance, objects express certain aspects of a person's identity" (12–13).

Chapter 4: Sui Sin Far and the Wisdom of the New

1. In "'We Wear the Mask': Sui Sin Far as One Example of Trickster Authorship," Annette White-Parks argues that the name "Sui Sin Far" was more than a pseudonym: "I purposefully use 'Sui Sin Far' to underline the personal choice this writer made to distinguish herself from the English-Canadian identity that most of her family maintained and to help bring to visibility the Chinese heritage for which she fought through her lifetime" (17). In her professional correspondence, Sui Sin Far most often used her birth

name, Edith Eaton, and in her early bylines she used the pseudonym "Sui Seen Far." Such a practice suggests the ways in which she carefully deployed her ethnic identity. My use of her name will change to reflect these strategic shifts.

2. See James Clifford, *The Predicament of Culture: Twentieth-Century Ethnography, Literature, and Art.*

3. Rather than the "'free' oscillation between or among chosen identities," the "materialist concept of hybridity" conveys that the histories of forced-labor migrations, racial segregation, economic displacement, and internment are left in the material traces of "hybrid" cultural identities; these hybridities are always in the process of, on the one hand, being appropriated and commodified by commercial culture and, on the other, of being rearticulated for the creation of oppositional "resistance cultures" (Lowe 82).

4. I am indebted here to Lisa Lowe's analysis of the critical inheritance of cultural definitions and traditions as well as the racial formation of Asian American cultures. See especially *Immigrant Acts* 65–69.

5. For the name translation, see Ling 41.

6. Born in Cheshire, England, to an English father, Edward Eaton, and a Chinese mother, Grace Trepesis (or Trefusius), Edith Eaton (1865–1914) moved with her family to Hudson City, New York, in 1871 or 1872 and settled in Montreal, Canada, in 1873 or 1874 (White-Parks, "Sui Sin Far" 17–19). Edith worked as a journalist for the *Montreal Star* and briefly for *Gall's Daily News Letter* in Kingston, Jamaica, where she wrote under the pseudonym "Fire Fly" (Ferens 69). Edith's first articles appeared in the Montreal magazine *Dominion Illustrated* in 1888. She adopted the first variation of her pseudonym, Sui Seen Far, in stories she published in the *Lotus* and *Fly Leaf* in 1896. Suffering long-term ill effects from rheumatic fever, which she contracted as a child, she was advised by her doctor to move west, and in 1898 she moved to San Francisco where she worked as a typist for the Canadian Pacific Railway (Ling 28). Two years later, she moved to Seattle where she remained for approximately ten years. Spending several months in Los Angeles, she published under the male pseudonym Wing Sing (Ferens 186). Using a letter of introduction from the Montreal Chinese community, she became involved with Seattle's Chinese community, which numbered 438 in 1900, about 1 percent of Seattle's total population (Ling 28).

7. In 1900 there were 89,863 Chinese in the United States, concentrated primarily on the West Coast (C. Wu 17). Due to open hostility from white communities and discriminatory renting practices as well as the support system provided by the Chinatown Benevolent Associations or Six Companies, most Chinese lived in Chinatowns at the turn of the century. The majority of these immigrants were men, sojourners who intended to earn their fortune and return to China. This fact, in addition to the expense of the journey and discriminatory U.S. immigration policies, created a vast disparity in the ratio of Chinese men to women in the United States—in 1900, among the 25,767 Chinese, only 3,471 were females (Tsai 40). The Page Law (1875), which denied entry to Chinese, Japanese, and Mongolian contract laborers, prostitutes, and felons, worked to intimidate all Chinese women from emigrating (Peffer 42). Many Chinese women were rejected during or refused to undergo the demeaning interrogation and cross-examination by U.S. immigration officials stationed in Hong Kong (Peffer 32). The Chinese Exclusion Act of 1882 not only prevented Chinese laborers from entering the country but also provided the rationale for excluding Chinese women. The court decision *Re Ah Moy* (1883) declared that the wife of a Chinese laborer took the status of her husband and could therefore be denied entry (Takaki 41). The Scott Act of 1888 prevented Chinese laborers who had temporarily

left the United States from returning, while the Geary Act of 1892 continued the exclusion of Chinese immigrants established in the 1882 act and required the Chinese to hold certificates of residence within one year or else face deportation (C. Wu 16). Congress reaffirmed these exclusion laws in 1902 and denied the Chinese in the United States the possibility of naturalization (17). The San Francisco earthquake in April 1906, however, allowed Chinese men both to strengthen their status in this country and to make immigration possible for their wives. Because municipal records were destroyed during the quake, Chinese men could claim San Francisco as their birthplace and as citizens could legally bring their wives to the United States (Takaki 234). During the period from 1907 to 1922, one out of every four Chinese immigrants was female (235).

8. In April 1896, the *Fly Leaf* was taken over by Elbert Hubbard's *Philistine* (Mott 4:646).

9. See Nina Baym, *Woman's Fiction: A Guide to Novels by and about Women in America, 1820–1870.* Sui Sin Far's construction of her life history has many parallels to the traditional "overplot" (12) that Baym identifies in nineteenth-century women's fiction: the heroine as initially "a poor and friendless child" who, if not an orphan, "thinks herself to be one" (35); as a child she is abused by those in power over her, her "success in life [is] entirely a function of her own efforts and character" (35); the heroine is depicted as "a social product" (36); while discerning in her personal relationships with men, she finds people in her community who "support, advise, and befriend her" (38); the novels ultimately criticize marketplace values as they chart a path to Christian belief (45).

10. Eaton's relationship with author and editor Charles Lummis appears to have been the most fruitful of her literary contacts, but even that was fairly limited. A mentor to Austin, Gilman, and other writers and reformers, Lummis edited the *Land of Sunshine* (later *Out West*) in which some of Sui Sin Far's early work appeared (see White-Parks, "Sui Sin Far" 86).

11. This and subsequent references to "The Inferior Woman" refer to the 1912 version in *Mrs. Spring Fragrance.*

12. She had expressed a similar perspective some fifteen years earlier in the *Gall's Daily News Letter:* "I am perhaps even more weary of the fuss about 'Woman's Rights' 'Woman's Sphere' 'Woman's Mission' and so forth, this calling to arms as it were of many wives, mothers and daughters, who, perhaps, would feel better and happier if they spent less time abroad meddling in other people's affairs, and more time at home quietly and unostentatiously doing their duty amongst those with whom Providence has cast their lot" (Fire Fly, "The Woman about Town").

13. Like Sui Sin Far, Adachi Kinnosuke also stresses the fact that strong images of Chinese women existed before the revolution, most notably in the guise of the empress dowager: "As a matter of historical fact, the new woman of China is not quite new. The position of women among the Chinese has always been high. The late Empress Dowager, who, in her time, received a deal of free advertisement, not of the kindliest brand . . . —the Imperial Lady was no more a freak and exception among the dowager empresses of China than she was a monster" (73). Eaton appeared to share these sentiments. In a letter to Charles Lummis in September 1900, she writes, "Europeans and Americans are forever talking about the way the Chinese women are kept down. Isn't it strange that the greatest person in China—the one who has the most influence—should be a woman. And the white people howl over the fact and don't like it at all. What do they want?" (letter in Southwest Museum Library, Los Angeles).

14. In "The New and the Old," a brief story that appeared in *The Westerner's* series (1909), the young hero rejects filial reverence and devotion to strike out on his own. Wanting a business that "would call for a telephone and electric lights," he starts his own employment agency (37). In "The Story of a Forty-Niner," the scholar protagonist whose sedentary life had made him "nervous and irritable" (18) comes to America for essentially an activity cure, "the new life brought with renewed health and strength" (19). Sui Sin Far often depicted China as a kind of neurasthenic patient needing American vitality.

15. The revolutionary movement offered another avenue for nationalist sentiment. Led by Sun Yat-sen, the revolutionaries advocated a constitutional republic like the American governmental system but incorporating Confucian ideas. In 1895, the revolutionaries staged the Canton revolt but were forced to flee the country when it failed. They continued to carry out an anti-Manchu movement abroad (Chong 17–18). According to Annette White-Parks, evidence exists that Edith Eaton met Sun Yat-sen. She cites an article printed in the *Montreal Gazette* (n.d.): "captioned 'Sun Yat Sen Paid Visit to Montreal,' its description of Sun Yat Sen's secret visit to Montreal in the early part of the century includes the following: 'Amongst the few who were in the secret of the Doctor being here was the late Miss Edith Eaton, a clever literary lady, . . . She had the entry to Sun Yat Sen's suite of rooms for herself and a few selected friends" (White-Parks, "Sui Sin Far," 139 n. 52).

16. Lowe defines the title of her book *Immigrant Acts* as an attempt "to name the *contradictions* of Asian immigration, which at different moments in the last century and a half of Asian entry into the United States have placed Asians 'within' the U.S. nation-state, its workplaces, and its markets, yet linguistically, culturally, and racially marked Asians as 'foreign' and 'outside' the national polity" (8).

Chapter 5: Mary Johnston, Ellen Glasgow, and the Evolutionary Logic of Progressive Reform

1. See Alice Payne Hackett, *Fifty Years of Best Sellers, 1895–1945*; and Dorothy M. Scura, *Ellen Glasgow: The Contemporary Reviews*, xvii–xxvii.

2. Glasgow's work, of course, has received much more scholarly attention over the years than has Johnston's. Recently, however, southern historian Marjorie Wheeler has offered extensive analysis of Johnston's political work in the Virginia suffrage campaign (Wheeler, *New Woman of the New South: The Leaders of the Woman Suffrage Movement in the Southern States*). The only literary critic to treat these two writers together is Anne Goodwyn Jones in *Tomorrow Is Another Day: The Woman Writer in the South, 1859–1936*.

3. According to Paul M. Gaston, although the term originated in 1862, it did not come into wide usage until ten years later when *Atlanta Constitution* editor Henry Grady became the "chief apostle" of the New South movement. For Grady, the goal of the New South was to achieve prosperity by copying the economy of the North through crop diversification, railroad construction, and industrial development. C. Vann Woodward locates the origin of the New South after Reconstruction when the growth of railroads and factories suggested a new era of prosperity (23–50). According to George Brown Tindall in *The Emergence of the New South: 1913–1945*, for white Southerners the New South emerges in 1913, the year the southern-born Woodrow Wilson became president and reintegrated southern whites into the political and economic process of the nation. As Woodward points out, 1913 was widely celebrated by African Americans as the Year of Jubilee, the

fiftieth anniversary of emancipation, which ironically marked the fact that, apart from a small black elite, blacks had made little material progress (368).

4. As Nancy Cott points out in *The Grounding of Modern Feminism,* the word "feminism" began to appear frequently about 1910, at the height of the suffrage movement: "The meaning of Feminism (capitalized at first) also differed from the woman movement. It was both broader and narrower: broader in intent, proclaiming revolution in all the relations of the sexes, and narrower in the range of its willing adherents. As an *ism* (an ideology) it presupposed a set of principles not necessarily belonging to every woman—nor limited to women" (3). In two respects, Johnston's and Glasgow's use of the term corresponds to Cott's working definition of feminism, with its three essential components: firstly, opposing sex hierarchy; secondly, presupposing that women's condition is socially constructed (i.e., "historically shaped by human social usage rather than simply predestined by God or nature"); and, finally, perceiving women not only as a biological sex but also as a social grouping (4–5). While Johnston and Glasgow see women's roles as socially constructed and sex as a social grouping, they, like Hopkins, suggest that women are more advanced on a moral hierarchy of the sexes, and therefore should do the sexual selecting.

5. Johnston and Glasgow reflect, then, the concerns of the prevailing forward-looking Lost Cause movement. As Gaines Foster argues in *Ghosts of the Confederacy: Defeat, the Lost Cause, and the Emergence of the New South, 1865 to 1913,* memorialization of the Confederate cause and its soldiers both alleviated fears that loss brought with it dishonor and paved the way for the reconciliation necessary for rebuilding efforts (6). Vehement detractors of the Old South, such as Henry Watterson of Kentucky and Walter Hines Page of North Carolina, were, according to Foster, in the minority: "Most southerners . . . worried that the social changes they only dimly perceived but apparently feared they could not avoid would somehow undermine southern character. They focused most intently on 'commercialism,' a vaguely defined anxiety that the new order entailed . . . a scramble 'for personal, pecuniary, and political advancement, without regard to honor and integrity, or the interest and rights of others'" (85).

6. Johnston's journal is in the Mary Johnston Papers, accession no. 3588, no. 21, University of Virginia, Charlottesville.

7. In *The Descendant,* Michael Akershem, the illegitimate son of poor whites in Virginia, becomes the editor of the *Iconoclast* and proclaims religion useless, society worthless, and marriage a fake. When he meets Rachel Gavin, a woman who initially wants an artistic career rather than romance, he eventually falls in love and they live together unmarried. Their relationship is eventually doomed, however, as Akershem's moral and psychological state decline.

8. Also present at the meeting were Glasgow's sister Cary Glasgow McCormick, Kate Langley Bosher, Mary Pollard Clarke, Adele Clark, and Edith Clark Cowles. On Nov. 27, 1909, the Equal Suffrage League of Virginia was organized and Mrs. Valentine was elected president (Charlotte Jean Shelton 11–12).

9. Money is emphasized throughout the text as Hagar carefully demonstrates her literary earnings. Johnston may be stressing to her readers that employed women would contribute to the tax base while reminding readers that while Johnston, herself, is not allowed to vote, she is required to pay taxes (Shelton 18).

10. Ronald L. Numbers and Lester D. Stephens note that while "[n]o region in the world has won greater notoriety for its hostility to Darwinism," the South did find many supporters of evolution among the "educated classes" (123, 137).

11. Contrary to Bert Bender's findings in *The Descent of Love: Darwin and the Theory of Sexual Selection in American Fiction, 1871–1926*, these novels do not focus on sexual selection, nor do they present a "dark" image of sexual love.

12. While Lester Ward began to develop his alternative to evolutionary theory between 1888 and 1890 in a series of discussions with, among others, Elizabeth Cady Stanton, Phoebe Couzins, Jennie June, and N. P. Willis, as well as in a published exchange of letters with British writer Grant Allen, his fully developed gynecocentric theory appeared some years later in *Pure Sociology* (Ward 297–98).

13. Johnston's father appears to have embraced the New South ethic. Once a major in the Confederate Army, he became a lawyer, state legislator, and president of the Georgia Pacific Railroad Company (Wheeler, *New Women* 42).

14. In *The Promise of the New South*, Ayers argues that the railroad was central to the South's economic development: "From the end of Reconstruction to the end of the century the South built railroads faster than the nation as a whole.... [B]y 1890, nine of every ten Southerners lived in a railroad county. The construction of a railroad touched people all up and down the track" (9).

15. Patrick Geddes and J. Arthur Thomson, *The Evolution of Sex* (1908). To explain sex differences, Geddes and Thomson employ a metabolic argument: the nutritive, passive female organism (egg) is "anabolic" while the active, potentially destructive organism (sperm) is "katabolic" (94, 120). Johnston reported first reading Geddes and Thomson on Jan. 17, 1910.

16. Recent historians have explored the South's role as a tourist destination after 1870. With the development of the railroad, resorts like West Virginia's White Sulphur Springs and Virginia's Warm Springs, Hot Springs, and Healing Springs became health retreats for "neurasthenic" northern visitors. See Nina Silber, *The Romance of Reunion: Northerners and the South, 1865–1900*, 66–92; and Atwood, "'Saratoga of the South': Tourism in Luray, Virginia, 1878–1905" in Ayers and Willis, *The Edge of the South: Life in Nineteenth-Century Virginia*.

17. In March 1910, Johnston read August Weismann's *Germ Plasm* (1893), which maintained that the body was unable "to influence the genetic information passed on to the next generation" (Bowler 41). Beginning in the 1880s, Weismann launched a full attack on the Lamarckian assertion of the inheritance of acquired characteristics and would be credited with founding the "neo-Darwinist" movement (Peter J. Bowler, *The Eclipse of Darwinism*, 41).

18. Not readily conceivable by the senses, the fourth dimension may be determined by objective methods of science but only realized by those able to imagine a reality beyond themselves. According to C. Howard Hinton's *The Fourth Dimension*, which Johnston read in October 1912, perceiving the fourth dimension is evidence in itself of a higher civilized state: "With the greater development of man there comes a consciousness of something more than all the forms in which it shows itself. There is a readiness to give up all the visible and tangible for the sake of those principles and values of which the visible and tangible are the representation. The physical life of civilised man and of a mere savage are practically the same, but the civilised man has discovered a depth in his existence, which makes him feel that that which appears all to the savage is a mere externality and appurtenage to his true being" (Hinton 1).

19. Francis worked for the company for more than sixty-three years, and the president of the company, Joseph Reid Anderson, was his uncle (Raper 16–17). Located on five acres

between the James River and the Kanawha Canal, it was the South's largest iron works in the nineteenth century and depended upon a large slave labor force housed on company grounds (Dew 19).

20. Glasgow reminds her readers that electricity, like the train, is a sign of the change facing the South, and she links this change with a concomitant social upheaval if the values of the Old and New South are not merged. In Glasgow's *The Ancient Law,* even though Emily Brooke's demeanor suggests "unconsciously generations of social courtesy—of racial breeding" (29) and her nature "elemental motherhood," she is often represented as having "radiant energy" (57). Light shines from her: "[W]hat impressed him most was the quality of radiant energy which revealed itself in every line of her face and figure—now sparkling in her eyes, now dimpling in her cheek, now quickening her brisk steps across the floor, and now touching her eyes and mouth like an edge of light" (28). Similarly, the circuit of affection between Daniel and his daughter Alice, with its incestuous overtones, suggests the disastrous consequences of unbridled energy. Alice seems to have none of the tempering qualities that regulate the direction and force of her energy. She races too fast in her buggy, runs off with her lover, and eventually forges a check to cover her extravagant tastes. During her elopement, she stays at a hotel flooded with a "dazzling glare of electric light," which reminds Daniel of the period in his life when he too was amid such light (373).

21. In *Modernism, Technology, and the Body,* Tim Armstrong sees electricity as one of the predominant tropes to describe the deployment of desire in the late-nineteenth- and early-twentieth-century marketplace. He reads the critically disputed end of *Sister Carrie* as the logical evolution of Carrie's electric self: "That is the real scandal of *Sister Carrie,* that a human being should became [*sic*] a system for sustaining and disseminating desire" (26).

22. She is also the namesake of Gabriel Pendleton, which again indicates the remnants of the Old South in her character.

Chapter 6: Willa Cather and the Fluid Mechanics of the New Woman

1. Much work has been done on Cather's relationship to the West. In Susan Rosowski's recent book, *Birthing a Nation: Gender, Creativity, and the West in American Literature,* for example, she argues that "Cather conceived of the West as female nature slumbering, awakening, and roaring its independence. In her stories, and culminating in *O Pioneers!,* she gave women's fantasies to the West and cast their domestic materials on an epic scale; in doing so she reclaimed materiality for women, rewrote the captivity myth into a story of liberation, and divorced the plot of sexuality from its gendered confinements" (79). See also Judith Fryer, *Felicitous Space: The Imaginative Structures of Edith Wharton and Willa Cather.*

2. See also the work of Guy Reynolds, who is careful to point out how Cather rejected the nativist elements in American progressivism: "Against the narrowly Protestant idealism of the progressives, Cather places her own multicultural vision" (16).

3. In "Willa Cather and the Bicycle," Virgil Albertini suggests that Louise Pound, the woman with whom many scholars believe Cather had her first lesbian relationship, may be a prototype for Tommy. Like Tommy, Pound was an avid cyclist and athlete (16–17).

4. In *Bicycles, Bangs, and Bloomers,* Patricia Marks writes, the "New Woman on a bicycle . . . exercised power . . . changing the conventions of courtship and chaperonage, of marriage and travel" (174).

5. Cather seems to foreclose the possibility of Miss Jessica's response even before the ride. As "a maiden most discreet," Miss Jessica is so reticent to express her feelings about Jay Harper that Tommy wonders "if she were capable of having any at all" ("Tommy" 66–67).

6. See Gilbert and Gubar, *No Man's Land,* 2:174.

7. I disagree somewhat with the distinction that Susan Rosowski makes between these two female characters: "The spirituality of Winifred is conveyed through colors of white and silver, references to the night, moon, and stars, and a cool temper of restraint and stillness; the physicality of Hilda through colors of yellow and gold, references to the day, sun, and fire, and a warm temper of intensity and movement; the energy of Bartley by the bridge that must unite the two" (*Voyage Perilous* 35). I argue that through water imagery both women are, to some extent, placed in a continuum of New-Woman-like sexual turbulence.

8. The critical debate surrounding this novel focuses on how one reads Bartley's failure and the circumstances leading up to it. Cecilia Tichi reads the novel as evidence of Cather's dismay concerning the ascendancy of the engineer over the artist in American culture (*Shifting Gears* 171–80). Elizabeth Ammons likewise sees the novel as Cather's critique of a dehumanizing ethic of industrial progress and, by extension, the "underlying values of conquest and rugged masculinity" of the engineer as hero ("Engineer" 754). Even as Marilee Lindemann notes the ambiguities in Bartley's character and ultimately reads the novel as a sign of Cather's "ambivalence towards the emergence of modern America that haunts all of her major works of fiction" (Introduction xxxi), she sees Cather offering a clear indictment of Bartley's sexual misconduct (xxxii). Yet as Susan Rosowski points out, given the relentless pace of her editorial work at *McClure's,* Cather would have, in some respects, identified with Alexander (*The Voyage* 39). Jonathan Goldberg takes such an identification reading further by claiming that Bartley Alexander acts as Cather's "surrogate" (4). Noting that Alexander's desire for Hilda is also a desire for his own young self, Goldberg argues "that Cather represents her own desire through a cross-gendered same-sex scenario. . . . A plot that looks heterosexual houses lesbian desire that is also figured as male-male desire" (12). I would like to shift the debate by focusing my discussion on the role of Winifred and Hilda as they suggest both the anxieties of female-identified New Woman sexuality and Cather's critique of the gear-and-girder age.

9. Irigaray defines fluidity as

> unending, potent and impotent owing to its resistance to the countable; . . . it enjoys and suffers from a greater sensitivity to pressures; . . . it changes—in volume or in force, for example—according to the degree of heat; . . . it is, in its physical reality, determined by friction between two infinitely neighboring entities—dynamics of the near and not of the proper, movements coming from the quasi contact between two unities hardly definable as such . . . and not energy of a finite system; . . . it allows itself to be easily traversed by flow by virtue of its conductivity to currents coming from other fluids or exerting pressure through the walls of a solid; . . . it mixes with bodies of a like state, sometimes dilutes itself in them in an almost homogeneous manner, . . . it is already diffuse "in itself," which disconcerts any attempt at static identification. (111)

10. In her introduction to the 1977 University of Nebraska edition of *Alexander's Bridge,* Bernice Slote mentions but does not elaborate on the significance of the water imagery in the novel (Murphy 106). Sharon O'Brien offers somewhat more analysis of the water imagery in *Alexander's Bridge:*

Bartley's method of construction . . . reveals dominance and subordination, not the integration of opposites. His bridges seem to represent union since they link opposite shores, yet they span and subdue rivers—an image of form arching over passion, control precariously bridging the unconscious. Rivers—often underground rivers—are Cather's recurrent metaphors for unconscious energies; . . . In *Alexander's Bridge,* however, the engineer who forces the wrong design on his river has not "[given] himself absolutely" to his subject, as Alexandra Bergson gives herself to the land. Instead, Bartley strives to maintain control and dominance, and so his formal designs—imposed by the ego rather than arising from the unconscious—are weak. (391)

I agree with O'Brien that Bartley's inability to cope with the stress of the river leads to his downfall, while Alexandra is able to integrate the two elements. I would disagree with her reading, however, on three points. The fluid element is more precisely defined as feminine than O'Brien suggests. Cather gives that fluid-feminine-sexuality element destructive qualities. In other words, there is no easy dichotomy of a negative masculine and a positive female aesthetic. And finally, the ending of the novel does not simply represent Bartley's inability to "'give himself absolutely' to his subject," that is, to give himself over to the river and the unconscious it represents, but rather to incorporate the fluid as he subdues it. As I hope to demonstrate later in this chapter, Alexandra Bergson, like Bartley Alexander, struggles to exert control and dominance over the land even as she embraces a kind of fluid mechanics in doing so.

11. See also Joseph Urgo, "Willa Cather's Political Apprenticeship at *McClure's* Magazine." Urgo notes that the text of "Gompers and Burns on Unionism and Dynamite" is "bordered on the left and right by sidebars into which representations of bridges have been drawn. The architecture of the page is thus framed by industrial images, while the pages chronicle the human forces that lay stress to the represented phenomena" (65).

12. See Cather's preface to the 1922 edition of *Alexander's Bridge* and her 1931 essay written for the *Colophon.* Both essays are included in the appendix of Marilee Lindemann's 1997 edition of *Alexander's Bridge* (94–100).

13. Sharon O'Brien argues, "In her second novel Cather dramatically revises *Alexander's Bridge* when she turns Alexander into Alexandra: replacing her failed masculine hero with her triumphant heroine, she creates an artist-conqueror who achieves her creative designs by letting them emerge from the soil, not by seeking to subdue nature through force" (392). For Lindemann, both novels exhibit "an ambivalent fascination with the chaotic force of illicit sexuality, a fascination that ultimately leads to the elimination of threat and the restoration of a conservative social order" (49). Jonathan Goldberg reads the connection quite differently: "The 'failure' of the first novel is the desire realized in the second. Or, to put this more exactly, it is the desire of the first—Bartley's for Hilda—that is embodied in Alexandra" (4).

14. For feminist readings, see, most notably, Ellen Moers, Sharon O'Brien, Judith Fryer, Gilbert and Gubar, Hermione Lee, Janis Stout, Louise Westling, and Marilee Lindemann. Moers explores the female erotics and mysticism of Cather's landscapes (258–60). More reluctant to identify Alexandra exclusively by her relationship to the land, O'Brien argues that by "[c]hallenging the traditional culture-nature dichotomy in which men are aligned with culture, women with nature, Cather portrays Alexandra both as connected to nature and as separate from it, a subject with will, imagination, and desire who shapes the land as she is shaped by it" (434). Fryer focuses on Alexandra's rejection of patriarchal cultural assumptions in favor of a precise "authentic" rendering of her frontier experience: "In

O Pioneers! the whole complex range of women's experience and imagination—words, gestures, the making of things—is primary" (259). For Gilbert and Gubar, the journey west undermines rather than solidifies male authority making way for the primacy of female experience: "Cather creates a mythic America which is girlhood, for she tells the story of the gender dislocation fostered by immigration into the wilderness, a dislocation that results in the death of the father, the diminution of the son, and the empowerment of the daughter with the concomitant centrality of female work" (184). Lee and Stout likewise focus on Alexandra's subversion of male authority. According to Lee, "Just as the older brothers ineffectually try to contain Alexandra in a traditional, subordinate role ... so Frank wants to bend 'dat woman' to his will. Alexandra survives by transcending all 'roles,' and by taking over the land which had been, up to then, male property" (114). Stout argues that "[t]hrough the voice of Alexandra, Cather ... asserts her commitment to equality of the sexes" (115). For Westling, by contrast, "Cather's impulses toward a positive female agency fail to break out of a masculinist network of codes.... [T]he lesbian eroticism that connects Alexandra to her land finally serves the same purpose of masking and justifying exploitation that heterosexual eroticism serves for male writers" (70).

15. Evidence suggests that Cather would have been well aware of the rise in sexology discourse that pathologized lesbianism. According to Carroll Smith-Rosenberg, such discourse grew increasingly common in the 1890s after the publication of Krafft-Ebing's *Psychopathia Sexualis* in 1886 and reached a fervor in the first decades of the twentieth century as resistance to suffrage grew (265–80). In 1892, Cather wrote to her intimate friend Louise Pound decrying the fact that friendships between women had been deemed unnatural (Stout 55).

16. Cather's use of the fluid is undoubtedly influenced by her reading of William James early in her career when she claimed to be a "devoted disciple" of his work (Seibel 202). In the late nineteenth century, James offered a new conception of the mind as a "free water of consciousness" (195) where to survive we must select some information and suppress the rest (203). Language served as the "by product" of selective attention, filtering and familiarizing experience, but, at the same time, the key was not to become too closed off to the confusing fluid (Ruddick, "Fluid Symbols" 339–40). To be dynamic, the mind had to adopt a kind of "plasticity" in order to assimilate the new (quoted in "Fluid Symbols" 340). For Cather, the (white) New Woman would most likely retain that crucial balance.

17. This passage reiterates, in some respects, Annette Kolodny's conclusions concerning women's relationship to the prairie: "women reveal themselves healed, renewed, revitalized—and even psychically reborn—in a country, as Margaret Fuller put it, 'such ... as I had never seen, even in my dreams'" (8). Tom Quirk suggests that this passage may have been inspired by Cather's reading of Henri Bergson's *Creative Evolution* (Quirk 134).

18. Similarly, in *The Song of the Lark,* Wunsch would compare Thea to a "glass full of sweet-smelling, sparkling Moselle wine. He seemed to see such a glass before him in the arbor, to watch the bubbles rising and breaking, like the silent discharge of energy in the nerves and brain, the rapid florescence in young blood" (30). The key difference, however, is that Thea is able, unlike the less assimilable Bohemian ethnics, to manage that dangerous intoxicant.

19. See Gelfant (xxviii–xxix), Wiesenthal (53), and Westling (69).

20. I am indebted to bell hooks's reading of *The Cook, the Thief, His Wife, and Her Lover* in her chapter "Eating the Other" of *Black Looks.*

21. Harold Wilson argues that while the muckrakers accepted social Darwinism, they also affirmed Christian social teaching (308).

22. In "Full-Blooded Writing and Journalistic Fictions: Naturalism, the Female Artist, and Willa Cather's *Song of the Lark,*" Amy Ahearn makes a persuasive case for the naturalistic origins the novel.

Conclusion

1. Consider, for example, Dale Bauer's argument that in Wharton's later fiction Wharton engages a wide range of social and political issues—including eugenics, fascism, Bolshevism, and mass culture—in a fashion that allows her to interrogate her "own values by imagining real alternatives to [her] own" (9).

BIBLIOGRAPHY

Adams, Henry. "The Dynamo and the Virgin." *The Education of Henry Adams,* ed. Ernest Samuels. Boston: Houghton Mifflin, 1973.

Adams, John H., Jr. "Rough Sketches: A Study of the Features of the New Negro Woman." *Voice of the Negro* (Aug. 1904): 323–26.

———. "Rough Sketches: 'The New Negro Man.'" *Voice of the Negro* (Oct. 1904): 447–52.

Ahearn, Amy. "Full-Blooded Writing and Journalistic Fictions: Naturalism, the Female Artist and Willa Cather's *The Song of the Lark.*" *American Literary Realism* 33 (2001): 143–56.

Albertini, Virgil. "Willa Cather and the Bicycle." *Platte Valley Review* 15, no. 1 (1987): 12–22.

Ammons, Elizabeth. *Conflicting Stories: American Women Writers at the Turn into the Twentieth Century.* New York: Oxford University Press, 1992.

———. "The Engineer as Cultural Hero and Willa Cather's First Novel, *Alexander's Bridge.*" *American Quarterly* 38, no. 5 (1986): 746–60.

———. "The New Woman as Cultural Symbol and Social Reality: Six Women Writers' Perspectives." In *1915, the Cultural Moment: The New Politics, the New Woman, the New Psychology, the New Art, and the New Theater in America,* ed. Adele Heller and Lois Rudnick. New Brunswick: Rutgers University Press, 1991. 82–97.

Anargyros, S. "Turkish Trophies." Advertisement. *Life,* Sept. 26, 1901.

Antin, Mary. *The Promised Land.* Boston: Houghton Mifflin Co., 1912.

Ardis, Ann. *New Women, New Novels: Feminism and Early Modernism.* New Brunswick: Rutgers University Press, 1990.

Armstrong, Tim. *Modernism, Technology, and the Body: A Cultural History.* Cambridge: Cambridge University Press, 1998.

Atherton, Gertrude. *Patience Sparhawk and Her Times.* New York: John Lane, 1897.

Atwood, Elizabeth. "'Saratoga of the South': Tourism in Luray, Virginia, 1878–1905." In *The Edge of the South: Life in Nineteenth-Century Virginia,* ed. Edward L. Ayers and John C. Willis. Charlottesville: University Press of Virginia, 1991.

Austin, Mary. *A Woman of Genius.* Old Westbury, N.Y.: Feminist Press, 1985.

———. *Earth Horizon.* New York: Riverside Press, 1932.

Ayers, Edward L. *The Promise of the New South: Life after Reconstruction.* New York: Oxford University Press, 1993.

Banner, Lois W. *American Beauty.* Chicago: University of Chicago Press, 1984.

Banta, Martha. *Imaging American Women: Idea and Ideals in Cultural History.* New York: Columbia University Press, 1987.

————. *Taylored Lives: Narrative Productions in the Age of Taylor, Veblen, and Ford.* Chicago: University Chicago Press, 1993.

Bardes, Barbara, and Suzanne Gossett. *Declarations of Independence: Women and Political Power in Nineteenth-Century American Fiction.* New Brunswick: Rutgers University Press, 1990.

Bauer, Dale M. *Edith Wharton's Brave New Politics.* Madison: University of Wisconsin Press, 1994.

Baym, Nina. *Woman's Fiction: A Guide to Novels by and about Women in America, 1820–1870.* Ithaca: Cornell University Press, 1978.

Behling, Laura L. *The Masculine Woman in America, 1890–1935.* Urbana: University of Illinois Press, 2001.

Bender, Bert. *The Descent of Love: Darwin and the Theory of Sexual Selection in American Fiction, 1871–1926.* Philadelphia: University of Pennsylvania, 1996.

Bennett, Johnstone. Photograph. n.d. Merriman Scrapbooks. Curtis Theatre Collection. University of Pittsburgh Library System.

Benstock, Shari. *No Gifts from Chance: A Biography of Edith Wharton.* New York: Scribner's, 1994.

Berg, Allison. *Mothering the Race: Women's Narratives of Reproduction, 1890–1930.* Urbana: University of Illinois Press, 2002.

Bergson, Henri. *Creative Evolution.* New York: Random House, 1944.

Berkson, Dorothy. "'A Goddess behind a Sordid Veil': The Domestic Heroine Meets the Labor Novel in Mary E. Wilkins Freeman's *The Portion of Labor.*" In *Redefining the Political Novel: American Women Writers, 1797–1901.* Knoxville: University of Tennessee Press, 1995.

Betts, Lillian. "The New Woman." *Outlook* 12 (1895): 587.

Bingham, Edwin R. *Charles F. Lummis, Editor of the Southwest.* San Marion, Calif.: Huntington Library, 1955.

Blankley, Elyse. "Beyond the 'Talent of Knowing': Gertrude Stein and the New Woman." In *Critical Essays on Gertrude Stein,* ed. Michael J. Hoffman. Boston: Hall, 1986. 196–209.

Bone, Charles, Rev. "The Awakening of the Women of China." *Independent* (Sept. 18, 1913): 669–70.

"Books of the Week." *Providence Sunday Journal,* June 4, 1899. In Kate Chopin's *The Awakening,* ed. Margaret Culley. New York: Norton, 1976.

Bowler, Peter J. *The Eclipse of Darwinism: Anti-Darwinian Evolution Theories in the Decades around 1900.* Baltimore: Johns Hopkins University Press, 1983.

Braithwaite, William Stanley. "Negro America's First Magazine." *Negro Digest* (Dec. 1947): 21–26.

Brodhead, Richard H. *Cultures of Letters: Scenes of Reading and Writing in Nineteenth-Century America.* Chicago: University of Chicago Press, 1993.

Bronner, Simon J. *Consuming Visions: Accumulation and Display of Goods in America, 1880–1920.* New York: Norton, 1989.

Bruce, John E. Papers. New York Public Library.

Buhle, Mary Jo. *Women and American Socialism, 1870–1920.* Urbana: University of Illinois Press, 1981.

Burgess-Ware, M. Louise. "Bernice, the Octoroon." *Short Fiction by Black Women, 1900–1920,* ed. Henry Louis Gates Jr., coll. Elizabeth Ammons. New York: Oxford University Press, 1991. 250–75.

Butler, Judith. *Bodies That Matter: On the Discursive Limits of "Sex."* New York: Routledge, 1993.

———. *Gender Trouble: Feminism and the Subversion of Identity.* New York: Routledge, 1990.

Byrne, Kathleen D., and Richard C. Snyder. *Chrysalis: Willa Cather in Pittsburgh, 1896–1906.* Pittsburgh: Historical Society of Western Pennsylvania, 1980.

Carby, Hazel. *Reconstructing Womanhood: The Emergence of the Afro-American Woman Novelist.* New York: Oxford University Press, 1987.

Cash, Floris Loretta Barnett. "Womanhood and Protest: The Club Movement among Black Women, 1892–1922." Ph.D. diss. State University of New York, 1986. Ann Arbor: UMI, 1997. ATT 8704374.

Cassel. "New Woman Club Rules." Cartoon. *Life,* Dec. 2, 1897, 464.

Cather, Willa. *Alexander's Bridge.* New York: Oxford University Press, 1997.

———. "Behind the Singer Tower." 1912. *Twenty-four Stories,* comp. Sharon O'Brien. New York: Signet, 1988. 277–91.

———. "The Bohemian Girl." 1912. *Twenty-four Stories,* comp. Sharon O'Brien. New York: Signet, 1988. 292–340.

———. *Calendar of Letters.* Lincoln: University of Nebraska Press, 2002.

———. "Eric Hermannson's Soul." 1900. *Twenty-four Stories,* comp. Sharon O'Brien. New York: Signet, 1988. 92–117.

———. *The Kingdom of Art: Willa Cather's First Principles and Critical Statements, 1893–1896,* ed. Bernice Slote. Lincoln: University of Nebraska Press, 1966.

———. *O Pioneers!* Lincoln: University of Nebraska Press, 1992.

———. *The Song of the Lark.* Lincoln: University of Nebraska Press, 1978.

———. "Tommy the Unsentimental." 1896. *Twenty-four Stories,* comp. Sharon O'Brien. New York: Signet, 1988. 62–71.

———. *The Troll Garden.* Lincoln: University of Nebraska Press, 1983.

———. *The World and the Parish: Willa Cather's Articles and Reviews, 1893–1902,* ed. William M. Curtin. 2 vols. Lincoln: University of Nebraska Press, 1970.

Cella, C. Ronald. *Mary Johnston.* Boston: Twayne, 1981.

Charles Scribner's Sons. "Edith Wharton's new novel concentrates upon the social topics of the moment—especially divorce." Advertisement. *Boston Evening Transcript,* Oct. 25, 1913.

Chong, Key Ray. *Americans and Chinese Reform and Revolution, 1898–1922.* Lanham: University Press of America, 1984.

Chopin, Kate. *The Awakening,* ed. Margaret Culley. New York: W. W. Norton, 1976.

Christy, Howard Chandler. *The American Girl.* New York: Moffat, Yard, and Co., 1906.

Chu, Patricia Press. *Assimilating Asians: Gendered Strategies of Authorship in Asian America.* Durham: Duke University Press, 2000.

Clarke, Michael Tavel. "These Days of Large Things: The Culture of Size in America, 1865–1930" Ph.D. diss. University of Iowa, 2001.

Clifford, James. *The Predicament of Culture: Twentieth-Century Ethnography, Literature, and Art.* Cambridge: Harvard University Press, 1988.

Collins, James H. "The Eternal Feminine." *Printers' Ink* (June 26, 1901): 3–5.

"The Colored Magazine in America." *Crisis* (Nov. 5, 1912): 33–35.

Connoly, Louise. "The New Woman." Letter to the editor. *Harper's Weekly.* June 7, 1913: 6.

Cooper, Anna Julia. *A Voice from the South.* New York: Oxford University Press, 1988.

Cooper, John Milton, Jr. *The Warrior and the Priest: Woodrow Wilson and Theodore Roosevelt.* Cambridge: Belknap Press of Harvard University Press, 1983.

Cott, Nancy F. *The Grounding of Modern Feminism.* New Haven: Yale University Press, 1987.

Crawford, Robert. "A Cultural Account of 'Health': Self-Control, Release, and the Social Body." In *Issues in the Political Economy of Health Care,* ed. John McKinlay. New York: Methuen, 1985. 60–103.

Cutter, Martha J. *Unruly Tongue: Identity and Voice in American Women's Writing, 1850–1930.* Jackson: University Press of Mississippi, 1999.

Darwin, Charles. *The Descent of Man, and Selection in Relation to Sex.* 1871; Princeton: Princeton University Press, 1981.

———. *The Descent of Man, and Selection in Relation to Sex.* Down, Beckenham, Kent, 1874, http://www.gutenberg.org/dirs/etext00/dscmn10.txt (accessed Mar. 6, 2005).

———. *The Origin of Species.* New York: Penguin, 1958.

Davis, Richard Harding. *Soldiers of Fortune.* New York: Charles Scribner's Sons, 1897.

De Koven, Anna. "The Athletic Woman." *Good Housekeeping* (Aug. 1912): 148–57.

DeKoven, Marianne. *Rich and Strange: Gender, History, and Modernism.* Princeton: Princeton University Press, 1991.

Deland, Margaret. "The Change in the Feminine Ideal." *Atlantic Monthly* (Mar. 1910): 289–302.

Den Tandt, Christophe. "Amazons and Androgynes: Overcivilization and the Redefinition of Gender Roles at the Turn of the Century." *American Literary History* 8, no. 4 (Winter 1996): 639–64.

Dew, Charles B. *Ironmaker to the Confederacy: Joseph R. Anderson and the Tredegar Iron Works.* New Haven: Yale University Press, 1966.

Dickinson, Robert L. "Bicycling for Women from the Standpoint of the Gynecologist." *American Journal of Obstetrics and Diseases of Women and Children* 21 (1895): 25–37.

Dijkstra, Bram. *Idols of Perversity: Fantasies of Feminine Evil in Fin-de-Siècle Culture.* New York: Oxford University Press, 1986.

Dixon, Thomas. *The Leopard's Spots: A Romance of the White Man's Burden—1895–1900.* New York: Doubleday, 1902.

Doan, Laura L. *Old Maids to Radical Spinsters: Unmarried Women in the Twentieth-Century Novel.* Urbana: University of Illinois Press, 1991.

Donovan, Josephine. *After the Fall: The Demeter-Persephone Myth in Wharton, Cather, and Glasgow.* University Park: Pennsylvania State University Press, 1989.

Douglas, Mary. *Purity and Danger: An Analysis of the Concepts of Pollution and Taboo.* London: Routledge and Kegan Paul, 1978.

Downey, Fairfax. *Portrait of an Era as Drawn by C. D. Gibson: A Biography.* New York: Scribner's, 1936.

Doyle, Don. *New Men, New Cities, New South: Atlanta, Nashville, Charleston, Mobile, 1860–1910.* Chapel Hill: University of North Carolina Press, 1990.

Dreiser, Theodore. *Jennie Gerhardt,* ed. James L. W. West III. New York: Penguin Books, 1994.

Du Bois, W. E. B. *The Correspondence of W. E. B. Du Bois: Selections, 1877–1934,* ed. Herbert Aptheker. Amherst: University of Massachusetts Press, 1973.

DuCille, Ann. *The Coupling Convention: Sex, Text, and Tradition in Black Women's Fiction.* New York: Oxford University Press, 1993.

Dupree, Ellen. "Jamming the Machinery: Mimesis in *The Custom of the Country.*" *American Literary Realism, 1870–1910* 22, no. 2 (1990): 5–16.

———. "The New Woman, Progressivism, and the Woman Writer in Edith Wharton's *The Fruit of the Tree.*" *American Literary Realism, 1870–1910* 31, no. 2 (1999): 44–62.

Eastman Kodak Co. "Folding Pocket Kodak." Advertisement. *Life,* Mar. 27, 1902.

Edison, Thomas A. "The Woman of the Future." *Good Housekeeping Magazine* (Oct. 1912): 436–44.

"Editorial and Publishers' Announcements." *Colored American Magazine* (May 1900): 60–64.

E. F. E. "Mary Johnston's Feminist Novel." *Boston Evening Transcript* (Oct. 25, 1913): 8.

Ellis, Havelock. "Sexual Inversion in Women." *Alienist and Neurologist: A Quarterly Journal of Scientific, Clinical, and Forensic Psychiatry and Neurology* 16 (1896): 141–58.

Eltzbacher, O. "The Yellow Peril." *Living Age* (July 23, 1904): 223–35.

"The Face of Romance and the Face of Reality." *New York World,* Aug. 16, 1895.

Felski, Rita. *The Gender of Modernity.* Cambridge: Harvard University Press, 1995.

Ferber, Edna. *Roast Beef, Medium.* Urbana: University of Illinois Press, 2001.

Ferens, Dominika. *Edith and Winnifred Eaton: Chinatown Missions and Japanese Romances.* Urbana: University of Illinois Press, 2002.

Finck, Henry T. "The Evolution of Sex in Mind." *The Independent* 53 (1901): 3059–64.

Finnegan, Margaret. *Selling Suffrage: Consumer Culture and Votes for Women.* New York: Columbia University Press, 1999.

Fire Fly [Edith Eaton]. "The Girl of the Period." *Gall's Daily News Letter,* Jan. 19, 1897.

———. "The Woman about Town." *Galls Daily News Letter,* Dec. 14, 1896, 27.

Fisher, Dexter. Foreward to *American Indian Stories.* Lincoln: University of Nebraska Press, 1985.

Fleissner, Jennifer. *Women, Compulsion, Modernity: The Movement of American Naturalism.* Chicago: University of Chicago Press, 2004.

Foster, Gaines M. *Ghosts of the Confederacy: Defeat, the Lost Cause, and the Emergence of the New South, 1865 to 1913.* New York: Oxford University Press, 1987.

Fox, James. *Five Sisters: The Langhornes of Virginia.* New York: Simon and Schuster, 2000.

F. P. C. Wax. Advertisement. *Life,* Mar. 17, 1904, 275.

Franklin Heirloom Dolls. "The Gibson Girl Bride Doll." Advertisement. *Star,* Sept. 22, 1992, 21.

Freeman, Mary Wilkins. *The Portion of Labor.* 1901. Ridgewood, N.J.: Gregg Press, 1967.

Fryer, Judith. *Felicitous Space: The Imaginative Structures of Edith Wharton and Willa Cather.* Chapel Hill: University of North Carolina Press, 1986.

Gaines, Kevin K. "Black Americans' Racial Uplift Ideology as 'Civilizing Mission': Pauline E. Hopkins on Race and Imperialism." In *Cultures of United States Imperialism,* ed. Amy Kaplan and Donald E. Pease. Durham: Duke University Press, 1993. 443–55.

———. *Uplifting the Race: Black Leadership, Politics, and Culture in the Twentieth Century.* Chapel Hill: University of North Carolina Press, 1996.

Garvey, Ellen Gruber. *The Adman in the Parlor: Magazines and the Gendering of Consumer Culture, 1880s to 1910.* Oxford: Oxford University Press, 1996.

Gaston, Paul M. *The New South Creed: A Study in Southern Mythmaking.* New York: Knopf, 1970.

Gates, Henry Louis, Jr. "The Trope of a New Negro and the Reconstruction of the Image of the Black." *Representations* 24 (1988): 129–55.

Geddes, Patrick, and Arthur J. Thomson. *The Evolution of Sex.* 1889; New York: Walter Scott Publishing Co., 1908.

Gelfant, Blanche H. Introduction to *O Pioneers!* by Willa Cather. New York: Penguin, 1989. vii–xxxvi.

Gere, Anne Ruggles. *Intimate Practices: Literacy and Cultural Work in U.S. Women's Clubs, 1880–1920.* Urbana: University of Illinois Press, 1997.

Gibson, Charles Dana. *Americans.* New York: Scribner's, 1900.

———. *The Education of Mr. Pipp.* New York: Scribner's, 1899.

———. *Everyday People.* New York: Scribner's, 1904.

———. "Girls Will Be Girls." Cartoon. *Life,* July 8, 1897, 30–31.

———. "In Days to Come Who Will Look after This Boy?" Cartoon. *Life,* June 4, 1896, 458–59.

———. "One of the Disadvantages of Being in Love with an Athletic Girl." *Life,* May 22, 1902, 446–47.

———. *Other People.* New York: Scribner's, 1911.

———. *Sketches and Cartoons.* New York: R. H. Russell, 1898.

———. *The Social Ladder.* New York: Scribner's, 1902.

———. "St. Valentines No." *Life,* Feb. 5, 1903, cover.

———. *The Weaker Sex.* New York: Scribner's, 1903.

Gibson, Prof., and Mrs. J. L. *Golden Thoughts on Chastity and Procreation.* Cincinnati: W. H. Ferguson, 1904.

Giddings, Paula. *When and Where I Enter: The Impact of Black Women on Race and Sex in America.* New York: W. Morrow, 1984.

Gilbert, Sandra M., and Susan Gubar. *No Man's Land: The Place of the Woman Writer in the Twentieth Century*, vol. 2. New Haven: Yale University Press, 1989.

Gilman, Charlotte Perkins. *The Man-Made World or Our Androcentric Culture.* New York: Charlton Co., 1911.

———. "Personal Problems." *The Forerunner.* July 1910. *Project Gutenberg,* comp. Christopher Hapka. Jan. 2002. http://www.ibiblio.org/gutenberg/etext02/forer10.txt.

———. *What Diantha Did.* New York: Charlton Co., 1910.

———. *Women and Economics,* ed. Carl N. Degler. New York: Harper Torchbooks, 1966.

Gilman, Sander, ed. *Degeneration: The Dark Side of Progress.* New York: Columbia University Press, 1985.

Glasgow, Ellen. *The Ancient Law.* New York: Doubleday, Page and Co., 1908.

———. *A Certain Measure: An Interpretation of Prose Fiction.* New York: Harcourt, Brace and Co., 1938.

———. *The Descendant.* New York: Harper and Brothers, 1897.

———. *Letters of Ellen Glasgow,* ed. Blair Rouse. New York: Harcourt, 1958.

———. *Life and Gabriella: The Story of a Woman's Courage.* Garden City, N.Y.: Doubleday, Page and Co., 1916.

———. Preface to *Virginia.* New York: Scribner's, 1938. ix–xxi.

———. *Virginia.* New York: Doubleday, 1913.

———. *Voice of the People.* New York: Doubleday, 1900.

———. *The Woman Within.* New York: Harcourt, 1954.

Glenn, Susan A. *Daughters of the Shtetl: Life and Labor in the Immigrant Generation.* Ithaca: Cornell University Press, 1990.

Godbold, Stanly E. *Ellen Glasgow and the Woman Within.* Baton Rouge: Louisiana State University Press, 1972.

Godden, Richard. *Fictions of Capital: The American Novel from James to Mailer.* Cambridge: Cambridge University Press, 1990.

Goldberg, Jonathan. *Willa Cather and Others.* Durham: Duke University Press, 2001.

Goodman, Susan. *Ellen Glasgow: A Biography.* Baltimore: Johns Hopkins University Press, 1998.

Grand, Sarah. "The New Aspect of the Woman Question." *North American Review* (Mar. 1894): 270–76.

Grant, Robert. "Charles Dana Gibson: The Man and His Art." *Collier's Weekly* (Nov. 29, 1902): 8–9.

———. *Unleavened Bread.* New York: Scribner's, 1900.

Gregoire, Marie. "The Bathing Suit Beautiful." *Collier's Weekly* (Aug. 2, 1902): 14.

Hackett, Alice Payne. *Fifty Years of Best Sellers, 1895–1945.* New York: R. R. Bowker Co., 1945.

Haller, John S., Jr. *Outcasts from Evolution: Scientific Attitudes of Racial Inferiority, 1859–1900.* Carbondale: Southern Illinois University Press, 1971.

Hanmer, Trudy J. "A Divine Discontent: Mary Johnston and Woman Suffrage in Virginia." M.A. thesis. University of Virginia, 1972.

Harbaugh, William H. *The Writings of Theodore Roosevelt.* Indianapolis: Bobbs-Merrill, 1967.

Hawley, Ellis W. *The New Deal and the Problem of Monopoly.* Princeton: Princeton University Press, 1996.

Heller, Adele, and Lois Rudnick, eds. *1915, the Cultural Moment: The New Politics, the New Woman, the New Psychology, the New Art, and the New Theatre in America.* New Brunswick: Rutgers University Press, 1989.

Hendrick, Burton. "The Skulls of Our Immigrants." *McClure's* 35 (1910): 36–50.

Hennessy, Rosemary. *Materialist Feminism and the Politics of Discourse.* New York: Routledge, 1993.

"Here Is the New Woman." *New York World,* Aug. 18, 1895, n.p.

Hine, Darlene Clark. *Black Women in America: An Historical Encyclopedia.* Brooklyn: Carlson, 1993.

Hinton, C. Howard. *The Fourth Dimension.* London: Swan Sonnenschein, 1906.

Hirata, Lucie Cheng. "Chinese Immigrant Women in Nineteenth-Century California." In *Women of America: A History,* ed. Carol Ruth Berkin and Mary Beth Norton. Boston: Houghton Mifflin, 1979.

"Ho! For the Suffragettes!" Cartoon. *Life,* Jan. 12, 1911, 141.

Hofstadter, Richard. *Social Darwinism in American Thought 1860–1915.* Philadelphia: University of Pennsylvania Press, 1945.

hooks, bell. *Black Looks: Race and Representation.* Boston: South End Press, 1992.

Hopkins, Pauline. *Contending Forces.* Carbondale: Southern Illinois University Press, 1978.

———. "Famous Men of the Negro Race: Booker T. Washington." *Colored American Magazine* (Oct. 1901): 436–41.

———. *Hagar's Daughter: A Story of Southern Caste Prejudice.* 1901–2. In *The Magazine Novels of Pauline Hopkins,* ed. Henry Louis Gates Jr. New York: Oxford University Press, 1988. 2–284.

————. *Of One Blood.* 1902–3. In *The Magazine Novels of Pauline Hopkins,* ed. Henry Louis Gates Jr. New York: Oxford University Press, 1988. 439–621.

————. *Winona.* 1903. In *The Magazine Novels of Pauline Hopkins,* ed. Henry Louis Gates Jr. New York: Oxford University Press, 1988. 285–437.

————. "Women's Department." June 1900: 118–23.

Houghton Mifflin Company. "A Great Novelist's Plea for the Emancipation of Women." *Boston Evening Transcript* (Oct. 25, 1913): 8.

Irigaray, Luce. *This Sex Which Is Not One.* Ithaca: Cornell University Press, 1985.

James, William. *Selected Writings,* ed. G. H. Bird. Rutland, Vt.: Charles E. Tuttle, 1995.

Jeffreys, Sheila. *The Spinster and Her Enemies: Feminism and Sexuality, 1880–1930.* North Melbourne, Australia: Spinifex Press, 1985.

Jewett, Sarah Orne. "Tom's Husband." In *Novels and Stories.* New York: First Library of America, 1996.

Johnson, Abby Arthur, and Ronald Mayberry Johnson. "Away from Accommodation: Radical Editors and Protest Journalism, 1900–1910." *Journal of Negro History* 62 (1977): 325–38.

Johnston, Mary. *Hagar.* Charlottesville: University Press of Virginia, 1994.

————. "'Tea and Metaphysics': Excerpts from Mary Johnston's Diary." *Ellen Glasgow Newsletter* (Oct. 1983): 2–9.

————. "The Woman's War." *Atlantic Monthly* (Apr. 1910): 559–70.

Jones, Anne Goodwyn. *Tomorrow Is Another Day: The Woman Writer in the South, 1859–1936.* Baton Rouge: Louisiana State University Press, 1981.

Kaplan, Amy. *The Anarchy of Empire in the Making of U.S. Culture.* Cambridge: Harvard University Press, 2002.

Kassanoff, Jennie A. "Corporate Thinking: Edith Wharton's *The Fruit of the Tree.*" *Arizona Quarterly* 53, no. 1 (1997): 25–59.

————. "'Fate Has Linked Us Together': Blood, Gender, and the Politics of Representation in Pauline Hopkins's *Of One Blood.*" In *The Unruly Voice: Rediscovering Pauline Elizabeth Hopkins,* ed. John Cullen Gruesser. Urbana: University of Illinois Press, 1996.

Katzman, David M. *Seven Days a Week: Women and Domestic Service in Industrializing America.* New York: Oxford University Press, 1978.

Kellogg, Vernon L. *Darwinism To-Day.* London: Holt, 1908.

Kemble, Edward. "Pardon me, Miss Saffron." *Life,* Oct. 5, 1899, cover.

Kennedy, David M. *Birth Control in America: The Career of Margaret Sanger.* New Haven: Yale University Press, 1973.

Kibler, M. Alison. *Rank Ladies: Gender and Cultural Hierarchy in American Vaudeville.* Chapel Hill: University of North Carolina Press, 1999.

Kinnosuke, Adachi. "The New Woman in China and Japan." *American Review of Reviews* (July 1912): 71–77.

Kitchelt, Florence Ledyard Cross. "An Excerpt from the Journal of Florence Ledyard Cross Kitchelt." Apr. 3, 1901. *The Booker T. Washington Papers,* vol. 6, ed. Louis R. Harlan and Raymond W. Smock. Urbana: University of Illinois Press, 1977. 84–85.

Knupfer, Anne Meis. *Toward a Tenderer Humanity and a Nobler Womanhood: African American Women's Clubs in Turn-of-the-Century Chicago.* New York: New York University Press, 1996.

Koch, Robert. "Gibson Girl Revisited." *Art in America* 53, no. 1 (1965): 70–73.

Kolodny, Annette. *The Land before Her: Fantasy and Experience of the American Frontiers, 1630–1860.* Chapel Hill: University of North Carolina Press, 1984.

Kraditor, Aileen S. *The Ideas of the Woman Suffrage Movement, 1890–1920.* New York: W. W. Norton and Co., 1981.

Krafft-Ebing, Richard von. *Psychopathia Sexualis: A Medico-Forensic Study.* New York: G. P. Putnam's Sons, 1965.

LaChiusa, Chuck. "Evelyn Rumsey Cary." June 2001. Preservation Coalition of Erie County. Dec. 17, 2002. http://bfn.org/preservationworks/hist/essays/panwho/carye/carye.html.

Leach, William. *Land of Desire: Merchants, Power, and the Rise of a New American Culture.* New York: Pantheon, 1993.

Lears, Jackson. *No Place of Grace: Antimodernism and the Transformation of American Culture 1880–1920.* New York: Pantheon, 1981.

Lebsock, Suzanne. "Woman Suffrage and White Supremacy: A Virginia Case Study." In *Visible Women: New Essays on American Activism,* ed. Nancy A. Hewitt and Suzanne Lebsock. Urbana: University of Illinois Press, 1993. 62–100.

Lee, Hermione. *Willa Cather: Double Lives.* New York: Pantheon, 1989.

Lee, Yan Phou. "The Chinese Must Stay." In *Racism, Dissent, and Asian Americans from 1850 to the Present,* ed. Philip S. Foner and Daniel Rosenberg. Westport: Greenwood Press, 1993. 113–18.

Lemmah, L. "The New God." *Fly Leaf* (Jan. 1896): 21–23.

Lewis, R. W. B. *Edith Wharton: A Biography.* New York: Harper and Row, 1975.

"*Life*'s Suffragette Contest." *Life,* Dec. 8, 1910, 1050.

Lindemann, Marilee. Introduction to *Alexander's Bridge,* by Willa Cather. New York: Oxford University Press, 1997. vii–xxxvii.

———. *Willa Cather: Queering America.* New York: Columbia University Press, 1999.

Ling, Amy. *Between Worlds: Women Writers of Chinese Ancestry.* New York: Pergamon Press, 1990.

Lissak, Rivka Shpak. *Pluralism and Progressives: Hull House and the New Immigrants, 1890–1919.* Chicago: University of Chicago Press, 1989.

Lock, Robert Heath. *Recent Progress in the Study of Variation Heredity, and Evolution.* London: John Murray, Albemarle Street, 1906.

Locke, Alain. "The New Negro." In *The New Negro,* ed. Alain Locke. New York: Touchstone, 1997. 3–16.

Lowe, Lisa. *Immigrant Acts: On Asian American Cultural Politics.* Durham: Duke University Press, 1996.

Lury, Celia. *Consumer Culture.* New Brunswick: Rutgers University Press, 1996.

Lutz, Tom. *American Nervousness, 1903.* Ithaca: Cornell University Press, 1991.

MacComb, Debra Ann. "New Wives for Old: Divorce and the Leisure-Class Marriage Market in Edith Wharton's *The Custom of the Country.*" *American Literature* 68, no. 4 (1996): 765–97.

Magruder, Julia. "The Typical Woman of the New South." *Harper's Bazaar* (Nov. 3, 1900): 1685–87.

Marchalonis, Shirley. *College Girls: A Century in Fiction.* New Brunswick: Rutgers University Press, 1995.

Marks, Patricia. *Bicycles, Bangs, and Bloomers.* Lexington: University Press of Kentucky, 1990.

Marschall, Richard E. "Life." In *American Humor Magazines and Comic Periodicals,* ed. David E. E. Sloane. New York: Greenwood Press, 1987.

Matthews, Pamela. *Ellen Glasgow and a Woman's Traditions.* Charlottesville: University Press of Virginia, 1994.

McCracken, Grant. *Culture and Consumption: New Approaches to the Symbolic Character of Consumer Goods and Activities.* Bloomington: Indiana University Press, 1988.

McCullough, Kate. *Regions of Identity: The Construction of America in Women's Fiction, 1885–1914.* Stanford: Stanford University Press, 1999.

Michaels, Walter Benn. "The Souls of White Folk." In *Literature and the Body: Essays on Populations and Persons,* ed. Elaine Scarry. Baltimore: Johns Hopkins University Press, 1986.

———. "Corporate Fiction: Norris, Royce, and Arthur Macen." In *Reconstructing American Literary History,* ed. Sacvan Bercovitch. Cambridge: Harvard University Press, 1986.

"Miss Willard on the 'New Woman.'" *Woman's Signal,* Sept. 17, 1896, 181.

Mixon, Wayne. *Southern Writers and the New South Movement, 1865–1913.* Chapel Hill: University of North Carolina Press, 1980.

Moers, Ellen. *Literary Women.* New York: Oxford University Press, 1963.

Montgomery, Mauren E. *Displaying Women: Spectacles of Leisure in Edith Wharton's New York.* New York: Routledge, 1998.

Moody, Winfield Scott. "Daisy Miller and the Gibson Girl." *Ladies' Home Journal* 21 (Sept. 1904): n.p.

Moses, Wilson Jeremiah. *The Golden Age of Black Nationalism 1850–1925.* Hamden: Archon Books, 1978.

Mott, Frank Luther. *A History of American Magazines, 1885–1905,* vol. 4. Cambridge: Harvard University Press, 1957.

Mowry, George E. *The Era of Theodore Roosevelt, 1900–1912.* New York: Harper and Brothers, 1958.

Murphy, John J. *Critical Essays on Willa Cather.* Boston: G. K. Hall and Co., 1984.

National Park Service. "Booker T. Washington: The Oaks." ParkNet. Apr. 7, 2000. http://www.cr.nps.gov/museum/exhibits/tuskegee/btwoaks.htm (accessed Jan. 13, 2003).

Nettels, Elsa. *Language and Gender in American Fiction: Howells, James, Wharton, and Cather.* Charlottesville: University Press of Virginia, 1997.

Newman, Louise Michele. *White Women's Rights: The Racial Origins of Feminism in the United States.* New York: Oxford University Press, 1999.

"A New Note in Fiction." *New York Times,* July 7, 1912, 405.

"The New Power and Woman." *Independent* (Feb. 6, 1902): 356–58.

Newton, Esther. "The Mythic Mannish Lesbian: Radclyffe Hall and the New Woman." In *Hidden from History: Reclaiming the Gay and Lesbian Past,* ed. Martin Bauml Duberman, Martha Vicinus, and George Chauncey Jr. New York: Penguin, 1989. 281–93.

"The New Woman." Advertisement for *The Country Gentleman. Ladies' Home Journal* (Oct. 1913).

"The New Woman." *National Labor Tribune,* Aug. 26, 1897, n.p.

"The New Woman." *Woman's Tribune,* June 8, 1895, 90.

Numbers, Ronald L., and Lester D. Stephens. "Darwinism in the American South." In *Disseminating Darwinism: The Role of Place, Race, Religion, and Gender,* ed. Ronald L. Numbers and John Stenhouse. Cambridge: Cambridge University Press, 1999. 123–43.

Nye, David. *Electrifying America: Social Meanings of a New Technology, 1880–1940.* Cambridge: MIT Press, 1990.

Oates, Stephen B. *To Purge This Land with Blood: A Biography of John Brown.* New York: Harper Torchbooks, 1970.

O'Brien, Sharon. *Willa Cather: The Emerging Voice.* New York: Oxford University Press, 1987.

Otten, Thomas J. "Pauline Hopkins and the Hidden Self of Race." *ELH* 59 (1992): 227–56.

Ouida. "The New Woman." *North American Review* (May 1894): 610–19.

Page, Thomas Nelson. "The Lynching of Negroes—Its Cause and Its Prevention." *North American Review* 178 (1904): 33–48.

———. *Social Life in Old Virginia before the War.* New York: Scribner's, 1897.

Painter, Nell. *Standing at Armageddon: The United States, 1877–1919.* New York: W. W. Norton, 1987.

Parrott, Angie. "'Love Makes Memory Eternal': The United Daughters of the Confederacy in Richmond, Virginia, 1897–1920." In *The Edge of the South: Life in Nineteenth-Century Virginia,* ed. Edward L. Ayers and John C. Willis. Charlottesville: University Press of Virginia, 1991.

Patterson, Martha H. "'kin' o' rough jestice fer a parson': Pauline Hopkins's *Winona* and the Politics of Reconstructing History." *African American Review* 32, no. 3 (1998): 445–60.

Peffer, George Anthony. "Forbidden Families: Emigration Experiences of Chinese Women under the Page Law, 1875–1882." *Journal of American Ethnic History* 6 (1986): 28–46.

Peiss, Kathy. *Cheap Amusements: Working Women and Leisure in Turn-of-the-Century New York.* Philadelphia: Temple University Press, 1986.

Pickens, Donald K. *Eugenics and the Progressives.* Nashville: Vanderbilt University Press, 1968.

Pierce, Charles W. "How Electricity Is Taught at Tuskegee." *Colored American Magazine* 7 (Sept. 1904): 666–73.

Pollard, Percival. "One Failure to Forget." *Fly Leaf* (Feb. 1896): 19–24.

Porcher, Frances. "Kate Chopin's Novel." *Mirror* 9 (May 4, 1899): 6.

Potter, Henry C., Rt. Rev. "Mother and Child." *Harper's Monthly Magazine* 104 (1901): 101–4.

Preston, Claire. *Edith Wharton's Social Register.* New York: St. Martin's, 2000.

"Publisher's Annoucement." *New York Times Book Review* (July 7, 1912): 405.

Quirk, Tom. *Bergson and American Culture: The Worlds of Willa Cather and Wallace Stevens.* Chapel Hill: University of North Carolina Press, 1990.

Raper, J. R. *Without Shelter: The Early Career of Ellen Glasgow.* Baton Rouge: Louisiana State University Press, 1971.

Reynolds, Guy. *Willa Cather in Context: Progress, Race, Empire.* London: Macmillan Press, 1996.

Rief, Michelle. "Thinking Locally, Acting Globally: The International Agenda of African American Clubwomen, 1880–1940." *Journal of African American History* 89 (2004). Academic Search Premier. http://www.mckendree.edu/library/default.htm (accessed Mar. 15, 2005).

Riley, Glenda. *Inventing the American Woman: A Perspective on Women's History 1865 to the Present.* Arlington Heights, Ill.: Harlan Davidson, 1986.

Rosenberg, Rosalind Lee. *Beyond Separate Spheres: Intellectual Roots of Modern Feminism.* New Haven: Yale University Press, 1982.

Rosowski, Susan J. *Birthing a Nation: Gender, Creativity, and the West in American Literature.* Lincoln: University of Nebraska Press, 1999.

————. *The Voyage Perilous: Willa Cather's Romanticism.* Lincoln: University of Nebraska Press, 1986.

Ruddick, Lisa. "Fluid Symbols in American Modernism: William James, Gertrude Stein, George Santayana, and Wallace Stevens." In *Allegory, Myth, and Symbol,* ed. Morton W. Bloomfield. Cambridge: Harvard University Press, 1981.

Rudnick, Lois. "The New Woman." In *1915, the Cultural Moment: The New Politics, the New Woman, the New Psychology, the New Art, and the New Theater in America,* ed. Adele Heller and Lois Rudnick. New Brunswick: Rutgers University Press, 1991. 69–81.

Russett, Cynthia Eagle. *Darwin in America: The Intellectual Response, 1865–1912.* San Francisco: W. H. Freeman and Co., 1976.

————. *Sexual Science: The Victorian Construction of Womanhood.* Cambridge: Harvard University Press, 1989.

Russo, Mary. "Female Grotesques: Carnival and Theory." In *Feminist Studies Critical Studies,* ed. Teresa de Lauretis. Bloomington: Indiana University Press, 1986. 213–29.

Said, Edward W. *Orientalism.* New York: Vintage, 1978.

Salem, Dorothy. *To Better Our World: Black Women in Organized Reform, 1890–1920.* Brooklyn: Carlson, 1990.

Sanborn, F. B. *The Life and Letters of John Brown, Liberator of Kansas, and Martyr of Virginia.* Boston: Roberts Brothers, 1891.

Satter, Beryl. *Each Mind a Kingdom: American Women, Sexual Purity, and the New Thought Movement, 1875–1920.* Berkeley: University of California Press, 1999.

Schrager, Cynthia D. "Pauline Hopkins and William James: The New Psychology and the Politics of Race." In *The Unruly Voice: Rediscovering Pauline Elizabeth Hopkins,* ed. John Cullen Gruesser. Urbana: University of Illinois Press, 1996. 182–209.

Schriber, Marysue. "Darwin, Wharton, and 'The Descent of Man': Blueprints of American Society." *Studies in Short Fiction* 17 (1980): 31–39.

Scott, Anne Firor. *The Southern Lady: From Pedestal to Politics, 1830–1930.* Chicago: University of Chicago Press, 1970.

Scura, Dorothy M., ed. *Ellen Glasgow: The Contemporary Reviews.* Cambridge: Cambridge University Press, 1992.

Seibel, George. "Miss Willa Cather from Nebraska." *New Colophon* 2 (Sept. 1949): 195–208.

Shelton, Charlottte Jean. "Woman Suffrage and Virginia Politics, 1909–1920." M.A. thesis. University of Virginia, 1969.

Showalter, Elaine. *Sexual Anarchy: Gender and Culture at the Fin de Siècle.* New York: Viking, 1990.

Silber, Nina. *The Romance of Reunion: Northerners and the South, 1865–1900.* Chapel Hill: University of North Carolina Press, 1993.

Simms, Joseph. *Physiognomy Illustrated; or, Nature's Revelations of Character.* New York: Murray Hill Publishing, 1887.

Sklar, Martin J. *The Corporate Reconstruction of American Capitalism, 1890–1916: The Market, the Law, and Politics.* Cambridge: Cambridge University Press, 1988.

————. *The United States as a Developing Country: Studies in U.S. History in the Progressive Era and the 1920s.* Cambridge: Cambridge University Press, 1992.

Small, Maynard, and Company. "The Prize on Sylvia's Head is $500." Advertisement. *Life,* Mar. 13, 1902.

Smith, Howard. *Economic History of the United States.* New York: Ronald Press Company, 1955.

Smith, Theophus H. *Conjuring Culture: Biblical Formations of Black America.* New York: Oxford University Press, 1994.

Smith-Rosenberg, Carroll. *Disorderly Conduct: Visions of Gender in Victorian America.* New York: Oxford University Press, 1985.

Sochen, June. *The New Woman in Greenwich Village, 1910–1920.* New York: New York Times Book Co., 1972.

"Some Fresh Suggestions about the New Negro Crime." *Harper's Weekly* (Jan. 23, 1904): 120–21.

Somerville, Siobhan. "Passing through the Closet in Pauline E. Hopkins's *Contending Forces.*" *American Literature* 69 (1997): 139–66.

Spencer, Herbert. *The Principles of Biology,* vol. 2. London: Williams and Norgate, 1899.

Spillers, Hortense. "Mama's Baby, Papa's Maybe: An American Grammar Book." In *Black, White, and in Color: Essays on American Literature and Culture.* Chicago: University of Chicago Press, 2003. 203–229.

Steele, Phyllis Eileen. "Hungry Hearts, Idle Wives, and New Women: The American Novel Re-examines Nineteenth-Century Domestic Ideology, 1890–1917." Ph.D. diss. University of Iowa, 1993.

Stein, Gertrude. *Fernhurst, Q.E.D., and Other Early Writings.* New York: Liveright, 1996.

Stepan, Nancy Leys, and Sander L. Gilman. "Appropriating the Idioms of Science: The Rejection of Scientific Racism." In *The Bounds of Race: Perspectives on Hegemony and Resistance,* ed. Dominick LaCapra. Ithaca: Cornell University Press, 1991. 72–103.

Stokes, Mason. *The Color of Sex: Whiteness, Heterosexuality, and the Fictions of White Supremacy.* Durham: Duke University Press, 2001.

Stout, Janis P. *Willa Cather: The Writer and Her World.* Charlottesville: University Press of Viriginia, 2000.

Sui Seen Far [Edith Eaton]. "The Chinese Woman in America." *Land of Sunshine* (Jan. 1897): 59–64.

———. "The Gamblers." *Fly Leaf* (Feb. 1896): 14–18.

———. "The Story of Iso." *Lotus* (Aug. 1896): 117–19.

Sui Sin Far [Edith Eaton]. "The Chinese in America." *Westerner* (May 10, 1909): 24–25.

———. "Chinese Workmen in America." *Independent* (July 3, 1913): 56–58.

———. "Inferior Woman." *Hampton's Magazine* (May 1910): 727–31.

———. "Leaves from the Mental Portfolio of an Eurasian." *Independent* (Jan. 21, 1909): 125–32.

———. "Leung Ki Chu and His Wife." *Los Angeles Express,* Oct. 22, 1903, n.p.

———. *Mrs. Spring Fragrance.* New York: McClurg, 1912.

———. "The New and the Old." *Westerner* (June 10, 1909): 36–38.

———. "The Reform Party." *Westerner* (Aug. 1909): 26.

———. "Scholar or Cook." *Westerner* (May 1909): 26.

———. "The Story of a Forty-Niner." *Westerner* (July 1909): 18–19.

———. "The Story of Wah." *Westerner* (May 1909): 25–26.

———. "Sui Sin Far, the Half Chinese Writer, Tells of Her Career." *Boston Globe,* May 5, 1912, 6.

Susman, Warren. *Culture as History: The Transformation of American Society in the Twentieth Century.* New York: Pantheon Books, 1984.

Takaki, Ronald. *Strangers from a Different Shore: A History of Asian Americans.* Penguin: 1989.

Tate, Claudia. "Allegories of Black Female Desire; Or, Rereading Nineteenth-Century Sentimental Narratives of Black Female Authority." In *Changing Our Own Words: Essays on Criticism, Theory, and Writing by Black Women,* ed. Cheryl Wall. New Brunswick: Rutgers University Press, 1989. 98–126.

———. *Domestic Allegories of Political Desire: The Black Heroine's Text at the Turn of the Century.* New York: Oxford University Press, 1992.

Tayleur, Eleanor. "The Negro Woman—Social and Moral Decadence." *Outlook* 30 (Jan. 1904): 266–71.

"The Tenth Annual Report of the Tuskegee Woman's Club." 1905. *The Booker T. Washington Papers,* vol. 8, eds. Louise R. Harlan and Raymond W. Smock. Urbana: University of Illinois Press, 1979. 475.

Terborg-Penn, Rosalyn. *African American Women in the Struggle for the Vote, 1850–1920.* Bloomington: Indiana University Press, 1998.

Thayer and Chandler. "Gibson Pyrography." Advertisement. *Life,* Sept. 5, 1901.

Thelan, David P. *Robert M. La Follette and the Insurgent Spirit.* Madison: University of Wisconsin Press, 1985.

Thomspon, Maurice. "Is the New Woman Really New?" In *Chap-Book Essays.* Chicago: Herbert Stone and Co., 1896. 223–50.

Tichi, Cecelia. "Women Writers and the New Woman." In *Columbia Literary History of the United States,* ed. Emory Elliot. New York: Columbia University Press, 1988. 589–606.

———. *Shifting Gears: Technology, Literature, Culture in Modernist America.* Chapel Hill: University of North Carolina Press, 1987.

Ticknor, Caroline. "The Steel-Engraving Lady and the Gibson Girl." *Atlantic Monthly* (July 1901): 107–8.

Tindall, George Brown. *The Emergence of the New South, 1913–1945.* Baton Rouge: Louisiana State University Press, 1967.

Todd, Ellen Wiley. *The 'New Woman' Revised: Painting and Gender Politics on Fourteenth Street.* Berkeley: University of California Press, 1993.

Torgovnick, Marianna. *Gone Primitive: Savage Intellects, Modern Lives.* Chicago: University of Chicago, 1990.

Trachtenberg, Alan. *The Incorporation of America: Culture and Society in the Gilded Age.* New York: Hill and Wang, 1982.

Trimberger, Ellen Kay. "The New Woman and the New Sexuality: Conflict and Contradiction in the Writings and Lives of Mabel Dodge and Neith Boyce." In *1915, The Cultural Moment: The New Politics, the New Woman, the New Psychology, the New Art, and the New Theater in America,* ed. Adele Heller and Lois Rudnick. New Brunswick: Rutgers University Press, 1991. 98–115.

Trustee Company of Seattle. "The Wealth That *Grows*—in Seattle." Advertisement. *Westerner* (May 1909): 25.

Tsai, Shih-Shan Henry. *The Chinese Experience in America.* Bloomington: Indiana University Press, 1986.

Tutwiler, Carrington C., Jr. *Ellen Glasgow's Library.* Charlottesville: Bibliographical Society of the University of Virginia, 1967.

Urgo, Joseph R. "Willa Cather's Political Apprenticeship at *McClure's* Magazine." In *Willa Cather's New York: New Essays on Cather in the City,* ed. Merrill Maguire Skaggs. Cranbury, N.J.: Associate University Press, 2000. 60–74.

Veblen, Thorstein. *The Theory of the Leisure Class.* New York: Viking, 1899.

Walsh, George E. "Electricity in the Household." *Independent* 53 (1901): 556–59.

Ward, Lester F. "Our Better Halves." *Forum* 6 (November 1888): 274–75.

———. *Pure Sociology: A Treatise on the Origin and Spontaneous Development of Society.* New York: Macmillan, 1919.

Washington, Booker T. *Character Building: Being Addresses Delivered on Sunday Evenings to the Students of Tuskegee Institute.* New York: Doubleday, Page, and Co., 1902.

———. *Up from Slavery,* ed. William L. Andrews. New York: Oxford University Press, 1995.

Washington, Booker T., N. B. Wood, and Fannie Barrier Williams. *A New Negro for a New Century.* Chicago: American Publishing House, 1900.

Washington, Josephine T. "Impressions of a Southern Federation." *Colored American Magazine* 7 (1904): 676–80.

Washington, Margaret Murray. "An Account of Addresses by Washington and Mrs. Washington Delivered at Charleston." Sept. 12, 1898. In *The Booker T. Washington Papers,* vol. 4, ed. Louis R. Harlan and Raymond W. Smock. Urbana: University of Illinois Press, 1977.

———. "Club Work among Negro Women." In *Progress of a Race or the Remarkable Advancement of the American Negro,* ed. J. L. Nichols, A.B., and William Crogman, LL.D. Naperville, Ill.: J. L. Nichols & Co., 1925. 177–209.

———. "The Gain in the Life of Negro Women." *Outlook* (Jan. 1904): 271–74.

———. "The New Negro Woman." *Lend a Hand* (Oct. 1895): 254–60.

———. "To Ednah Dow Littlehale Cheney." Jan. 13, 1901. In *The Booker T. Washington Papers,* vol. 6, ed. Louis R. Harlan and Raymond W. Smock. Urbana: University of Illinois Press, 1977. 11–12.

———. "To Ednah Dow Littlehale Cheney." Nov. 23, 1896. *The Booker T. Washington Papers,* vol. 4, ed. Louis R. Harlan. Urbana: University of Illinois Press, 1975. 237–39.

Washington, Mary Helen. *Invented Lives: Narratives of Black Women 1860–1960.* New York: Anchor Press, 1987.

Weingarten Bros. "W.B. Erect Form." Advertisement. *Ladies' Home Journal* (Nov. 18, 1901): 33.

Wenzell, Albert Beck. "The American Girl Who Marries an Oriental Must Be Prepared for Real Changes in Her Home Life." *Life,* Jan. 30, 1896, 78–79.

Westling, Louise Hutchings. *The Green Breast of the New World: Landscape, Gender, and American Fiction.* Athens: University of Georgia Press, 1996.

Wharton, Edith. *A Backward Glance.* New York: Appleton, 1938.

———. *The Collected Short Stories of Edith Wharton,* vol. 1, ed. R. W. B. Lewis. New York: Scribner's, 1968.

———. *The Custom of the Country.* New York: Scribner's, 1913.

———. *French Ways and Their Meaning.* New York: Appleton, 1919.

———. *The Fruit of the Tree.* New York: Scribner's, 1907.

———. *The House of Mirth,* ed. Elizabeth Ammons. New York: W. W. Norton, 1990.

———. *The Letters of Edith Wharton,* ed. R.W.B. Lewis and Nancy Lewis. New York: Scribner's, 1988.

———. *The Reef.* New York: Collier Books, 1987.

———. *Sanctuary.* New York: Scribner's, 1903.

Wheeler, Marjorie. *New Women of the New South: The Leaders of the Woman Suffrage Movement in the Southern States.* New York: Oxford University Press, 1993.

———. "The Woman Suffrage Movement in the Inhospitable South." In *Votes for Women!:*

The Woman Suffrage Movement in Tennessee, the South, and the Nation, ed. Marjorie Spruill Wheeler. Knoxville: University of Tennessee Press, 1995.

White, William Allen. "The Story of Georgie Don't." *Good Housekeeping* 37 (1903): 406.

White-Parks, Annette. *Sui Sin Far/Edith Maude Eaton: A Literary Biography.* Urbana: University of Illinois Press, 1995.

———. "'We Wear the Mask': Sui Sin Far as One Example of Trickster Authorship." In *Tricksterism in Turn-of-the-Century American Literature,* ed. Elizabeth Ammons and Annette White-Parks. Hanover: University Press of New England, 1994. 1–19.

Wiesenthal, C. Susan. "Female Sexuality in Willa Cather's 'O Pioneers!' and the Era of Scientific Sexology: A Dialogue between Frontiers." *Ariel* 20, no. 1 (1990): 41–63.

Willard, Carla. "Timing Impossible Subjects: The Marketing Style of Booker T. Washington." *American Quarterly* 53, no. 4 (2001): 624–69.

Williams, Deborah Lindsay. *Not in Sisterhood: Edith Wharton, Willa Cather, Zona Gale, and the Politics of Female Authorship.* New York: Palgrave, 2001.

Williams, Fannie Barrier. "The Club Movement among Colored Women of America." *A New Negro for a New Century,* ed. Booker T. Washington, N. B. Wood, and Fannie Barrier Williams. Chicago: American Publishing House, 1900. 379–405.

———. "The Clubs and Their Location in all the States of the National Association of Colored Women and Their Mission." In *A New Negro for a New Century,* ed. Booker T. Washington, N. B. Wood, and Fannie Barrier Williams. Chicago: American Publishing House, 1900. 406–28.

———. "The Women's Part in a Man's Business." *Voice of the Negro* (Nov. 1904): 543–47.

Wilson, Harold. *McClure's Magazine and the Muckrakers.* Princeton: Princeton University Press, 1970.

Winston, Ella. "Foibles of the New Woman." *Forum* 21 (1896): 186–92.

Wolf, Emma. *The Joy of Life.* Chicago: A. C. McClurg, 1896.

Wolff, Cynthia Griffen. *A Feast of Words: The Triumph of Edith Wharton.* 2nd ed. New York: Oxford University Press, 1995.

Woloch, Nancy. *Women and the American Experience.* New York: Knopf, 1987.

Woodward, C. Vann. *Origins of the New South, 1877–1913.* Baton Rouge: Louisiana State University Press, 1971.

Wu, Cheng-Tsu. *"Chink!": A Documentary History of Anti-Chinese Prejudice in America.* New York: Straight Arrow Books, 1972.

Wu, William F. *The Yellow Peril: Chinese Americans in American Fiction 1850–1940.* Hamden: Archon Books, 1982.

Wyckoff, Peter. *Wall Street and the Stock Markets: A Chronology (1644–1971).* Philadelphia: Chilton Book Company, 1972.

Yaeger, Patricia. *Dirt and Desire: Reconstructing Southern Women's Writing, 1930–1990.* Chicago: University of Chicago Press, 2000.

Young Men's Congressional Club. "Here and There." *Colored American Magazine* (May 1900): 57–58.

———. "Young Men's Congressional Club Mock Trial." *Colored American Magazine* (Aug. 1900): 144–45.

Zitkala-Ša. *American Indian Stories.* Lincoln: University of Nebraska Press, 1985.

INDEX

Page numbers in italics refer to illustrations.

MARTHA H. PATTERSON is an associate professor at McKendree University in Lebanon, Illinois. She is currently working on a book about the American New Woman, 1915–1930.

The University of Illinois Press
is a founding member of the
Association of American University Presses.

———————————————————————————

Composed in 10.5/13 Adobe Minion
by Jim Proefrock
at the University of Illinois Press
Manufactured by Thomson-Shore, Inc.

University of Illinois Press
1325 South Oak Street
Champaign, IL 61820-6903
www.press.uillinois.edu